Stanley Leathes

A Short Hebrew Grammar

Stanley Leathes

A Short Hebrew Grammar

ISBN/EAN: 9783741172861

Manufactured in Europe, USA, Canada, Australia, Japa

Cover: Foto ©Andreas Hilbeck / pixelio.de

Manufactured and distributed by brebook publishing software (www.brebook.com)

Stanley Leathes

A Short Hebrew Grammar

A

SHORT PRACTICAL

HEBREW GRAMMAR;

WITH AN APPENDIX,

CONTAINING

THE HEBREW TEXT OF GENESIS I.—VI., AND PSALMS I.—VI.,
GRAMMATICAL ANALYSIS, AND VOCABULARY.

BY THE

REV. STANLEY LEATHES, M.A.,

PROFESSOR OF HEBREW, KING'S COLLEGE, LONDON.

LONDON:
JOHN MURRAY, ALBEMARLE STREET.
1868.

LEIPZIG: W. DRUGULIN, 22, KÖNIGSSTRASSE.

TO

EDWARD BYLES COWELL, ESQ., M.A.

IN TOKEN OF A VALUED FRIENDSHIP OF MANY YEARS.

ERRATA.

In pages 53, 203, 224, READ *teshng* FOR *teshng*.
In page 130, READ wehyeh FOR wehyeh.

PREFACE.

After some years experience in teaching Hebrew the writer found that, in spite of the many existing works on Hebrew Grammar, a chief impediment consisted in the want of a compendious manual, which might be at once sufficiently elementary for beginners and at the same time not too elementary for the more advanced student. It was in the hope of doing something towards supplying this want that the present attempt originated.

It must be understood that the object of it is not in any way to supersede or compete with larger and more pretentious works on Hebrew Grammar, but to present in a concise and intelligible form the principal facts of the language.

Everything therefore of the nature of theory is studiously avoided, and results only are given, without reference to anterior principles upon which they may be explained, since these are stated differently by different writers and to discuss them here would have been foreign to the purpose of the work. But special care has been taken to furnish the student with rules and observations that may be of practical use to him, as well as with numerous examples, paradigms and tables of various kinds to facilitate constant reference.

In one respect however this book will be found to differ from all previous works and that is in the *method adopted to express Hebrew words in English letters.*

Most persons have felt the desirableness of doing this, however difficult they may have found it. There is no recognised method and no two scholars adopt the same method. In almost all, if not all, cases, the plan followed must be acknowledged an inconvenient, awkward and unsuccessful one. The reason it has been so is twofold.

1. The habit of the English printer to express all foreign words in Italics. This at once deprived him of a resource ready to his hand which might have been utilised; for the cases in which Hebrew and English words printed together in the same type could be mistaken for each other are very few, and the mixed use of Italics as here adopted would have served to distinguish them in almost every instance.

2. The attempt was made to represent the *pronunciation* of the Hebrew in English letters;

which owing to the essential diversity of the two alphabets could not but be a task of considerable difficulty. Nothing of the kind is done here: but the letters of the Hebrew alphabet are represented by constant equivalents in English, to which the commonly received power is assigned in the alphabetical Table on the third page.

It must therefore be distinctly understood that the English correspondents of the Hebrew words, here met with, are in no case intended to express the sound of those words except according to the scheme of pronunciation which they uniformly follow, and which they are used, arbitrarily though appropriately, to represent.

According to this scheme the Student can indeed feel no doubt as to the pronunciation; on the contrary it will be marked for him with unfailing accuracy; but the expression of the sound is kept subordinate to the exact representation of the Hebrew characters which, by the simple expedient of Italic types, is attained in every case, without ambiguity, and without any awkward collocation of letters.

By this method, first published in "the Guardian" of March 6. 1867, any Hebrew word can be expressed in English characters with minute exactness, and the greatest attainable simplicity, and any word so written can be restored to its original Hebrew form, with perfect ease and certainty. In fact, the system of *transliteration*, so successfully pursued, and universally adopted, in the case of the Sanskrit, an Aryan language, is here applied for the first time to the Shemitic Hebrew. A slight modification of the same system would render it applicable to other members also of the Shemitic family, the Chaldee, Syriac and even Arabic. An end it must be confessed long desired, but hitherto inadequately realised.

This little book is intended to aid the student, with or without other assistance, to read the scriptures of the Old Testament in the original language with intelligence and precision: if it succeeds in doing so, the writer's object will have been attained and his trouble in preparing it amply rewarded.

It can hardly be needful to add that, as many Grammars have been consulted, many proofs of obligation to other writers may frequently be discovered, though it is hoped that there will occasionally be tokens also of original and independent work.

A
HEBREW GRAMMAR.

CHAPTER I.

THE ALPHABET.

1. There are in Hebrew twenty-two letters, of the following Forms, Names and Powers:

Form.	Name.	Power.
א	'Alef	' not sounded
ב	Beyth	b or v
ג	Gimel	g as in go
ד	Daleth	d
ה	He'	h
ו	Waw	w
ז	Za-yin	z
ח	Heyth	h guttural as ch in the German Buch
ט	Teyth	t
י	Yod	y
כ or ך	Kaf	k
ל	Lamed	l
מ or ם	Meym	m
נ or ן	Nun	n
ס	Samek	s
ע	Ga-yin	g not sounded
פ or ף	Pe	p or f
צ or ץ	Zadey	z as ts in nuts or the German z.
ק	Kof	k a peculiarly hard k
ר	Reysh	r
ש	Shin	sh
ש	Sin	s
ת	Taw	t or th as in thin.

(כ ,מ ,נ ,פ ,צ when final)

2. It will be seen that while some Hebrew letters, as Beyth, Pe' and Taw, have two sounds and therefore stand for two or more letters in English, according to circumstances which will be explained hereafter, other English letters as h, k, s and z, are represented by two in Hebrew, which, though in most cases differing in sound, cannot be well distinguished by our alphabet.

This difference is here denoted by the use of *Italic* letters.

In like manner the Italic vowels here used are the long vowels for the sound of which see the next ch.

The other letters are sounded exactly like their English equivalents given in the Table.

3. The letters are read from right to left.

They are all consonants.

Some of them as א and ע have no sound but that of the vowel which is written beneath them, as אָדָם 'adam, *man*; עֵדֶן *geden, Eden*. The ' and *g* must however be used to express their *silent* power as consonants.

4. Some of them as אהוי are at times absorbed in the sound of the vowel which precedes or accompanies them, as בָּא ba', *he came;* לֹא lo', *not;* פֶּה peh, *mouth;* לוֹ lo, *to him;* לוּ lu, *if;* לִי li, *to me.* For this reason they are called *quiescent* letters.

5. Every consonant is either (1) followed by a vowel as תֹהוּ *tohu, desolation*, so forming an *open* syllable; or (2) completes the (*close*) syllable formed by the preceding vowel and consonant, as גַם gam, *also;* or (3) is followed by Shĕwa, *see the next ch.*, as בְּ bĕ, *in*: thus, בְּרֵאשִׁית bĕre'shith, *in the beginning.*

6. Every syllable therefore begins with a consonant; the only exception, if it be one, is in the case

of a word beginning with ו *u*, *and*, which is in itself a complete syllable. Shĕwa and its compounds are not reckoned as syllables.

7. Five of them assume a different form, when they occur at the end of a word. *See the Table.* But once or twice these forms are interchanged. Is. ix. 6. Neh. ii. 13. Job. xxxviii. 1.

8. Six of them בגדכפת when initial have a point inserted in them which is called soft Dagesh (ch. ii.). In this case ב is sounded b; פ p; and ת t; otherwise ב is v, פ is f, ת is th. The sound of the other three letters is not affected by this point. These six letters are called *aspirates*.

9. As words are not divided in printing or writing Hebrew, some of the letters are occasionally spread out to fill up a line when there is not room for the next word, thus ר, ם &c.

10. The letters אהחע are gutturals, and בומף are labials.

11. Care must be taken not to confound ב and כ; ג and נ; ר, ד and ך; ה, ח and ת; י, ו, ן and ן; ש and ש; ס and ם; ע, צ and ק.

CHAPTER II.

THE VOWELS &c.

1. The vowels in Hebrew are expressed by certain marks placed, with two exceptions, *beneath* the letters. These marks are called the Points. Their form, name and power will be seen in the following Table:

Form.	Name.	Power.		Expressed by
ָ	*Kamez*	a, as in Father		a
ֵ	*Zerey*	a.i, - - Pain		e
ִי	Long *Hirik*	ee, - - Seen		i
וֹ	*Holem*	o, - - Bone		o
וּ	*Shurek*	oo, - - Root		u
ַ	Patha*h*	a, - - Fat		a
ֶ	Segol	e, - - Bed		e
ִ	Short *Hirik*	i, - - Tin		i
ָ	*Kamez Hatuf*	o, - - Not		o
ֻ	*Kibbuz*	u, - - Full		u
ְ	Shĕwa	e, ⎫	Begin	ĕ
ֲ	*Hatef* Patha*h*	a, ⎬ all very short	Alone	ă
ֱ	*Hatef* Segol	e, ⎭	Begin	ĕ
ֳ	*Hatef Kamez*	o,	Collecting	ŏ

It must be borne in mind that the *Italic* vowels always stand for *long* vowels in Hebrew, except in the case of *Hatef* Segol which is a very short one.

2. The Hebrew vowels are always sounded *after* the letter to which they are affixed: except in the case of *Furtive* Patha*h* which is so called when found under a final ה, ח, or ע that is preceded by a long vowel as רוּחַ rua*h*, *spirit*.

3. A short vowel does not commonly stand in an open syllable. 2 Sam. i. 26 &c. A long vowel can never stand in a close syllable, without an accent. Such forms as those in Ps. lxxxi. 2. cii. 5 &c. are anomalous.

4. Long *Hirik* is usually followed by a Yod which is absorbed in the sound of it. Yod also sometimes follows *Kamez*, Patha*h*, Segol, and Zer*e*y and is then absorbed in their sound or coalesces with it as a diphthong, as חַי *hay*, חֵי *hay*, עָלֶיהָ *galeyha*, מֵימֵי *meymey*.

5. The W*a*w in *H*olem and Shure*k* is only the medium of the vowel and has no consonantal sound. *H*olem may also be written without W*a*w, Shure*k* cannot, but *K*ibbu*z* with an accent is sometimes put for Shure*k*. Sometimes Yod follows W*a*w as גּוֹי *goy* *a nation*, גָּלוּי *galuy*, *revealed*; and sometimes W*a*w follows Yod, as עָלָיו *galayw*, *upon him*. In the former case a sort of diphthong is formed, in the latter the Yod is not sounded.

6. *Alef* having no relation to a previous vowel is said to be *otiose* as חֵטְא *het'*, *sin*; הֵבִיא *hevi'*, *he brought in*.

7. *Kamez* is not *Kamez* but *Kamez Hatuf* when it comes (1) before silent Shĕwa (see 13) and forms an unaccented syllable with the following letter as חָכְמָה *h*okmah, *wisdom* (but חֲכָמָה *h*akêmah,

she was wise); or (2) before Dagesh forte and is not accented, as בָּתִּים *bottim, houses;* or (3) when it is in a close final syllable without the accent, as וַיָּקָם *wayyakom, and he arose;* or (4) when it comes before another *Kamez Hatuf,* not final, as פָּעָלְךָ *pogolka, thy work;* or (5) before *Hatef Kamez* as פָּעֳלוֹ *pogolo, his work,* or (6) is shortened from an original *Holem,* as in the two anomalous words קָדָשִׁים *kodashim, holy things,* from קֹדֶשׁ *kodesh,* שָׁרָשָׁיו *shorashayw, his roots,* from שֹׁרֶשׁ *shoresh.* The last three cases apply only to Segolates (ch. viii.).

8. If Sh*i*n is preceded by a letter without a vowel *H*olem is implied in the Sh*i*n as מֹשֶׁה Mosheh, *Moses.*

If *Si*n is not final and has no vowel *H*olem is implied as שֹׂנֵא *sone', hating.*

Sh*i*n with two points beginning a syllable is read sho, as שֹׁמֵר *shomer, keeping.*

*Si*n with two points ending a syllable is read *os,* as יִרְפֹּשׂ *yirpos, he will tread down.*

9. W*a*w with *H*olem and a vowel besides is a consonant, as הֹוָה *howah, calamity.*

A point in W*a*w is not Shurek but Dagesh (15.) when the W*a*w has a vowel under it, as צִוָּה *ziwwah, he commanded.*

W*a*w preceded by a vowel or Shëwa is consonantal, as עָוֹן *gawon, iniquity;* עֵדְוֹת *gedwoth, precepts.*

10. Shëwa means *nothing* or *emptiness* and is the sign which is placed under a letter which has no vowel of its own. Shëwa is always to be understood beneath every unpointed letter except אהוי, and is written in every final ך that has no other vowel, and with every final consonant that has no vowel and is preceded by silent Shëwa as פָּקַדְתְּ *pakadt.*

In one case Shĕwa is written in a final consonant not preceded by Shĕwa, viz. in the 2. pers. fem. sing. Past of verbs whose 3rd radical is a guttural, as שָׁלַחַתְּ, and this is because the second Pathaḥ stands for *Hatef* Pathaḥ (iii. 3.).

The case of the pronoun of 2. pers. fem. sing. אַתְּ hardly needs to be mentioned. It probably stands for אַתִּי.

11. The compounds of Shĕwa are only used regularly with gutturals, for these letters do not commonly take simple Shĕwa.

Compound Shĕwa when found with other letters is anomalous e. g. Gen. ii. 12 and xxix. 8 Cf. xxvii. 38 Jer. xxii. 20 &c.

Gutturals anomalously take simple Shĕwa see a remarkable case Ex. xv. 6.

12. Shĕwa is sometimes silent and sometimes sounded. It is *sounded* or vocal (1) Whenever it begins a word, as בְּרֵאשִׁית; or (2) comes after a long vowel without the tone, as בְּנֵי; or (3) after Metheg (commonly), as וַיְהִי; or (4) after another Shĕwa if not final, as יִפְקְדוּ; or (5) is under the first of two double letters, in verbs, as הַלְלוּ; or (6) under Dagesh not final, as פָּקְדוּ.

13. Shĕwa is *silent* in all other cases merely marking the division of the syllables, as מַלְכִּי malki, *my king*.

14. Every vocal and every compound Shĕwa stands, with the consonant to which it belongs, at the beginning, and every silent Shĕwa at the end, of a syllable. The only exception is in the case of words ending with two Shĕwas, as פְּקַדְתְּ. But two Shĕwas cannot stand at the beginning of a syllable.

15. Dagesh is a point which may be inserted in any letter but a guttural or ר and has the effect of doubling it: but when inserted in one of the six aspirates its effect is twofold. (1) It either doubles the letter (hard Dagesh or Dagesh forte), as סִפֵּר sapper; or (2) in the case of ב, פ, ת, alters its sound, as מַרְבֶּה marbeh. The effect of Dagesh is imperceptible in the other three letters, where its use is practically formal, as מַלְכִּי malki. Soft Dagesh in ג, ד, כ is expressed by a dot beneath the g, d, k.

16. There is also a euphonic use of Dagesh by which after a word ending in a vowel or quiescent letter it is inserted in the first letter of the following word, as הוֹשִׁיעָה נָּא hoshigah nna'. This use of Dagesh is even found in ר, Job. xxxiii. 21, Jer. xxxix. 12. So מַה־זֶּה or, contracted, מֶּה Ex. iv. 2. מַה־לָּכֶם, contracted, מַלָּכֶם Is. iii. 15 &c.

17. Dagesh in a letter which is preceded and followed by a vowel is always hard, as סִפֵּר sipper: and also in any medial letter having Shĕwa but not preceded by Shĕwa, as פִּקְרוּ. In all other cases it is soft merely altering the sound of the letter or else being practically formal. Dagesh therefore in the first or last letter of a word is always soft. When it doubles the letter it also alters the sound if the letter is susceptible of such change, as סִפֵּר sipper, *not* siffer.

18. Mapp*i*k is a point in a final ה shewing that it retains its consonantal sound and is not merely absorbed in a preceding vowel. It is here expressed by ḥ.

19. Ma*k*kaf is a mark like a hyphen, and is used to *connect* words together. Zere*y* before Ma*k*kaf

becomes Segol and *Holem* becomes *Kamez;* because Ma*kk*af deprives the previous word of its accent (ii. 3). In spite of Ma*kk*af the sense is sometimes broken; thus the substantive verb is understood, or the subject joined to the predicate by Ma*kk*af. Prov. xix. 6.

20. As a general rule the *tone* or *accent* is laid on the last syllable of a word, but it sometimes falls on the last but one; e. g. in words with two Segols, or two Pathahs, or with Zerey Segol, or Holem Segol; in the words אֵלֶּה, הֵמָּה, אֲנַחְנוּ; in nouns with the affixes מוֹ, ־ֵינוּ, ־ֶיהָ, ־ֶיךָ, ־ִיךְ, ־ֵיו, ־ָה, ־ֵהוּ. In the 3. fem. sing. and the 3. plur. Past of hollow verbs (xi) and verbs of double radical, as קָמָה, סָבְבוּ; in the verbal terminations תָּ, תִּי, נוּ, נָה; and in the verbal affixes הוּ, הָ, נִי, נוּ, ־ֵנִי, ־ֶנָּה, ־ֵם, מוֹ. Furtive Patha*h* (2), or local or paragogic ה (xii. 18), does not affect the accent. But if ה paragogic is preceded by Shew*a* it takes the accent as אֶשְׁמְרָה, אֶשְׁמֹר; שָׁמְרָה/שֹׁמֵר. The accent sometimes serves to distinguish words otherwise alike, e. g. בִּינָה is a noun Prov. i. 2, but בִּינָה is a verb. Ps. v. 2. So שָׁבוּ Jonah iii. 10 is from שׁוּב, but שָׁבוּ/ Gen. xxxiv. 29 from שׁבה. Occasionally the accent is thrown back when the next word has a distinctive accent e. g. Gen. i. 5, Ps. ii. 12 &c. Cf. Num. xxiii. 23. where the last word but one has a distinctive accent. Dual nouns also and the apocopated futures, Kal and Hi*f*g*i*l, of verbs in ה have the accent penultimate.

21. The *accents* in the Hebrew Bible may safely be neglected by the student till far advanced in the language. The exceptions are 'Ethna*h*, Sillu*k* and Metheg of which the two first always lengthen the vowel they accompany which is then said to be *in*

pause. 'Ethna*h* divides every verse into two parts. Sillu*k* is always found with the last word of it and nowhere else. Metheg is like Sillu*k* in form, but is always subsidiary to some other accent. There may be more than one Metheg in the same word. Metheg stands with the vowel preceding a compound Shĕ́wa and remains when that Shĕwa has passed away as יַעֲמֹד, יָעְמְדוּ. Also with the long vowel before the tone if followed by vocal Shĕwa as הָיְתָה. Also with the second syllable before the tone, if an open one; if not with the third syllable before the tone, if open. Also before implied Dagesh. Metheg is also found sometimes with Patha*h* or short *Hirik* in a close syllable next before the tone Gen. i. 11. In such a case it does not make Shĕwa vocal. (12) Of two similar accents in a word the former takes the tone Gen. i. 2.

The foregoing rules will be best exemplified by the first chapter of Genesis which according to the method here adopted is written as follows.

Bĕre'shíth bara' 'ĕlohím 'eth hashshamayim wĕ'eth ha'arez. 2. Wĕha'arez hayĕthah thohu wavohu wŏ*h*oshek *g*al-pĕne*y* thĕhom wĕrua*h* ĕlohím mĕra*h*efeth *g*al-pĕne*y* hammayim. 3. Wayyo'mer ĕlohím yĕhí or wayĕhí 'or. 4. Wayyar' 'ĕlohím 'eth-ha'or ki-tov wayyavdel 'ĕlohím beyn ha'or uveyn ha*h*oshek. 5. Wayyikra' 'ĕlohím la'or yom wŏla*h*oshek kara' layĕlah wayĕhí *g*erev wayĕhí-voker yom 'e*h*ad. 6. Wayyo'mer 'ĕlohím yĕhí raki*ng* bĕthok hammayim wihí mavdíl beyn mayim lamayim. 7. Wayyagas 'ĕlohím 'eth-haraki*ng* wayyavdel beyn hammayim 'ásher mi*tt*a*h*ath laraki*ng* uveyn hammayim ásher me*g*al laraki*ng* wayĕhí-ken. 8. Wayyikra' 'ĕlohím laraki*ng* shamayim wayĕhí-*g*erev wayĕhí-voker yom sheni. 9. Wayyo'mer 'ĕlohim yikkawu hammayim mittahath hashshamayim 'el-makom 'chad wĕthera'ch hayyabbashah wayĕhi-ken. 10. Wayyikra' 'ĕlohim layyabbashah 'erez ulĕmikwch hammayim kara' yammim wayyar' 'ĕlohim ki-tov. 11. Wayyo'mer 'ĕlohim tadshe' ha'arez deshe' gesev mazriag zerag gez pĕri gosch pĕri lĕmino ăsher zargo-vo galha'arez wayĕhi-ken. 12. Wattoze ha'arez deshe' gesev mazriag zerag lĕminehu wĕgez gosch-pĕri 'ăsher zargo-vo lĕminehu wayyar' 'ĕlohim ki-tov. 13. Wayĕhi gerev wayĕhi voker yom shĕlishi. 14. Wayyo'mer 'ĕlohim yĕhi mĕ'oroth birkiag hashshamayim lĕhavdil beyn hayyom uveyn hallayĕlah wĕhayu lĕ'othoth ulĕmogadim ulĕyamim wĕshanim. 15. Wĕhayu lim'oroth birkiag hashshamayim lĕha'ir gal-ha'arez wayĕhi-ken. 16. Wayyagas 'ĕlohim 'ethshĕney hammĕ'oroth haggĕdolim 'eth-hamma'or haggadol lĕmemsheleth hayyom wĕ'eth-hamma'or hakkaton lĕmemsheleth hallayĕlah wă'eth hakkokavim. 17. Wayyitten otham 'ĕlohim birkiag hashshamayim lĕha'ir gal-ha'arez. 18. Wĕlimshol bayyom uvallayĕlah ulĕhavdil beyn ha or uveyn hahoshek wayyar' ĕlohim ki-tov. 19. Wayĕhi-gerev wayĕhivoker yom rĕvigi. 20. Wayyo'mer 'ĕlohim yishrĕzu hammayim sherez nefesh hayyah wĕ-gof yĕgofef galpĕney rĕkiag hashshamayim. 21. Wayyivra' 'ĕlohim 'eth-hattanninim haggĕdolim we'eth kol-nefesh hahayyah haromeseth 'ăsher sharĕzu hammayim lĕminehem wĕ'eth kol-gof kanaf lĕminehu wayyar' 'ĕlohim ki-tov. 22. Wayĕvarek 'otham 'ĕlohim le'mor pĕru urĕvu umil'u 'eth-hammayim bayyammim wĕhagof yirev ba'arez. 23. Wayĕhi-gerev wayĕhi-voker yom hămishi. 24. Wayyo'mer 'ĕlohim toze' ha'arez nefesh hayyah lĕm'nah bĕhemah waremes we'hayotho-'erez lĕminah wayĕhî-ken. 25. Wayyagas 'ĕlohim 'eth-ħayyath ha'arez lĕmînah wĕ'eth-habbĕhemah lĕmînah wĕ'eth ḳol-romes ha'adamah lōmînehu wayyar' ĕlohim ḳi-tov. 26. Wayyo'mor 'ĕlohim nagăseh 'adam bŏzalmenu ḳidmuthenu wŏyirdu vidgath hayyam uvŏgof hashshamayim uvabbĕhemah uvĕkol-ha'arez uvĕkolharemes haromes gal-ha'arez. 27. Wayyivra' 'ĕlohim 'eth-ha'adam bĕzalmo bĕzelem 'ĕlohim bara' 'otho zakar unŏkevah bara' 'otham. 28. Wayŏvarek 'otham 'ĕlohim wayyo'mer lahem 'ĕlohim pĕru urŏvu umil'u 'eth-ha'arez wĕkivshuha urŏdu bidgath hayyam uvŏgof hashshamayim uvĕkol-ħayyah haromeseth galha'arez. 29. Wayyo'mer 'ĕlohim hinneh nathattí lakem 'eth-ḳol-gesev zoreag zerag 'asher gal-pĕney ḳol-ha'arez wĕ'eth-ḳol-hagez 'asher-bo pĕri-gez zoreag zarag lakem yihyeh le'oklah. 30. Ulĕkol-ħayyath ha'arez ulĕkol-gof hashshamayim ulĕkol romes galha'arez 'asher-bo nefesh ħayyah 'eth-ḳol-yerek gesev lĕ'oklah wayĕhî-ken. 31. Wayyar' 'ĕlohim eth-ḳolăsher gasah wĕhinneh-tov mĕ'od wayĕhî-gerev wayĕhîvoker yom hashshishshi.

The student will do well to learn to read the Hebrew characters and to understand the principles of syllabication by the aid of this specimen which is written in English letters. It will also facilitate his progress if he practices writing it back again in Hebrew characters.

CHAPTER III.

RULES AFFECTING SHĔWA, DAGESH AND THE GUTTURALS.

1. If one Shĕwa follows another the first becomes short *Hirik*, *Pathah*, or *Segol*, as דִּבְרֵי for דְּבְרֵי, בְּנֵי for בְּנְפֵי, נֶגְדִּי for נְגְדִּי, אֹיִבְךָ for אֹיְבְךָ, לִפְקֹד for לְפְקֹד (ii. 14.).

This however is not the case when the first Shĕwa is silent by position as יִקְרוּ.

2. If a compound Shĕwa follows a simple Shĕwa the simple Shĕwa is changed to the Pathah, Segol or *Kamez*, with which it is compounded, as יַאֱסֹף for יְאֱסֹף, לַעֲבֹד for לְעֲבֹד, בַּעֲבֹד for בְּעֲבֹד, יַעֲמֹד for יְעֲמֹד, &c.

3. If simple Shĕwa follows compound Shĕwa the compound Shĕwa is changed to its Pathah, Segol or *Kamez*, thus נֶעְמְדוּ becomes נֶעֲמְדוּ (ii. 11.), then נַעֲמְדוּ (iii. 2), then finally נַעַמְדוּ. So נַעֲרֹךְ for נֶעֱרֹךְ, תִּצְעַקְנָה for תִּצְעֲקְנָה and similarly שְׁמַעְתְּ for שְׁמָעַתְּ in verbs of the 3rd guttural.

It must be understood that the last only of these forms in every case is met with; the others are merely given to shew how the ultimate forms arise.

4. The omission or insertion of soft *Dagesh* occasions great difficulty to the early student of Hebrew. The following practical rules must be borne in mind.

1) Dagesh must always be inserted in an *initial* aspirate if the preceding word ends in a non-quiescent letter, or diphthong, or Mapp*ik*, as בְּרֵאשִׁית בָּרָא; or though ending in a vowel has a disjunctive accent and is therefore not closely connected with the next word in sense, as בְּצַלְמוֹ בְּעֶלֶם, Gen. i. 27. but וַיִּהְרֵּ֑ן, v. 7; also when two aspirates begin a word even though preceded by a conjunctive accent, as Josh. viii. 24, Is. x. 9. In like manner it is generally inserted after יְהוָֹה and יֱהוִֹה because these words were read by the Jews, אֲרֹנָי and אֱלֹהִים, respectively.

2) Dagesh also as a rule is inserted in an aspirate when it *begins a syllable* that is when it comes after silent Shĕw*a*, as פָּקַדְתָּ (ii. 13.) except

α. The Shĕw*a* stands for an original *Kamez*, *Zerey* or *Holem* as מַלְכֵי from מְלָכִים; כְּתָפוֹת from יַעֲבְרוּ ;בְּתֵפוֹת from יַעֲבֹד or: β. has become silent from the prefixing of ל, כ, ב, to a noun, as בִּדְבָרְךָ, not בְּלִבַב .בִּלְבָב not בְּדְבָרְךָ. The reason of this is that though the *slight vowel* in the first syllable represents the former of two Shewas yet the second of them is treated as if it were still vocal; in which case the following aspirate ceasing to be initial could not carry Dagesh.

3) If however the particles ב כ ל are prefixed to an infinitive mood, the Dagesh is inserted, as לִשְׁבֹּן. This is the normal rule, but there are many exceptions, e. g. we find בִּנְפֹל and בְנֹפֹל, but לִנְפֹל. Cf. Jer. i. 10, xviii. 7, xxxi. 28; Ps. xl. 15, where however some read Dagesh &c. &c.

4) Imperatives do not take Dagesh as פְּקָרִי (exceptions occur Is. xlvii. 2, Jer. x. 17, Cf. xii. 9) neither do they with ה paragogic as שִׁבְכָה; neither do infini-

tives with an affix as רָדְפוּ. To this last however there are some exceptions. Cf. Is. xxix. 16 &c.

5) Dagesh is inserted in Segolate nouns before all the affixes in the Singular but not in the constructive plural or before the grave affixes (v. 5) as מַלְכִּי, מַלְכָּם but מַלְכֵי, מַלְכֵיכֶם. Exceptions to the first are found Job. xxix. 4; Ps. cxvi. 14. Cf. 18; to the second Is. v. 10; Cant. viii. 6; Ps. lxxvi. 4; Ezek. xvii. 9. With ה paragogic, Dagesh is inserted in nouns, as הַנֶּגְבָּה Gen. xiii. 1.

6) Dagesh is not inserted after a silent Shĕwa which has become silent in consequence of the previous vowel being put for a compound Shĕwa as יַעְמְדוּ, not הוּ, from נֶעֶמְדוּ, which according to iii. 3 cannot stand. As above in 2),9, the Shĕwa affects the following consonant as if it were still vocal depriving it of Dagesh.

7) But Dagesh is inserted when a simple Shĕwa has been substituted for a compound Shĕwa, as יַחְפֹּץ Deut. xxv. 7.

8) The affixes ךָ, כֶם, כֶן, never take Dagesh (but ךְ in certain cases becomes ךּ with Dagesh forte and once it has Dagesh lene *as well as* the Epenthetic Nun, Jer. xxii. 24); neither does an aspirate before וּ as עַבְדוּת, מַלְכוּת etc. (exceptions are found Num. xxxii. 14; 1 Sam. xx. 30); neither does the word בֶּגֶד *a garment*, before the affixes.

5. שְׁתַּיִם, שְׁתַּיִם and שְׁתֵּי are the only words which take Dagesh after vocal Shĕwa.

6. In some cases hard Dagesh is omitted as שָׁלְחָה for שָׁלְּחָה *she sent*, Ezek. xvii. 7; xxxi. 4 &c. Thus it is very frequently omitted (but not from an aspirate) when the Shĕwa that follows it would be

2

vocal especially if under a letter that is repeated as הַלְלוּ. So we have הַיְאֹר and הַלְוִיִם but anomalously. Cf. Ps. lxxiv. 7; Eccles. vii. 28, 29, &c.

7. Sometimes Dagesh forte is anomalously inserted as in Ex. ii. 3; Hos. iii. 2.

8. נ with silent Shĕwa is elided and its absence marked by Dagesh as יִפֹּל for יִנְפֹּל.

9. As Dagesh cannot stand in a guttural or ר the preceding vowel requires compensation for its omission. Thus before a guttural, Patha*h* with Dagesh becomes *Kamez* as אֶבֶן *a stone*, הָאֶבֶן *the stone*, (see 14) instead of Patha*h* under the He' and Dagesh in the Alef. In like manner Segol or *Hirik* becomes *Zerey*; and *K*ibbu*z*, *H*olem, before a guttural, as מֵעַל for מִן עַל and מְבֹרָךְ for Beyth *K*ibbu*z* and Dagesh in the Reysh. But Dagesh is found in ר Ezek. xvi. 4; Prov. xiv. 10.

10. But ה and ח, not pointed with *Kamez*, dispense with this compensation as חָשַׁךְ, תָהוּא. So הַחָכְמָה because here the vowel is *Kamez Hatuf*. In such cases Dagesh is said to be *implied*. But we have הָחַי Gen. vi. 19, and הָהֵם *passim*.

11. Patha*h* before a guttural with implied Dagesh frequently becomes Segol as יֶחְנָם, הֶעָרִים, הֶהָרִים.

12. Gutturals having *Kamez* change Patha*h* to Segol, especially ח, as הֶחָכָם הָחָג. Also in dissyllables with ה and ע if the tone is ultimate as in the two instances given in 11. While if the tone is penultimate the vowel is *Kamez* as הָעָלָם and so in monosyllables as הָהָר.

13. The interrogative particle הֲ before Shĕwa and gutturals with any vowel but *Kamez* becomes

הַ as Job. viii. 3; xi. 7; 2 K. v. 26; before gutturals with *Kamez* it becomes הָ as Num. xi. 12; xiii. 18; Job. xiii. 25; Eccles. ii. 19. While in Judges vi. 31. and xii. 5. it even has *Kamez*. If a letter having Shĕw*a* follows the ה it frequently takes Dagesh, Gen. xvii. 17; xviii. 21 &c. and once when it has not Shĕw*a* Lev. x. 19.

14. The *definite article* in Hebrew is ה which is prefixed by Patha*h* followed by Dagesh and is the same for both genders and numbers as גַּן *a garden*, הַגַּן *the garden*, נָשִׁים *women*, הַנָּשִׁים *the women*.

a. Before a guttural (especially א) or ר the Patha*h* becomes *Kamez* by 9, 10; and sometimes Segol if the guttural has *Kamez* by 12. Sometimes the article is prefixed by Patha*h* alone by 10 and sometimes the Dagesh is omitted especially if the first letter is *Yod* with Shĕw*a*. Cf. iii. 6.

CHAPTER IV.

RADICALS AND SERVILES. THE USE OF THE LEXICON.

1. The Parts of speech in Hebrew are four viz. Pronouns, Nouns (including adjectives), Verbs and Particles.

2. There are three numbers Singular, Dual, and Plural, but the dual is peculiar to nouns substantive.

3. There are two genders masculine and feminine which are marked in Verbs as well as Nouns and Pronouns. The feminine is commonly used where other languages would use the neuter as e. g. in Ps. cxviii. 23. An idiom which is preserved in Mark xii. 11.

4. The letters are either Radicals or Serviles. The *Radical* letters are those which form the root or primitive of a word which is commonly the 3. pers. sing. of the Past tense of the Verb. These roots mostly consist of three letters. The *servile* letters are those which are used in the inflexions and modifications of the root which take place in the course of declension and derivation.

Any of the serviles may be radical that is form part of a root or even the whole of it.

[Chap. IV.] RADICALS AND SERVILES. 21

But the radicals are never servile except in one case when a radical is substituted for a servile in a certain form of verbs as הִצְטַדֵּק. The serviles are comprised in the mnemonic words אֵיתָן מֹשֶׁה וְכָלֵב *Ethan Moses and Caleb*. All the other letters are radicals.

5. Words are commonly found in the Lexicon arranged alphabetically, but *under their roots*. This method of course assumes that the root is known. But as the beginner cannot know the root he experiences great difficulty in finding it. Indeed this is the most serious drawback he has to encounter at the outset.*

The following rules must be borne in mind at first.

1. If the student finds three radical letters in a word he may know that they constitute the root which will be found in the Lexicon, as מְרַחֶפֶת, see רחף.

2. But an initial Nun may have been lost, its absence being marked by Dagesh, he must therefore supply it and look for *this* word as יִבֹּל, see נבל.

3. A Yod, *Taw*, *Alef*, He', Nun, Meym, or the syllables מִי, נִח, הִת, אֶת, תִּח, יִת, and some others may

---

* I cannot forbear to add that the gain to the student of any of the Shemitic languages would be immense if the arrangement of words in the Lexicon according to their *permanent* letters were commonly adopted after the method proposed by Prof. Jarrett of Cambridge and carried out by him in his Hebrew Lexicon. It is not only the simplest method but also the most scientific because the one most completely in accordance with the genius of the language. For by it words of the same family are brought into juxtaposition instead of being widely separated according to mere alphabetical accident.

have been added on at the beginning of the root in which case these additions must first be taken away and the remainder of the word or part of it will constitute the root, thus נְפָק, see פקד, הִתְקַטֵל, see קטל &c.

4. The syllables ־ָה ־ֶה, ־ָ, ־ֵי, ־ֶם, ־ֶן, נָה ־ִי, ־ְ, or the letters Taw, Waw, Yod, and any of the pronominal affixes may have been added on to the end of the root in which case these also must be taken away and the remainder or part of it will form the root thus פְּקַדְתִּיהוּ, see פקד.

5. The conditions 3 and 4 may operate conjointly in the same word as תִּפְקְדֵנִי, see פקד.

6. A Waw or a Yod may be inserted between the second and third radicals; this happens in pass. participles of the first conjugation as פָּקוּד and in hollow verbs and verbs in Yod; see the paradigms.

7. The first letter of the root may disappear; this happens in the case of verbs beginning with Nun or Yod and in the verb לקח, see the paradigms.

8. The last letter of the root may disappear or be replaced by Yod; this happens in the case of verbs like גלה.

9. The syllables הוּ, תוּ, נִי, הוֹ, הֵי, &c. may have been added on at the beginning; this happens with hollow verbs and verbs in Yod; see the paradigms.

10. The syllables הִשׁ, הִצ, הִתּ, הִתְ, הַצ הַשׁ, הַתְ and הַה may have been added on at the beginning; this happens only in the case of certain verbs when in the Hithpa*gel.*

11. The prefixes ו, מ, ל, כ, ב, must of course be rejected before looking for the root.

12. The letters שׁ, ב, ל, א, in the middle of a word are radical.

13. Any of the letters האמנתי may be used as preformatives in derivation; these must be rejected in order to find the root.

These rules are only intended for mere *tirones*. The reason of them will appear afterwards. The only way of learning to use the Lexicon is to become thoroughly master of the grammar and especially of the Verbs.

CHAPTER V.

THE PRONOUNS.

1. The pronouns in Hebrew are either separate words or affixes.

The separate words are used when the Pronouns are put absolutely.

The affixes have the force of possessive pronouns when used with nouns and of the several objective cases of the personal pronouns when used with verbs and particles.

The separate Personal Pronouns are as follows:

    אֲנִי.   I.
    אַתָּה. m. אַתְּ f.   Thou.
    הוּא. m. הִיא. f. He. She. It.
    נַחְנוּ.   We.
    אַתֶּם. m. אַתֶּן. f. You.
    הֵם. m. הֵן. f.   They.

2. Other forms of them are:

I. אֲנִי in pause, and אָנֹכִי. Thou. m. אָתָּה in p., and אַתְּ. Thou. f. אָתְּ in p., and אַתִּי Judg. xvii. 1; 1 K. xiv. 2 &c.

She. הִיא. Sounded *hi*, only in the Pentateuch.

We. נַחְנוּ. Gen. xlii. 11; Num. xxxii. 32. אָנוּ Jer. xlii. 6.

You. f. אַתֵּנָה Gen. xxxi. 6; Ezek. xiii. 11, 20; xxxiv. 17; אַתֵּן Ezek. xxxiv. 31.

They. m. הֵמָּה. f. הֵנָּה.

3. The affixes for Nouns and Particles are as follows:

	For Singular nouns.	For Dual and Plural nouns.
My.	־ִי	־ַי
Thy. m.	ךָ, ־ְךָ ; ־ֶךָ in p.	־ֶיךָ
Thy. f.	־ֵךְ, ךְ	־ַיִךְ, ־ְיִךְ
His.	־ֹה, ־ֵהוּ, ו, הוּ	־ָיו, ־ָו, ־ֵיהוּ; poet.
Her.	־ָה, ־ֶהָ, הָ	־ֶיהָ
Our.	נוּ, ־ֵ	־ֵינוּ
Your. m.	כֶם, ־ְכֶם	־ֵיכֶם
Your. f.	־ְכֶן, כֶן	־ֵיכֶן
Their. m.	־ָם, הֶם; ־ָמוֹ poetically.	־ֵיהֶם; ־ֵימוֹ poet.
Their. f.	־ָן, הֶן, ־ָן	־ֵיהֶן

4. Variations of these forms are found Ps. cxxxix. 5; Ezek. v. 12; Nah. ii. 14; Job. xxii. 20; Ruth iii. 2; Ezek. xxiii. 48; 2 Sam. xxiii. 6; Gen. xli. 21; Ruth i. 19. The Yod in the affixes for plural nouns is sometimes omitted Gen. i. 21; Job. xlii. 10; Ex. xxxiii. 13; other plural forms are found Eccles. x. 17; Ps. cxvi. 12; Ezek. xli. 15 &c. Anomalously a sing. affix to a plural noun is found Ps. cxxxii. 12; Deut. xxviii. 59, and a plural affix instead of sing. is used Ps. ix. 15; Ezek. xvi. 31.

5. When a word ends with a consonant the vowel from of the affix must be taken. The affixes

כֶם, כֶן, הֶם, הֶן are called *grave* as having the tone. The others are called *light*.

6. The affixes for Verbs are as follows:

	For the Past Tense.	For the Future Tense.	For Future with Nun Epenthetic.
Me.	־ֵנִי	־ֵנִי	־ֶנִּי, ־ַנִּי
Thee. m.	ךָ, ־ְךָ; ־ֶךָ in p.	ךָ, ־ֶךָּ	־ֶךָּ, ־ַךָּ
Thee. f.	־ָךְ, ־ֵךְ, ־ֵךְ	־ֵךְ, ־ֵךְ, ־ִי־	
Him.	הוּ, ־ֵהוּ	הוּ, ־ֵהוּ	־ֶנּוּ
Her.	־ָהּ, ־ֶהָ, ־ָהּ	־ֶהָ	־ֶנָּה
Us.	־ֵנוּ, נוּ	־ֵנוּ	
You. m.	כֶם	כֶם	
You. f.	כֶן	כֶן	
Them. m.	־ָם, ־ֵם; ־ָמוֹ poet.	־ֵם, ־ֵם; מוֹ poet.	
Them. f.	־ָן, ־ֵן	־ֵן	

For the other separable pronouns see the Particles.

CHAPTER VI.

NOUNS.

1. Masculine nouns have no special terminations. Nouns denoting males and the proper names of nations, mountains, rivers and months are masculine.

2. Nouns denoting females, the double members of the body, the proper names of regions and cities, and those that end in הָ‎ or ת‎ servile are feminine.

3. The following are some exceptions עָקֵב‎ gakev, *the heel;* עַפְעַפַּיִם‎ gafgappayim, *the eyelids;* מוֹרָה‎ morah, *a razor;* לַיְלָה‎ layēlah, *night* and others, which are masculine.

4. Many nouns are used indifferently in either gender as אֶרֶץ‎ 'erez, *the earth,* גֶּפֶן‎ gefen, *a vine,* דֶּרֶךְ‎ derek, *a way,* לֶחֶם‎ lehem, *bread,* קֶשֶׁת‎ kesheth, *a bow,* תְּהוֹם‎ tēhom, *the deep,* אֶבֶן‎ even, *a stone,* אוֹת‎ 'oth, *a sign,* אֹרַח‎ 'orah, *a path,* אֵשׁ‎ 'esh, *fire,* הֵיכָל‎ heykal, *a temple,* לָשׁוֹן‎ lashon, *the tongue,* צָבָא‎ zava', *a host,* &c.

5. Many others as generic names of animals are used without distinction to express both genders as גָּמָל‎ gamal, *a camel,* חֲמוֹר‎ ḥamor, *an ass,* צֹאן‎ zo'n, *a flock,* שֶׂה‎ seh, *a lamb,* יוֹנָה‎ yonah, *a dove,* דְּבוֹרָה‎ dĕvorah, *a bee,* &c.

6. Feminine nouns and adjectives are formed from the masculine

1) by adding ה ָ— as מֶלֶךְ melek, *a king*, מַלְכָּה malkah, *a queen*, טוֹב tov, *good*, טִיבָה f.

2) by adding ת ֶ— as רֹמֵשׂ romes, *creeping*, רֹמֶשֶׂת romeseth, f.

3) by changing ִי— into יָה— as מֹאָבִי mo'avi, *a Moabite*, מֹאָבִיָה mo'aviyah f.

4) by changing ִי— into ִית— as שְׁלִישִׁי shelishi, *third*, שְׁלִישִׁית shelishith, f.

Some feminines take either (3) or (4) as מֹאָבִיָה or מֹאָבִית.

7. The dual is formed from the singular by adding ַיִם— as יָד yad, *a hand*, יָדַיִם yadayim, *two hands*.

8. The Plural is formed by adding ים— to masculine nouns as סוּס sus, *a horse*, סוּסִים susim, *horses*, and וֹת to feminine nouns as תּוֹרָה torah, *a law*, תּוֹרֹת toroth, *laws*.

9. Nouns and adjectives in ִי— take ים— or sometimes ִיִים— as גּוֹי goy, *a nation*, גּוֹיִם goyim, *nations, Gentiles*, לֵוִי lewi, *a Levite*, לְוִיִם lewiyim, *Levites*, so נָכְרִי nokri, *strange*, נָכְרִים nokrim, pl. נָקִי naki, *innocent*, נְקִיִּים nekiyim, pl. and עִבְרִי givri, *Hebrew* has commonly עִבְרִים but once Ex. iii. 18. עִבְרִיִּים.

10. The termination ָה— is changed into תַ— in the dual as שָׂפָה safah, *a lip*, שְׂפָתַיִם sefathayim, *two lips*. This change sometimes takes place in the plural as שְׂפָתוֹת sefathoth, *lips*.

11. The termination ֶה— is dropped in the dual and plural as מַחֲנֶה mahaneh, *a camp*, מַחֲנַיִם mahanayim, *two camps*, רֹעֶה rogeh, *a shepherd*, רֹעִים rogim, *shepherds*.

12. The terminations הָ— חָ— חֶ— are dropped in the plural as תְּהִלָּה *tĕhillah, praise,* תְּהִלּוֹת *tĕhilloth, praises,* תּוֹכַחַת *reproof* תּוֹכָחוֹת, but not in דַּעַת and קֶשֶׁת as דְּלָתוֹת; and אָמָה makes in the plural אֲמָהוֹת constr. אַמְהֹת.

13. The terminations ית— and וּת are changed in the plural into יוֹת— and יוֹת— as עִבְרִית *givrith, a Hebrew woman,* עִבְרִיּוֹת *givriyoth, Hebrew women,* מַלְכוּת *malkuth, a kingdom,* מַלְכֻיוֹת *malkuyyoth, kingdoms,* but some form it otherwise as חֲנִית *hănith, a spear,* חֲנִיתִים *hănithim, spears,* זְנוּת *zĕnuth, fornication,* זְנוּתִים *zĕnuthim.*

14. Many masculine nouns however form their plural in וֹת as אָב *'av, a father,* אָבוֹת *'avoth, fathers,* שֵׁם *shem, a name,* שֵׁמוֹת *shĕmoth, names.* These are too numerous to specify: they must be learnt from the Lexicon.

15. Many other nouns make their plural sometimes in ים— and sometimes in וֹת as יוֹם *yom, a day,* דּוֹר *dor, a generation,* נָהָר *nahar, a river,* שָׁנָה *shanah, a year,* עֶצֶם *gezem, a bone,* עֵת *geth, a time,* and many others which must be learnt by practice.

16. Some feminine nouns make their plural in ים—, as אִשָּׁה *'ishshah, a woman,* irreg. pl. נָשִׁים *women,* יוֹנָה *yonah, a dove,* לְבֵנָה *lĕvenah, a brick,* מִלָּה *millah, a word,* פִּילֶגֶשׁ *pilegesh, a concubine,* שִׁבֹּלֶת *shibboleth, a stream,* עִיר *gir, a city,* pl. עָרִים *garim* &c.

17. Some are found in the dual only as מֹאזְנַיִם *mo'zenayim, balances* &c.

18. Some nouns are collective as עוֹף *gof, fowl* or *fowls,* טַף *taf, child* or *children,* צֹאן *zo'n, flock* or *flocks,* &c.

19. Some nouns are used in the singular only as יַיִן yayin, *wine,* זָהָב zahav, *gold,* &c.

20. Some nouns are used in the plural only as מֵעִים m*egim, bowels,* חַיִּים ḥ*ayyim, life,* פָּנִים p*anim, face,* נְעוּרִים n*egurim, youth,* זְקֻנִים z*ekunim, old age,* &c.

21. Sometimes a dual termination is added on to a plural noun as at Is. xxii. 11; Ezek. xxvii. 5 and a mas. pl. constr. to a fem. plural Deut. xxxii. 13. Cf. xxxiii. 29; 1 Sam. xxvi. 12, &c.

22. A Chaldee plural ִין— for ִים— is found in a few places e. g. Prov. xxxi. 3; Ezek. xxvi. 18; 2 K. xi. 13; Lam. i. 4.

23. An anomalous plural form is found in a few places as, Am. vii. 1; Nahum iii. 17; Jer. xxii. 14; Zech. xiv. 5; Is. xix. 9, xx. 4. Cf. שַׂדַי, אֲדֹנָי &c.

CHAPTER VII.

THE CONSTRUCTIVE STATE AND NOUNS WITH AFFIXES.

1. Hebrew nouns have no distinction of case as in Latin, but the cases are expressed by prepositions as in English. The Nominative is called the Absolute and the Accusative the Objective case.

2. The noun which *precedes* a genitive case is said to be *in construction with* the latter noun.

3. Of two nouns so connected in Hebrew, the *first* is commonly altered in form, while the *second* remains unchanged, or in what is called its *absolute* state. Thus דָּבָר *davar, a word*, but דְּבַר יְהֹוָה *the word of the Lord*. In such a case דְּבַר is sometimes called the *antecedent* and יְהֹוָה the *consequent*.

4. The absolute and constructive forms of many nouns are the same and only to be distinguished by position.

5. Many nouns can be joined together in construction the second being the consequent to the first and the antecedent to the third and so on e. g. Is. x. 12; xxi. 17 &c.

6. Every noun in construction is supposed to be definite and therefore cannot take the article.

There are a few anomalous exceptions to this rule, see Gen. ii. 9, vi. 17; Ex. xxviii. 39; 2 K. xxiii. 17; Josh. iii. 14; 2 S. i. 19 &c. In all these cases we may suppose the noun that has the article to be repeated without it, as is the case in Ex. xxxviii. 21 or the two nouns may sometimes be regarded as being in apposition. Very anomalous is הַיֶתֶר Judg. xvi. 14 and הַמִּזְבֵּחַ 2 K. xvi. 14.

7. The following changes take place in nouns when in construction:

    1) ־ָה becomes ־ַה as מַחֲנֶה maḣăneh, *a camp*, מַחֲנֵה־דָן maḣăneh-dan, *the camp of Dan*.

    2) ־ָה becomes ־ַת as הוֹרָה *torah, a law*, הוֹרַת יְהוָה *toráth yĕhowah, the Law of the Lord*.

    3) The ־ַיִם of duals and ־ִים of plurals become ־ֵי as יָדַיִם *yadayim, the hands*, יְדֵי עֵשָׂו *yĕdey gesaw, the hands of Esau*, סוּסִים *susim, horses*, סוּסֵי אֵשׁ *susey 'esh, horses of fire*.

8. When a noun is in construction or an affix is added to it, it commonly undergoes some change in the vowel points, but no antepenultimate vowel is affected thereby. The following are the more important rules which govern this change.

9. A penultimate vowel followed by silent Shĕwa and without the tone is not changed as מֶרְכָּב *merkab, a chariot*, מֶרְכַּבְּי *my chariot*, קָדְקֹד *kodkod, crown of the head*, קָדְקֳרוֹ *his head*, &c.

10. In like manner a penultimate vowel followed by Dagesh is unchangeable as מַקֵּל *makkel, a staff*, כִּיּוֹר *kiyor, a furnace*, תְּהִלָּה *praise*, תְּהִלָּתִי *my praise*, &c.

11. Long *Hirik*, *Holem* and *Shurek* are unchangeable when final as בְּרִית *a covenant,* כּוֹס *a cup,* לְבוּשׁ *a garment,* &c. but

1) יוֹם *a day* makes its plural יָמִים and const. יְמֵי.

2) The following nouns change *Holem* to *Kibbuz* followed by Dagesh before any increment as עֹז *goz, strength,* עֻזּוֹ *guzzo, his strength.*

They are written in English letters both as practice for the student and to avoid a needless use of Hebrew type

'adom *red;* 'ayom *formidable;* 'efod *ephod;* gol *a bowl;* ḋov *bear;* hom *heat;* hok *law;* hartom *wise man;* ḳarḳov *brazier;* lĕ'om *people;* magoz *munition;* nakod *spotted;* sok *thicket;* gagol *round;* goz *strength;* geyrom *naked;* kardom *axe;* karsol *ancle;* rov *abundance;* rok *spittle;* sok *fence;* tom *integrity;* tof *tambourine.*

12. The following words take *Pathah* followed by Dagesh before any increment as גַּן *a garden;* גַּנּוֹ ganno *his garden;* 'ofan *wheel;* 'af *anger;* bad *fine linen;* bath *a measure;* gaw *back;* gal *heap;* gan *garden;* gaf *the top;* dak *poor;* dal *weak;* dak *thin;* hādas *myrtle;* had *sharp;* tal *dew;* taf *children;* kad *pitcher;* kaf *the palm;* mad *tunic;* maḥmad *object of desire;* sal *basket;* gaz *strong;* zav *litter;* kaw *line;* kal *light;* rav *many;* rak *tender;* sak *sackcloth.*

13. The following take short *Hirik* followed by Dagesh before any additional syllable as בַּת bath, *daughter;* בִּתּוֹ bitto, *his daughter;* 'at, *gently;* baz, *spoil;* bath, *daughter;* pl. banoth: gath, *winepress;* hath, *broken;* mad, *extent;* mas, *tribute;* mesav, *round about;* saf, *threshold;* path, *piece;* zad, *side.*

3

14. In the following words *Zerey* becomes short *Hirik* followed by Dagesh as אֵם 'em, *a mother;* אִמּוֹ 'immo, *his mother;* 'ev, *greenness;* 'em, *mother;* 'eth, *ploughshare;* gez, *a mowing;* hek, *the palate;* hen, *favor;* hez, *arrow;* lev, *heart;* magen, *shield;* nes, *banner;* gez, *goat;* geth, *time;* zel, *shadow;* ken, *nest;* kez, *end;* shen, *tooth.* But ḳen *base* makes ḳanno.

15. In these words *Kamez* is changed to Pathaḥ followed by Dagesh before any increment; as יָם yam, *a sea;* יַמִּים yammim, *seas.* 'ulam, *porch;* gag, *roof;* gamal, *camel;* zŏman, *a time;* hag, *feast;* ham, *hot;* yam, *sea;* maḥshak, *darkness;* merhak, *distance;* misgav, *refuge;* gam, *people;* zav, *litter;* katan, *little;* gakrav, *scorpion;* sha'ănan, *quiet;* tam, *upright.*

16. In these words *Kamez* is retained before the light affixes and becomes Shĕwa in constructive plural; as דָּם dam, *blood;* דָּמוֹ damo, *his blood;* dag, *fish;* dam, *blood;* dath, *law;* har, *mountain;* yad, *hand;* kovag, *helmet;* kokav, *star;* mishkan, *tabernacle;* golam, *eternity;* par, *bull;* sar, *prince;* shad, *breast.* But in dath, har and sar the *Kamez* is retained also in constructive Plural.

17. *Kamez* in a final syllable becomes Pathaḥ in construction in the singular and Shĕwa in construction in the plural; as כּוֹכָב kokav, *a star;* construct. sing. כּוֹכַב, constr. pl. כּוֹכְבֵי but the termination אָ‎ָ is not changed in constr. in the singular.

18. *Kamez* in a penultimate syllable becomes Shĕwa in construction in the singular and before any increment as מָקוֹם *a place,* מְקוֹם *the place of,* מְקוֹמִי *my place.* But *Kamez* remains unchanged in bavah, *pupil of the eye;* bamah, *high place;* bariaḥ,

bar; baruth, *food;* galuth, *captivity;* haguth, *meditation;* hazuth, *vision;* harash, *workman;* magen, *shield;* magoz, *refuge;* parash, *horseman;* parashah, *account;* kamah, *standing corn;* ragah, *evil;* rafch, *weak;* saris, *eunuch,* in pl.

19. Nouns of the form דָּבָר become דְּבַר in the singular in construction and before the grave affixes and דְּבָרִים in the Plural absolute and before the light affixes sing. and plur. In the plural construct and before the grave affixes דִּבְרֵי. So also *hazak, strong;* yevalim, *streams of water;* yashar, *upright;* kazav, *lie;* mashal, *proverb;* nataf, *drop;* rashag, *wicked.* But

כָּנָף kanaf, *wing,* makes in the plural construct and before the grave affixes כַּנְפֵי. So also *hadar, glory;* zanav, *tail;* hakam, *wise;* halal, *wounded;* nahar, *river;* ganaf, *branch.*

20. Nouns of the form of זָקֵן *zaken, old man,* make the pl. const. of the form of זִקְנֵי but some follow חָצֵר *hazer, village,* which makes חַצְרֵי.

21. It is a general rule that the grave affixes take the same vowels as the noun in construction whether in the singular, dual or plural.

22. *Segolate nouns.* Nouns of the same form as מֶלֶךְ or סֵפֶר and as קֶמַח or מֶצַח the last letter being a guttural and as נַעַר the middle letter being a guttural, are called Segolate nouns. Segolate nouns are unchanged in construction in the singular and become — ְ ָ in the plural absolute and before the light affixes.

1) In all other parts the following make — ְ ָ as חֵפֶץ hefez, *delight;* חֶפְצוֹ *his delight;* 'evel,

mourning; 'ezel, *near;* gelel, *dung;* het', *sin;* helev, *fat;* heled, *term of life;* helek, *portion;* hefez, *delight;* herem, *accursed thing;* neged, *before*; neked, *posterity;* gever, *passage;* gegel, *calf;* geder, *flock;* gezer, *help;* gerek, *value;* so likewise *h*ävereth, *companion.*

2) While the following make — ־ ־ָ as אֶרֶץ 'erez, *land;* אַרְצוֹ *his land;* all of the form of גֶּבֶר. 'even, *a stone;* 'eden, *a base;* 'ekef, *palm of the hand;* 'elef, *thousand;* 'efes, *end;* 'erez, *cedar;* 'erez, *the earth;* gefen, *vine;* deleth, *door;* derek, *way;* zerah, *rising;* zerag, *seed;* heder, *chamber;* hesed, *kindness;* herev, *sword;* teref, *prey;* yeled, *child;* yerah, *month;* kevel, *fetter;* kelev, *dog;* kesef, *silver;* kerem, *vineyard;* lehem, *bread;* melek, *king;* nefesh, *soul;* selag, *rock;* seranim, *lords;* geved, *servant;* gezem, *bone;* gerev, *evening;* garavim, *willows;* geres, *couch;* peleg, *division;* zelem, *likeness;* zelag, *rib;* zelag, *limping;* zemer, *wool;* kedem, *east;* kelag, *sling;* keren, *horn;* kerasim, *hooks;* kesheth, *bow;* keres, *plank;* regel, *foot;* rehem, *womb;* shelem, *peace-offering;* shemen, *oil;* telem, *furrow;* and so likewise yoneketh, *a sucker;* mishgeneth, *staff,* &c.

3) And the rest which are the most numerous class become — ־ ־ָ as סֵפֶר sefer, *a book;* סִפְרוֹ *his book,* &c. and likewise gevereth, *mistress;* yevemeth, *sister-in-law.*

23. Nouns of the form — ־ָ ־ or — ־ָ ־ָ the second or third letter being a guttural also have the peculiarities of Segolates specified above, and these become — ־ ־ָ before the singular affixes

as חֹדֶשׁ hodesh, *month;* חָדְשׁוֹ *his month;* פֹּעַל pogal, *work,* פָּעֳלוֹ *his work,* פָּעָלְךָ *thy work* (iii. 3).

In the plural absolute Shěwa becomes *Hatef Kamez* in hodesh, *month;* gomer, *sheaf;* gofel, *swelling;* sofer, *wild goat;* kodesh, *holiness,* and in this last also *Kamez Hatuf* but אֹהֶל *a tent,* makes אֹהָלִים, בֹּהֶן *the thumb,* בְּהֹנוֹת and גֹּרֶן *a floor,* גְּרָנוֹת and גֶּשֶׁם *rain,* once Ezek. xxii. 24. makes גָּשְׁמָהּ, סֹבֶךְ *thicket,* once Jer. iv. 7. makes סָבְכוֹ, סֹבֶל *burden,* three times Is. ix. 3, x. 27 and xiv. 25, makes סָבֳלוֹ, קֹמֶץ *handful,* three times Lev. ii. 2, v. 12, vi. 8, makes קֻמְצוֹ and גֹּדֶל *greatness,* once Ps. cl. 2, makes גָּדְלוֹ but otherwise גָּדְלוֹ &c.

In like manner נְחֹשֶׁת *brass,* becomes נְחֻשְׁתּוֹ and so with mahăloketh, *division;* malkodeth, *snare;* maskoreth, *wages;* mathkoneth, *fixed quantity.*

But gulgoleth, *skull;* soleth, *fine flour* and kĕ*'*oreth, *incense,* take *Kamez Hatuf,* as גֻּלְגָּלְתּוֹ but in Judges ix. 53. this becomes גֻּלְגָּלְתּוֹ.

24. Words of the forms —ֶ וּ —ַ and —ִ יְ— become —ְ וּ— and —ְ י— respectively either in construction or before an additional syllable; as מָוֶת maweth, *death;* מֵית מֹשֶׁה *the death of Moses;* בַּיִת bayith, *house;* בֵּיתִי *my house.*

But בַּיִת makes the plural בָּתִּים bottim, and in constr. בָּתֵּי.

25. גְּדִי gĕdi, *kid,* makes גְּדָיוֹ *his kid,* and גְּדָיִים *kids.*
    כְּלִי kĕli, *vessel,* makes כֵּלִים *vessels.*
    חֳלִי hŏli, *sickness,* makes חָלְיוֹ *his sickness,* and חֳלָיִים *sicknesses.*
    אַיָּלָה 'ayyalah, *antelope,* becomes in constr. אַיֶּלֶת.
    פֶּה peh, *mouth,* becomes פִּי in const. and before affixes and makes in the pl. פִּים and פִּיּוֹת.

עִיר *gir, city,* makes pl. עָרִים const. עָרֵי.
רֹאשׁ *ro'sh, head,* makes pl. רָשִׁים.
אִישׁ *'ish, man,* pl. אֲנָשִׁים const. אַנְשֵׁי.
אִשָּׁה *'ishshah, woman,* cr. אֵשֶׁת pl. נָשִׁים cr. נְשֵׁי.
שֶׂה *seh, sheep,* cr. שֵׂה, with aff. שֵׂיוֹ and שֵׂיהוּ

but these and many others must be learnt fully from the Lexicon.

26. From the foregoing rules it may be observed that the nouns in Hebrew are susceptible of the following general division

1) Those which do not change their vowels in inflection as מַלְאָךְ, בְּרִית, שִׁיר, &c.

2) Those which double their final consonant and in such cases shorten the previous vowel, as עַקְרָב, אֵם, בַּת, אַף, &c.

3) Those which shorten a final *Kamez* or *Zerey,* as מִפָּה, כּוֹכָב &c.

4) Those which shorten the penultimate vowel as שָׁלִישׁ, אָרוֹן &c.

5) Those which shorten both vowels, as דָּבָר, זָקֵן &c.

6) Segolate nouns, as מֶלֶךְ &c.

7) Nouns in ־ָה as רֹעֶה &c.

8) Feminine nouns, as מַלְכָּה &c.

Examples of nouns are given in the following chapter according to this general division; but it must be remembered that all the variations of the noun in Hebrew can only be learnt from the Lexicon.

CHAPTER VIII.

EXAMPLES OF NOUNS.

1. Those which do not change their vowels.

שִׁיר shir, *a song.* מַלְבּוּשׁ malbush, *raiment.*

	Sing.	Plur.	Sing.	Plur.
Abs.	שִׁיר	שִׁירִים	מַלְבּוּשׁ	מַלְבּוּשִׁים
Const.	שִׁיר	שִׁירֵי	מַלְבּוּשׁ	מַלְבּוּשֵׁי
My.	שִׁירִי	שִׁירַי	מַלְבּוּשִׁי	מַלְבּוּשַׁי
Thy. m.	שִׁירְךָ	שִׁירֶיךָ	מַלְבּוּשְׁךָ	מַלְבּוּשֶׁיךָ
Thy. f.	שִׁירֵךְ	שִׁירַיִךְ	מַלְבּוּשֵׁךְ	מַלְבּוּשַׁיִךְ
His.	שִׁירוֹ	שִׁירָיו	מַלְבּוּשׁוֹ	מַלְבּוּשָׁיו
Her.	שִׁירָהּ	שִׁירֶיהָ	מַלְבּוּשָׁהּ	מַלְבּוּשֶׁיהָ
Our.	שִׁירֵנוּ	שִׁירֵינוּ	מַלְבּוּשֵׁנוּ	מַלְבּוּשֵׁינוּ
Your. m.	שִׁירְכֶם	שִׁירֵיכֶם	מַלְבּוּשְׁכֶם	מַלְבּוּשֵׁיכֶם
Your. f.	שִׁירְכֶן	שִׁירֵיכֶן	מַלְבּוּשְׁכֶן	מַלְבּוּשֵׁיכֶן
Their. m.	שִׁירָם	שִׁירֵיהֶם	מַלְבּוּשָׁם	מַלְבּוּשֵׁיהֶם
Their. f.	שִׁירָן	שִׁירֵיהֶן	מַלְבּוּשָׁן	מַלְבּוּשֵׁיהֶן

2. Those which change the vowel and double the consonant.

	אֵם 'em, *a mother.*		מִשְׂגָּב misgav, *a fortress.*	
	Sing.	Plur.	Sing.	Plur.
Abs.	אֵם	אִמּוֹת	מִשְׂגָּב	מִשְׂגַּבִּים
Constr.	אֵם	אִמּוֹת	מִשְׂגַּב	מִשְׂגַּבֵּי
My.	אִמִּי	אִמּוֹתַי	מִשְׂגַּבִּי	מִשְׂגַּבַּי
Thy. m.	אִמְּךָ	אִמּוֹתֶיךָ	מִשְׂגַּבְּךָ	מִשְׂגַּבֶּיךָ
Thy. f.	אִמֵּךְ	אִמּוֹתַיִךְ	מִשְׂגַּבֵּךְ	מִשְׂגַּבַּיִךְ
His.	אִמּוֹ	אִמּוֹתָיו	מִשְׂגַּבּוֹ	מִשְׂגַּבָּיו
Her.	אִמָּהּ	אִמּוֹתֶיהָ	מִשְׂגַּבָּהּ	מִשְׂגַּבֶּיהָ
Our.	אִמֵּנוּ	אִמּוֹתֵינוּ	מִשְׂגַּבֵּנוּ	מִשְׂגַּבֵּינוּ
Your. m.	אִמְּכֶם	אִמּוֹתֵיכֶם	מִשְׂגַּבְּכֶם	מִשְׂגַּבֵּיכֶם
Your. f.	אִמְּכֶן	אִמּוֹתֵיכֶן	מִשְׂגַּבְּכֶן	מִשְׂגַּבֵּיכֶן
Their. m.	אִמָּם	אִמּוֹתֵיהֶם	מִשְׂגַּבָּם	מִשְׂגַּבֵּיהֶם
Their. f.	אִמָּן	אִמּוֹתֵיהֶן	מִשְׂגַּבָּן	מִשְׂגַּבֵּיהֶן

בֵּן ben, *a son*, makes in constr. בֶּן (but in Prov. xxx. 1 and always in the phrase "Joshua the son of Nun" בִּן) with affixes בְּנִי, בִּנְךָ, in plur. בָּנִים const. בְּנֵי.

בַּת bath, *a daughter*, makes בִּתִּי pl. בָּנוֹת const. בְּנוֹת.

3. Those which shorten the final vowel.

	כּוֹכָב kokav, *a star*.		מוֹפֵת mofeth, *a wonder*.	
	Sing.	Plur.	Sing.	Plur.
Abs.	כּוֹכָב	כּוֹכָבִים	מוֹפֵת	מוֹפְתִים
Constr.	כּוֹכַב¹	כּוֹכְבֵי	מוֹפֵת¹	מוֹפְתֵי
My.	כּוֹכָבִי¹	כּוֹכָבַי	מוֹפְתִי¹	מוֹפְתַי
Thy. m.	כּוֹכָבְךָ	כּוֹכָבֶיךָ	מוֹפֶתְךָ²	מוֹפְתֶיךָ
Thy. f.	כּוֹכָבֵךְ	כּוֹכָבַיִךְ	מוֹפְתֵךְ	מוֹפְתַיִךְ
His.	כּוֹכָבוֹ	כּוֹכָבָיו	מוֹפְתוֹ	מוֹפְתָיו
Her.	כּוֹכָבָהּ	כּוֹכָבֶיהָ	מוֹפְתָהּ	מוֹפְתֶיהָ
Our.	כּוֹכָבֵנוּ	כּוֹכָבֵינוּ	מוֹפְתֵנוּ	מוֹפְתֵינוּ
Your. m.	כּוֹכַבְכֶם	כּוֹכְבֵיכֶם	מוֹפֶתְכֶם	מוֹפְתֵיכֶם
Your. f.	כּוֹכַבְכֶן	כּוֹכְבֵיכֶן	מוֹפֶתְכֶן	מוֹפְתֵיכֶן
Their. m.	כּוֹכָבָם	כּוֹכְבֵיהֶם	מוֹפְתָם	מוֹפְתֵיהֶם
Their. f.	כּוֹכָבָן	כּוֹכְבֵיהֶן	מוֹפְתָן	מוֹפְתֵיהֶן

1. It will be seen that the *Kamez* is shortened in construction but retained before the light affixes while the *Zerey* is retained in construction and shortened before the affixes.

2. Some as אֹיֵב 'oyev, *an enemy*, make אֹיִבְךָ &c. In like manner cf. Ps. xxx. 2 and 13 in the case of verbs (iii. 1).

4. Those which shorten the penultimate vowel.

	אָדוֹן 'adon, a lord.		מֵלִיץ meliz, an interpreter.	
	Sing.	Plur.	Sing.	Plur.
Abs.	אָדוֹן	אֲדוֹנִים	מֵלִיץ	מְלִיצִים
Const.	אֲדוֹן	אֲדוֹנֵי	מְלִיץ	מְלִיצֵי
My.	אֲדוֹנִי	אֲדוֹנַי	מְלִיצִי	מְלִיצַי
Thy. m.	אֲדוֹנְךָ	אֲדוֹנֶיךָ	מְלִיצְךָ	מְלִיצֶיךָ
Thy. f.	אֲדוֹנֵךְ	אֲדוֹנַיִךְ	מְלִיצֵךְ	מְלִיצַיִךְ
His.	אֲדוֹנוֹ	אֲדוֹנָיו	מְלִיצוֹ	מְלִיצָיו
Her.	אֲדוֹנָהּ	אֲדוֹנֶיהָ	מְלִיצָהּ	מְלִיצֶיהָ
Our.	אֲדוֹנֵנוּ	אֲדוֹנֵינוּ	מְלִיצֵנוּ	מְלִיצֵינוּ
Your. m.	אֲדוֹנְכֶם	אֲדוֹנֵיכֶם	מְלִיצְכֶם	מְלִיצֵיכֶם
Your. f.	אֲדוֹנְכֶן	אֲדוֹנֵיכֶן	מְלִיצְכֶן	מְלִיצֵיכֶן
Their. m.	אֲדוֹנָם	אֲדוֹתֵיהֶם	מְלִיצָם	מְלִיצֵיהֶם
Their. f.	אֲדוֹנָן	אֲדוֹנֵיהֶן	מְלִיצָן	מְלִיצֵיהֶן

5. Those which shorten both vowels.

	דָּבָר davar, a word.		חָכָם hakam, a wise man.	
	Sing.	Plur.	Sing.	Plur.
Abs.	דָּבָר	דְּבָרִים	חָכָם	חֲכָמִים
Const.	דְּבַר	דִּבְרֵי	חֲכַם	חַכְמֵי
My.	דְּבָרִי	דְּבָרַי	חֲכָמִי	חֲכָמַי
Thy. m.	דְּבָרְךָ	דְּבָרֶיךָ	חֲכָמְךָ	חֲכָמֶיךָ
Thy. f.	דְּבָרֵךְ	דְּבָרַיִךְ	חֲכָמֵךְ	חֲכָמַיִךְ
His.	דְּבָרוֹ	דְּבָרָיו	חֲכָמוֹ	חֲכָמָיו
Her.	דְּבָרָהּ	דְּבָרֶיהָ	חֲכָמָהּ	חֲכָמֶיהָ
Our.	דְּבָרֵנוּ	דְּבָרֵינוּ	חֲכָמֵנוּ	חֲכָמֵינוּ
Your. m.	דְּבַרְכֶם	דִּבְרֵיכֶם	חֲכַמְכֶם	חַכְמֵיכֶם
Your. f.	דְּבַרְכֶן	דִּבְרֵיכֶן	חֲכַמְכֶן	ח׳ ׳ כֶן
Their. m.	דְּבָרָם	דִּבְרֵיהֶם	חֲכָמָם	חַכְמֵיהֶם
Their. f.	דְּבָרָן	דִּבְרֵיהֶן	חֲכָמָן	חַכְמֵיהֶן

The same continued.

	¹ זָקֵן zaken, an old man.		חָצֵר hazer, a village.	
	Sing.	Plur.	Sing.	Plur.
Abs.	זָקֵן	זְקֵנִים	חָצֵר	חֲצֵרִים
Constr.	זְקַן	זִקְנֵי	חֲצַר	חַצְרֵי
My.	זְקֵנִי	זְקֵנַי	חֲצֵרִי	חֲצֵרַי
Thy. m.	זְקֵנְךָ	זְקֵנֶיךָ	חֲצֵרְךָ	חֲצֵרֶיךָ
Thy. f.	זְקֵנֵךְ	זְקֵנַיִךְ	חֲצֵרֵךְ	חֲצֵרַיִךְ
His.	זְקֵנוֹ	זְקֵנָיו	חֲצֵרוֹ	חֲצֵרָיו
Her.	זְקֵנָהּ	זְקֵנֶיהָ	חֲצֵרָהּ	חֲצֵרֶיהָ
Our.	זְקֵנֵנוּ	זְקֵנֵינוּ	חֲצֵרֵנוּ	חֲצֵרֵינוּ
Your. m.	זְקֶנְכֶם	זִקְנֵיכֶם	חֲצַרְכֶם	חַצְרֵיכֶם
Your. f.	זְקֶנְכֶן	זִקְנֵיכֶן	חֲצַרְכֶן	חַצְרֵיכֶן
Their. m.	זְקֵנָם	זִקְנֵיהֶם	חֲצַרָם	חַצְרֵיהֶם
Their. f.	זְקֵנָן	זִקְנֵיהֶן	חֲצַרָן	חַצְרֵיהֶן

1. Words of this form sometimes become Segolates in construction, as כָּתֵף const. כֶּתֶף otherwise following זָקֵן, but some retain Zerey in pl. const. as שְׁנֵי, יְשֵׁנֵי &c.

6. Segolate nouns.

		מֶלֶךְ melek, *a king.*		סֵפֶר sefer, *a book.*	
		Sing.	Plur.	Sing.	Plur.
Abs.		מֶלֶךְ	מְלָכִים	סֵפֶר	סְפָרִים
Constr.		מֶלֶךְ	מַלְכֵי	סֵפֶר	סִפְרֵי
My.		מַלְכִּי	מְלָכַי	סִפְרִי	סְפָרַי
Thy.	m.	מַלְכְּךָ	מְלָכֶיךָ	סִפְרְךָ	סְפָרֶיךָ
Thy.	f.	מַלְכֵּךְ	מְלָכַיִךְ	סִפְרֵךְ	סְפָרַיִךְ
His.		מַלְכּוֹ	מְלָכָיו	סִפְרוֹ	סְפָרָיו
Her.		מַלְכָּהּ	מְלָכֶיהָ	סִפְרָהּ	סְפָרֶיהָ
Our.		מַלְכֵּנוּ	מְלָכֵינוּ	סִפְרֵנוּ	סְפָרֵינוּ
Your.	m.	מַלְכְּכֶם	מַלְכֵיכֶם	סִפְרְכֶם	סִפְרֵיכֶם
Your.	f.	מַלְכְּכֶן	מַלְכֵיכֶן	סִפְרְכֶן	סִפְרֵיכֶן
Their.	m.	מַלְכָּם	מַלְכֵיהֶם	סִפְרָם	סִפְרֵיהֶם
Their.	f.	מַלְכָּן	מַלְכֵיהֶן	סִפְרָן	סִפְרֵיהֶן

Segolate Nouns.

	חֵפֶץ ḥefez, delight.		פֹּעַל poḡal, work.	
	Sing.	Plur.	Sing.	Plur.
Abs.	חֵפֶץ	חֲפָצִים	פֹּעַל	פְּעָלִים
Const.	חֵפֶץ	חֶפְצֵי	פֹּעַל	פַּעֲלֵי
My.	חֶפְצִי	חֲפָצַי	פָּעֳלִי	פְּעָלַי
Thy. m.	חֶפְצְךָ	חֲפָצֶיךָ	פָּעָלְךָ	פְּעָלֶיךָ
Thy. f.	חֶפְצֵךְ	חֲפָצַיִךְ	פָּעֳלֵךְ	פְּעָלַיִךְ
His.	חֶפְצוֹ	חֲפָצָיו	פָּעֳלוֹ	פְּעָלָיו
Her.	חֶפְצָהּ	חֲפָצֶיהָ	פָּעֳלָהּ	פְּעָלֶיהָ
Our.	חֶפְצֵנוּ	חֲפָצֵינוּ	פָּעֳלֵנוּ	פְּעָלֵינוּ
Your. m.	חֶפְצְכֶם	חֲפָצֵיכֶם	פָּעָלְכֶם	פְּעָלֵיכֶם
Your. f.	חֶפְצְכֶן	חֲפָצֵיכֶן	פָּעָלְכֶן	פְּעָלֵיכֶן
Their. m.	חֶפְצָם	חֲפָצֵיהֶם	פָּעֳלָם	פְּעָלֵיהֶם
Their. f.	חֶפְצָן	חֲפָצֵיהֶן	פָּעֳלָן	פְּעָלֵיהֶן

	Segolate nouns cont.		7. Nouns in ה⸺ָ.	
	אֹזֶן 'ozen, *an ear.*		מַעֲשֶׂה ma*gásch*, a work.	
	Sing.	Dual.	Sing.	Plur.
Abs.	אֹזֶן	אָזְנַיִם	מַעֲשֶׂה	מַעֲשִׂים
Const.	אֹזֶן	אָזְנֵי	מַעֲשֵׂה	מַעֲשֵׂי
My.	אָזְנִי	אָזְנַי	מַעֲשִׂי	מַעֲשַׂי
Thy. m.	אָזְנְךָ	אָזְנֶיךָ	מַעֲשְׂךָ	מַעֲשֶׂיךָ
Thy. f.	אָזְנֵךְ	אָזְנַיִךְ	מַעֲשֵׂךְ	מַעֲשַׂיִךְ
His.	אָזְנוֹ	אָזְנָיו	מַעֲשֵׂהוּ[1]	מַעֲשָׂיו
Her.	אָזְנָהּ	אָזְנֶיהָ	מַעֲשֶׂיהָ[1]	מַעֲשֶׂיהָ
Our.	אָזְנֵנוּ	אָזְנֵינוּ	מַעֲשֵׂנוּ	מַעֲשֵׂינוּ
Your. m.	אָזְנְכֶם	אָזְנֵיכֶם	מַעֲשְׂכֶם	מַעֲשֵׂיכֶם
Your. f.	אָזְנְכֶן	אָזְנֵיכֶן	מַעֲשְׂכֶן	מַעֲשֵׂיכֶן
Their. m.	אָזְנָם	אָזְנֵיהֶם	מַעֲשָׂם	מַעֲשֵׂיהֶם
Their. f.	אָזְנָן	אָזְנֵיהֶן	מַעֲשָׂן	מַעֲשֵׂיהֶן

1. Nouns in ה⸺ָ prefer these affixes as being less harsh.

8. Feminine Nouns.

	שָׁנָה shanah, a year.		מַלְכָּה malkah, a queen.	
	Sing.	Plur.	Sing.	Plur.
Abs.	שָׁנָה	שָׁנוֹת	מַלְכָּה	מְלָכוֹת
Const.	שְׁנַת	שְׁנוֹת	מַלְכַּת	מַלְכוֹת
My.	שְׁנָתִי	שְׁנוֹתַי	מַלְכָּתִי	מַלְכוֹתַי
Thy. m.	שְׁנָתְךָ	שְׁנוֹתֶיךָ	מַלְכָּתְךָ	מַלְכוֹתֶיךָ
Thy. f.	שְׁנָתֵךְ	שְׁנוֹתַיִךְ	מַלְכָּתֵךְ	מַלְכוֹתַיִךְ
His.	שְׁנָתוֹ	שְׁנוֹתָיו	מַלְכָּתוֹ	מַלְכוֹתָיו
Her.	שְׁנָתָהּ	שְׁנוֹתֶיהָ	מַלְכָּתָהּ	מַלְכוֹתֶיהָ
Our.	שְׁנָתֵנוּ	שְׁנוֹתֵינוּ	מַלְכָּתֵנוּ	מַלְכוֹתֵינוּ
Your. m.	שְׁנַתְכֶם	שְׁנוֹתֵיכֶם	מַלְכַּתְכֶם	מַלְכוֹתֵיכֶם
Your. f.	שְׁנַתְכֶן	שְׁנוֹתֵיכֶן	מַלְכַּתְכֶן	מַלְכוֹתֵיכֶן
Their. m.	שְׁנָתָם	שְׁנוֹתֵיהֶם	מַלְכָּתָם	מַלְכוֹתֵיהֶם
Their. f.	שְׁנָתָן	שְׁנוֹתֵיהֶן	מַלְכָּתָן	מַלְכוֹתֵיהֶן

1. Segolate Feminines vary as their masculine forms, thus: עֶרְקָה const. צִרְקַת: הֶרְפָּה, const. הֶרְפַּת: הָרְבָּה const. הָרְבַּת. In other respects they follow the analogy of this noun.

2. Feminines ending in a double *Kamez*, as תִּפְאָרָה מִלְחָמָה &c. make in const. מִלְחֶמֶת, תִּפְאֶרֶת and with affix מִלְחַמְתִּי, תִּפְאַרְתִּי &c. but in some cases this const. is also an additional absolute form e. g. 1 S. xiii. 22; Ps. xcvi. 6 &c.

EXAMPLES OF NOUNS.

9. The following nouns are irregular:

a) מַיִם *water*, const. מֵי or מֵימֵי with affix מֵימַי &c.

b) אָב *a father*, const. אֲבִי (once אַב Gen. xvii. 5) with affix. אָבִיךָ, אָבִיו and אָבִיהוּ, אָבִיהָ, אָבִיהֶן, אֲבִיהֶם, אֲבִיכֶן, אֲבִיכֶם אָבִיט

plur. אָבוֹת const. אֲבוֹת with affix. אֲבוֹתַי, אֲבוֹתָם or אֲבוֹתֵיהֶם, אֲבוֹתֵיכֶם, אֲבוֹתֵינוּ, אֲבוֹתָיו, אֲבוֹתֶיךָ.

c) אָח *a brother*, const. אֲחִי, with affix. אָחִי, אָחִיךָ, אָחִיו or אֶחִיהוּ, אָחִיהָ, אָחִינוּ, אֲחִיכֶם, אֲחִיהֶם.

plu. אַחִים const. אֲחֵי, with affix אַחַי, in p. אֶחָיו, אָחִיךָ, אַחִיךְ, אָחִיו, אַחֶיהָ, אַחֵינוּ, אֲחֵיכֶם, אֲחֵיהֶם.

d) אָחוֹת *a sister*, const. אֲחוֹת with affix. אֲחוֹתִי, אֲחוֹתְךָ, אֲחוֹתֵךְ, אֲחוֹתוֹ, אֲחוֹתָהּ, אֲחוֹתֵנוּ, אֲחוֹתְכֶם, אֲחוֹתָם.

plu. with affix. אַחְיוֹתַי, אַחְיוֹתֶיךָ, אַחְיוֹתֵיכֶם or אַחְיוֹתָיו, אַחְיוֹתַי, אַחְיוֹתֵיהֶם.

e) חָם *a father-in-law*, is found with affixes חָמִיךְ, חָמִיהָ and

f) חָמוֹת *a mother-in-law*, with affixes חֲמוֹתֵךְ and חֲמוֹתָהּ.

g) גַּיְא or גַּיְא or גַּיְ *a valley*, makes const. גֵּיא or גֵּי plu. גֵּיאָיוֹת with affix. גֵּיאוֹתֶיךָ.

h) דָּם *blood*, makes דִּמְכֶם and

i) יָד *a hand*, makes יְדֵכֶם and יֶדְכֶם

k) שְׂלָו *a quail*, makes שַׂלְוִים

l) דְּלִי *a bucket*, makes דָּלְיָו

m) Some words of the form גְּזֵלָה, בְּרֵכָה &c. retain the *Zerey* in inflection as בְּרֵכַת but נְבֵלָה makes נִבְלַת, and once נְבֵלָתִי, Is. xxvi. 19.

n) The form —ֶ—ָ becomes —ְ—ַ before an affix, as פָּקָר, פִּקְרֵי.

o) פְּרִי *fruit*, makes פִּרְיוֹ, פֶּרְיְךָ, פֶּרְיֵךְ, פֶּרְיְכֶם, פִּרְיָהֶם and פִּרְיָם.

CHAPTER IX.

THE NUMERALS.

1. With numbers above ten there is no distinction between cardinals and ordinals.

2. To ten inclusive the numerals mark the masculine and feminine, the absolute and constructive state. From eleven to nineteen inclusive they mark the masculine and feminine only, while the tens have but one form for both genders and either state.

3. The cardinals generally stand *before* the noun they number (unless for emphasis as Gen. xxxii. 15, 16) and from 1 to 10 either in apposition or construction with it.

It is chiefly in the later books that the noun stands *first*, in apposition.* In every case the masculine form is mostly used with feminine nouns and the feminine form with masculine nouns Job. i. 2, 3; 1 Ch. xxv. 5 &c. except in the case of 1 and 2 when the numeral agrees in gender with the noun. Once or twice in construction 2 K. xii. 10; 2 Ch. xxiv. 8; Cf. Lev. xxiv. 22.

* When the noun stands in construction with the number it is generally as an ordinal 2 K. xviii. 1 &c.

4. From 3 to 10 inclusive the noun is put in the plural, for numbers above 10 the noun is put in the singular but there are some exceptions Ex. xxxvi. 23, Josh. vii. 21 &c. When a noun precedes a number above 10 it must stand in the plural 2 Ch. iii. 3.

5. In a number composed of hundreds tens and units the lower numbers may either precede or follow the higher. Cf. Gen. v. 18 and Ezra ii. 4. The latter mode prevails in the later books. When the tens precede or follow the units the conjunction ו must be used. In expressing thousands &c. the thousands stand first Num. iv. 48.

6. When numerals are used distributively they are repeated as שְׁנַיִם שְׁנַיִם *two and two*, i. e. by twos Gen. vii. 9 &c.

7. Numerals expressing the English *fold* are used in the dual as אַרְבַּעְתַּיִם 2 Sam. xii. 6.

8. They are occasionally found with an affix as שְׁנֵינוּ *both of us*, Gen. xxxi. 37. שְׁלָשְׁתְּכֶם *you three*, Num. xii. 4 &c.

9. We meet with a plural to *one* אֲחָדִים Gen. xi. 1 and a plural to *ten* עֲשָׂרוֹת *the chiefs of tens*, Ex. xviii. 25.

10. The construction of the ordinals is like that of adjectives. They are made feminine by adding ת, but the fem. of רִאשׁוֹן is רִאשׁוֹנָה.

Chap. XI.]   THE NUMERALS.   53

The following is a table of the Hebrew numerals with the corresponding alphabetical notation.

	Cardinals.				Ordinals.	
	Masculine.		Feminine.		Mas.	
	Abs.	Const.	Abs.	Const.		
1	אֶחָד	אַחַד	אַחַת \} אֶחָת	אַחַת	רִאשׁוֹן	א
2	שְׁנַיִם	שְׁנֵי	שְׁתַּיִם	שְׁתֵּי	שֵׁנִי	ב
3	שָׁלֹשׁ	שְׁלֹשׁ	שְׁלֹשָׁה	שְׁלֹשֶׁת	שְׁלִישִׁי	ג
4	אַרְבַּע		אַרְבָּעָה	אַרְבַּעַת	רְבִיעִי	ד
5	חָמֵשׁ	חֲמֵשׁ	חֲמִשָּׁה	חֲמֵשֶׁת	חֲמִישִׁי	ה
6	שֵׁשׁ		שִׁשָּׁה	שֵׁשֶׁת	שִׁשִּׁי	ו
7	שֶׁבַע	שְׁבַע	שִׁבְעָה	שִׁבְעַת	שְׁבִיעִי	ז
8	שְׁמֹנֶה		שְׁמֹנָה	שְׁמֹנַת	שְׁמִינִי	ח
9	תֵּשַׁע	תְּשַׁע	תִּשְׁעָה	תִּשְׁעַת	תְּשִׁיעִי	ט
10	עֶשֶׂר		עֲשָׂרָה	עֲשֶׂרֶת	עֲשִׂירִי	י

In 4. 6. 8. 10 the masc. abs. and constr. are alike.

Examples 1 שְׁנַיִם אֲנָשִׁים: 2 שָׂפָה אֶחָת: אִישׁ אֶחָד
שְׁתַּיִם נָשִׁים: 3 שְׁלֹשֶׁת יָמִים: שְׁלֹשָׁה בָּנִים: בָּנוֹת שָׁלֹשׁ:
עֲשָׂרָה שְׁקָלִים: עֲשָׂרָה יָמִים: עֶשֶׂר נָשִׁים 10 עֶשְׂרִים שָׁנָה 20.
עֶשְׂרִים וּשְׁתַּיִם שָׁנָה 22 &c.

Cardinals and Ordinals.

	For feminine nouns.		For masculine nouns.	
11	עַשְׁתֵּי ע׳ or אַחַד עָשָׂר		אַחַת עֶשְׂרֵה or עַשְׁתֵּי ע׳	יא
12	שְׁנֵים ע׳ or שְׁנֵי ע׳		שְׁתֵּים ע׳ or שְׁתֵּי ע׳	יב
13	שְׁלֹשָׁה ע׳		שָׁלֹשׁ ע׳	יג
14	אַרְבָּעָה ע׳		אַרְבַּע ע׳	יד
15	חֲמִשָּׁה ע׳		חָמֵשׁ ע׳	טו
16	שִׁשָּׁה ע׳		שֵׁשׁ ע׳	יו
17	שִׁבְעָה ע׳		שְׁבַע ע׳	יז
18	שְׁמֹנָה ע׳		שְׁמֹנֶה ע׳	יח
19	תִּשְׁעָה ע׳		תְּשַׁע ע׳	יט
20	עֶשְׂרִים	כ	400	אַרְבַּע מ׳	ת
21	אַחַד/אַחַת } וְעֶשְׂרִים	כא	500	חֲמֵשׁ מ׳	ר
30	שְׁלֹשִׁים	ל	600	שֵׁשׁ מ׳	ס
40	אַרְבָּעִים	מ	700	שְׁבַע מ׳	ן
50	חֲמִשִּׁים	נ	800	שְׁמֹנֶה מ׳	ף
60	שִׁשִּׁים	ס	900	תְּשַׁע מ׳	ץ
70	שִׁבְעִים	ע	1000	אֶלֶף	א
80	שְׁמֹנִים	פ	2000	אַלְפַּיִם	ב
90	תִּשְׁעִים	צ	3000	שְׁלֹשֶׁת אֲלָפִים	ג
100	מֵאָה, const. מְאַת	ק	10000	רִבּוֹא, עֲשֶׂרֶת א׳	י
200	מָאתַיִם	ר	20000	רִבֹּתַיִם, עֶשְׂרִים אֶלֶף	כ
300	שְׁלֹשׁ מֵאוֹת	ש	100000	מֵאָה א׳ or מְאַת א׳	ק

For examples of the use of the numerals, see Gen. v. &c.

CHAPTER X.

THE VERB.

1. The Verb has only two tenses a past and a future: but neither of these is used exclusively for the expression of past or future time. Some call the future a present and some an aorist.

There is also an Imperative mood.

The Infinitive is really a noun of action and takes the affixes like a noun. There are two participles one active the other passive each marking the feminine and the plural but both indeterminate as to time.

The past is sometimes a future and the future a past. The circumstances under which this happens will be explained afterwards.

2. The following is a model of the regular verb:

	Past Tense.			Future Tense.	
	Sing.	Plur.		Sing.	Plur.
3 m.	a. פָּקַד	פָּקְרוּ	3 m.	c. יִפְקֹד	b. יִפְקְרוּ
3 f.	פָּקְדָה		3 f.	c. תִּפְקֹד	c. תִּפְקֹדְנָה
2 m.	פָּקַרְתָּ	פְּקַרְתֶּם	2 m.	c. תִּפְקֹד	b. תִּפְקְרוּ
2 f.	פָּקַרְתְּ	פְּקַרְתֶּן	2 f.	b. תִּפְקְדִי	c. תִּפְקֹדְנָה
1	פָּקַרְתִּי	פָּקַרְנוּ	1	c. אֶפְקֹד	c. נִפְקֹד

Imperative mood.

	Sing.	Plur.
2 m.	פְּקֹד c	פִּקְדוּ b.
2 f.	פִּקְדִי b.	פְּקֹדְנָה c.

Infinitive mood.

Abs. פָּקוֹד constr. פְּקֹד c with affix פָּקְדִי

Participles.

	Active.	Passive.
S. m.	פֹּקֵד	פָּקוּד
f.	פֹּקֶדֶת or פֹּקְדָה	פְּקוּדָה
Pl. m.	פֹּקְדִים	פְּקוּדִים
f.	פֹּקְדוֹת	פְּקוּדוֹת

3. It must be borne in mind that Dagesh is inserted in the initial letter of this verb because it is an aspirate; when it ceases to be initial, it is omitted. In like manner when the 2d radical is an aspirate it takes Dagesh in the Future יִגְבֹּר בָּנַד &c.

a. Some verbs have Zerey here instead of Pathah as:

'afes, failed; zaken, was old; hamez, was sour; hanef, was profane; haser, lacked; hazev, cut; hafez, wished; harev, was dry; taher, was clean; tame', was polluted; yavesh, was dry; yare', feared; male', was full of; navel, wasted away; gayef, was weary; sane', hated; shafel, was low.

Some verbs have either Zerey or Pathah as:

'ahev or 'ahav, loved; gadal or gadel, was great; kaved or kavad, was heavy; karav or karev, was near; sha'el or sha'al, asked.

Some verbs have *H*olem instead of Patha*h* as: yagor, *feared;* yakol, *was able;* yakosh, *ensnared;* katon, *was small;* shakol, *was childless.*

These last form their Past tense as follows:

	Sing.		Plur.
3 m.	יָכֹל		יָכְלוּ
3 f.	יָכְלָה		
2 m.	יָכֹלְתָּ		יְכָלְתֶּם
2 f.	יָכֹלְתְּ		יְכָלְתֶּן
1	יָכֹלְתִּי		יָכֹלְנוּ

b. In pause the Shëwa of the second radical becomes *K*amez, *Z*erey or *H*olem according to the vowel of the verb.

c. Instead of *H*olem in the Future, Imperative, and Infinitive constructive, many verbs have Patha*h*.

4. The verbs which take Patha*h* are

1) Those whose third letter is ה, ח, ע.

2) All whose second letter is a guttural, except naham, *roared.*

3) Generally those with a neuter signification.

4) And the following:

'atar, *shut;* haraz, *cut;* lavash, *put on raiment;* nashal, *pulled off;* nashak, *kissed;* sathar, *concealed;* gathar, *entreated;* pazar, *urged;* pashat, *spread;* karam, *overlaid;* rakav, *rode.*

The rest have *H*olem.

5. The following verbs take sometimes *H*olem and sometimes Patha*h*:

gazar, *cut;* halak, *went;* halash, *weakened;* hafez, *delighted in;* shavath, *rested;* taraf, *tore.*

6. Verbs whose third letter is א have K'amez instead of Holem in the Future and Imperative.

7. Verbs whose third letter is ה have Segol instead of Holem in the Future and Zerey in the Imperative.

8. The first or simplest conjugation which is given above is called קַל i. e. *light* or *unencumbered*.

Besides this there are six other common forms or conjugations which are named from the corresponding forms of the verb פָּעַל *did* which has inconveniently been selected as the representative verb e. g.

    II. נִפְעַל   V. הִפְעִיל
    III. פִּעֵל   VI. הִפְעַל
    IV. פֻּעַל   VII. הִתְפַּעֵל

9. Besides these there are several others of less frequent occurrence whose names are as follows:

VIII. הָתְפָּעַל pass. of Hithp*ag*el. Num. i. 47, Cf. Deut. xxiv. 4, Is. xxxiv. 6.

IX. נִתְפָּעֵל an Aramaic form of Hithp*ag*el. Deut. xxi. 8, Prov. xxvii. 15.

X. אִתְפָּעֵל an Aramaic from of Ilithp*ag*el. Ps. lxxvi. 6, 2 Chr. xx. 35.

XI. and XII. פִּלְפֵּל and פֻּלְפַּל only belong to hollow verbs or verbs of doubled radical and correspond to Pi*g*el and Pu*g*al in other verbs Is. xxii. 17, 1 K. xx. 27 &c. &c.

XIII. הִתְפַּלְפֵּל Reflective of Pilpel. Esther iv. 4, Job. xxx. 14.

XIV. פָּעֲלַל Intensive. Ezek. xxviii. 23.

XV. פְּעֻלַל Pass. of do. Ps. vi. 3.

XVI. תִּפְעֵל Causal. Hos. xi. 3.

XVII. פְּעַלְעַל Intensive. Ps. xxxviii. 11. Cf. Prov. xxi. 8, Job. xvi. 16, Lam. i. 20; ii. 11.

No verb is found in all these conjugations. פעל itself is only found in Kal. קטל *killed* which is often given as the model verb is only found three times and in Kal. פקד *visited* is found in 8 conjugations.

10. The general relation of these forms to one another as regards meaning is as follows. The Lexicons will specify their signification more precisely in particular cases.

    II. Passive of I. or reflective Gen. iii. 10, Ps. lv. 13. Cf. Job. xxix. 10, 2 S. xx. 10 &c.

    III. Transitive when I. is not so, otherwise Intensive, Frequentative or Causal.

    IV. Passive of III.

    V. Causative; sometimes simply transitive.

    VI. Passive of V.

    VII. Reflective, Reciprocal (Gen. xlii. 1, Job. xli. 9) or Passive. Sometimes it implies *pretending* as Prov. xiii. 7 or *behaving like* 1 Sam. i. 14, xxi. 16, 2 Sam. xiii. 5. Sometimes the Hithp*agel* is merely passive. Prov. xxxi. 30, Lam. ii. 12, iv. 1, Micah vi. 16, Ezek. xix. 12, Gen. xxii. 18 &c.

11. The last syllable of the Future is sometimes shortened or rejected. The word is then said to be *apocopated*.

12. The syllable הָ— is sometimes added to the Future and Imperative. The Future is then hortative or inferential and the Imperative emphatic.

13. Paradigm of a Regular Verb.

The Past Tense. *he visited.*

	I.	II.	III.	IV.	V. פֻּעַל	VI.	VII.
Sing.							
3. m.	פָּקַד	פִּקֵּד	פֻּקַּד	הִפְקִיד	הָפְקַד	הִתְפַּקֵּד	נִתְפַּקֵּד
3. f.	פָּקְדָה	פִּקְּדָה	פֻּקְּדָה	הִפְקִידָה	הָפְקְדָה	הִתְפַּקְּדָה	נִתְפַּקְּדָה
2. m.	פָּקַדְתָּ	פִּקַּדְתָּ	פֻּקַּדְתָּ	הִפְקַדְתָּ	הָפְקַדְתָּ	הִתְפַּקַּדְתָּ	נִתְפַּקַּדְתָּ
2. f.	פָּקַדְתְּ	פִּקַּדְתְּ	פֻּקַּדְתְּ	הִפְקַדְתְּ	הָפְקַדְתְּ	הִתְפַּקַּדְתְּ	נִתְפַּקַּדְתְּ
1	פָּקַדְתִּי	פִּקַּדְתִּי	פֻּקַּדְתִּי	הִפְקַדְתִּי	הָפְקַדְתִּי	הִתְפַּקַּדְתִּי	נִתְפַּקַּדְתִּי
Plur.							
3	פָּקְדוּ	פִּקְּדוּ	פֻּקְּדוּ	הִפְקִידוּ	הָפְקְדוּ	הִתְפַּקְּדוּ	נִתְפַּקְּדוּ
2. m.	פְּקַדְתֶּם	פִּקַּדְתֶּם	פֻּקַּדְתֶּם	הִפְקַדְתֶּם	הָפְקַדְתֶּם	הִתְפַּקַּדְתֶּם	נִתְפַּקַּדְתֶּם
2. f.	פְּקַדְתֶּן	פִּקַּדְתֶּן	פֻּקַּדְתֶּן	הִפְקַדְתֶּן	הָפְקַדְתֶּן	הִתְפַּקַּדְתֶּן	נִתְפַּקַּדְתֶּן
1	פָּקַדְנוּ	פִּקַּדְנוּ	פֻּקַּדְנוּ	הִפְקַדְנוּ	הָפְקַדְנוּ	הִתְפַּקַּדְנוּ	נִתְפַּקַּדְנוּ

The Future Tense

	I.	II.	III.	IV.	V.	VI.	VII.
Sing. 3. m.							
3. f.							
2. m.							
2. f.							
1							
Plur. 3. m.							
3. f.							
2. m.							
2. f.							
1							

		Abs.	Const.	Act. m.	f.	Pass. m.	f.
Infinitive	I.	קָטֹל	קְטֹל	קֹטֵל	קֹטֶלֶת / קֹטְלָה	קָטוּל	קְטוּלָה
	II.	הִקָּטֵל				נִקְטָל	נִקְטֶלֶת / נִקְטָלָה
	III.	קַטֵּל		מְקַטֵּל	מְקַטֶּלֶת / מְקַטְּלָה		
	IV.	קֻטַּל				מְקֻטָּל	מְקֻטֶּלֶת / מְקֻטָּלָה
	V.	הַקְטִיל	הַקְטֵל	מַקְטִיל	מַקְטֶלֶת / מַקְטִילָה		
	VI.	הָקְטֵל				מָקְטָל	מָקְטֶלֶת / מָקְטָלָה
	VII.	הִתְקַטֵּל		מִתְקַטֵּל	מִתְקַטֶּלֶת / מִתְקַטְּלָה		

THE VERB.

Imperative.

	Sing. 2. m.	2. f.	Plur. 2. m.	2. f.
I.	קְטֹל	קִטְלִי	קִטְלוּ	קְטֹלְנָה
II.	הִקָּטֵל	הִקָּטְלִי	הִקָּטְלוּ	הִקָּטֵלְנָה
III.	קַטֵּל	קַטְּלִי	קַטְּלוּ	קַטֵּלְנָה
IV.	None			
V.	הִתְקַטֵּל	הִתְקַטְּלִי	הִתְקַטְּלוּ	הִתְקַטֵּלְנָה
VI.	None			
VII.	הַקְטֵל	הַקְטִילִי	הַקְטִילוּ	הַקְטֵלְנָה

The same in English Letters.

The Past Tense.

	I.	II.	III.	IV.	V.	VI.	VII.
Sing.							
3. m.	pakad	nikad	pikked	pukkad	hikkid	hokkad	hithpakked
3. f.	pakēdah	nikkēdah	pikkēdah	pukkēdah	hikkidah	hokkēdah	hithpakkēdah
2. m.	pakadta	nikadta	pikkadta	pukkadta	hikkadta	hokkadta	hithpakkadta
2. f.	pakadt	nikadt	pikkadt	pukkadt	hikkadt	hokkadt	hithpakkadt
1	pakadti	nikadti	pikkadti	pukkadti	hikkadti	hokkadti	hithpakkadti
Plur.							
3	pakēdu	nikēdu	pikkēdu	pukkēlu	hikkidu	hokkēdu	hithpakkēdu
2. m.	pĕkadtem	nikadtem	pikkadtem	pukkadtem	hikkadtem	hokkadtem	hithpakkadtem
2. f.	pĕkadten	nikadten	pikkadten	pukkadten	hikkadten	hokkadten	hithpakkadten
1	pakadnu	nikadnu	pikkadnu	pukkadnu	hikkadnu	hokkadnu	hithpakkadnu

Chap X.]   THE VERB.   65

The Future Tense.

	I.	II.	III.	IV.	V.	VI.	VII.
Sing.							
3. m.	yikod	yippaked	yefakked	yefukkad	yafkid	yofkad	yithpakked
3. f.	tikod	tippaked	tefakked	tefukkad	tafkid	tofkad	tithpakked
2. m.	tikod	tippaked	tefakked	tefukkad	tafkid	tofkad	tithpakked
2. f.	tikēdi	tippakēdi	tefakkēdi	tefukkēdi	tafkidi	tofkēdi	tithpakkēdi
1.	'ekod	'eppaked	'afakked	'afukkad	'afkid	'ofkad	'ethpakked
Plur.							
3. m.	yikōdu	yippakēdu	yefakkēdu	yefukkēdu	yafkidu	yofkēdu	yithpakkēdu
3. f.	tikodnah	tippakednah	tefakkednah	tefukkadnah	tafkednah	tofkadnah	tithpakkednah
2. m.	tikēdu	tippakēdu	tefakkēdu	tefukkēdu	tafkidu	tofkēdu	tithpakkēdu
2. f.	tikodnah	tippakednah	tefakkednah	tefukkadnah	tafkednah	tofkadnah	tithpakkednah
1.	nikod	nippaked	nefakked	nefukkad	nafkid	nofkad	nithpakked

5

66   THE VERB.   [Chap. X.

Imperative.

	I.	II.	III.	V.	VII.
Sing.					
2. m.	pĕkod	hippaked	pakked	hafked	hithpakked
2. f.	pikdi	hippakedi	pakkedi	hafkidi	hithpakkedi
Plur.					
2. m.	pikdu	hippakedu	pakkedu	hafkidu	hithpakkedu
2. f.	pĕkodnah	hippakednah	pakkednah	hafkednah	hithpakkednah

Infinitive.

	I.	II.	III.	V.	VI.	VII.
Abs.	pakod	hippaked	pakked	hafked-	hofkad	hithpakked
Constr.	pĕkod			hafkid		

Participle.

	I.	III.	V.	VI.	VII.
Act. m.	poked	mefakked	mafkid		mithpakked
f.	pokedah	mefakkedah	mafkidah		mithpakkedah
	pokedeth	mefakkedeth	mafkedeth		mithpakkedeth
Pass. m.	pakud	nifkad	mefukkad	mofkad	
f.	pĕkudah	nifkadah	mefukkadah	mofkadah	
		nifkedeth	mefukkedeth	mofkedeth	

13. Notes on the foregoing Paradigm.

a. For Patha*h* some verbs have *Zerey*, and some *H*olem, here. Those with *Zerey* mostly follow this paradigm but שׁאל makes שְׁאֵלְהֶם, and שְׁאֵלְתִיו is found. An example of those with *H*olem has been given.
b. Some few verbs have Patha*h*, Lam. ii. 9 &c. and some Segol here. Ps. l. 1 &c. Anomalous form Gen xli. 51.
c. Some verbs have *K*ibbu*z*, in VI, instead of *Kamez Hatuf*, throughout.
d. If the first radical is ר or ו, this ה becomes ר marked by Dagesh in the ו or ר, as רמה, הִרְדְּמָה; הִוְדְּתָה, זבה.

If ס, שׁ, or שׂ, the two letters are transposed, as סתר, הִסְתַּתֵּר.

If ט or ת, the ה is omitted and its omission marked by Dagesh, as חסה, הִסָּה; טמא, הִטַּמֵּא.
If צ, it is changed to ט and transposed, as צדק, הִצְטַדֵּק.
e. This *Zerey* is sometimes, but rarely, Patha*h*: Eccles. vii. 16.
f. Instead of *H*olem, some verbs have Patha*h*, throughout this tense. In a few places Sh*u*rek is found, Ex. xviii. 26, Ruth ii. 8, Prov. xiv. 3. Anomalous forms of 3. f. pl. occur Gen. xxx. 38, 1 Sam. vi. 12, Dan. viii. 22.
g. Instead of Segol, some verbs have short *Hirik*, here.
h. When apocopated *Hirik* becomes *Zerey* or Segol here.

5*

i. Anomalous forms of II. Inf. Gen. xxxi. 30. 1 S. xx. 28. Cf. 1 S. ii. 27. Jer. xxxii. 4. Ezek. xiv. 3. The ה is absorbed Prov. xxiv. 17.

k. The Participle is Past (Job. i. 14. Gen. xli. 1, xxvii. 33) Present (Is. v. 25, vi. 5) or Future (Ps. xxii. 32. Gen. xxv. 32) once in *Kal* it has *Hirik* instead of *Zerey* Ps. xvi. 5. Cf. 2 K. viii. 21. It takes the affixes either as a noun or as a verb e. g. we have רֹעִי Ps. xxiii. 1 and עֹשֵׂנִי Job. xxxii. 22, the latter commonly in an objective sense.

l. For *Kibbuz* we have *Kamez Hatuf* Nah. ii. 4. Cf. iii. 7 and sometimes the מ is dropped 2 K. ii. 10 &c.

m. Anomalous form מָלְכִי *reign thou*, f. Judg. ix. 10. חָשְׂפִי *make bare*, f. Is. xlvii. 2. So with ה par. שָׁפְטָה Lam. iii. 59. Ps. lxxxii. 8.

CHAPTER XI.

IRREGULAR VERBS.

1. Verbs subject to the following peculiarities are more or less irregular.

1) Verbs whose first letter is a guttural: as עמד.
2) Verbs whose second letter is a guttural: as בעק.
3) Verbs whose third letter is ה, ח or ע: as שמע.
4) Verbs whose first letter is Nun, נ: as נפל. Similar to these is לקח, *took*.
5) Verbs whose first letter is Yod, י: as ישב.
6) Verbs having Waw, ו or Yod, י for the second letter, these we shall call *hollow* verbs: as גיל, שוב.
7) Verbs having the second and third letters alike, these we shall call *double* verbs: as סבב.
8) Verbs whose third letter is א as מצא.
9) Verbs whose third letter is ה as גלה.
10) Verbs which fulfil more than one of these conditions and are therefore doubly irregular: as ירה &c.

It is common to speak of these several verbs according as they correspond to the type פעל, thus a verb of the 4th class will be called a verb פ"נ Pe' Nun, because in it Nun corresponds to Pe' in

*Pag*al. So a verb of the 7th class will be called a verb ע״ע with double *Gayin*, and a verb of the 9th class a verb ל״ה *Lamed He* &c. But this plan is not followed here.

2. In Verbs (1) whose first letter is a guttural a compound Shĕwa commonly takes the place of the simple Shĕwa wherever it is found under the first letter, thus יַעֲמֹד.

But sometimes the simple Shĕwa is retained, as יַחְפֹּץ.

In the six verbs אבד *perished*, אחז *seized*, אכל *ate*, אמר *said*, אבה *wished*, אפה *baked*, the first vowel of the Future *K'al* is *H*olem, thus

&c. תֹּאבַרְנָה, יֹאבְרוּ, תֹּאבַר, יֹאבַד
&c. תֹּאחַזְנָה, יֹאחֲזוּ, תֹּאחֵז, יֹאחֵז
&c. תֹּאמַרְנָה, יֹאמְרוּ, תֹּאמַר, יֹאמַר

In other respects these verbs follow the analogy of their class; thus אכל in Fut. II. is יַאֲכֵל &c.

In some cases the א is rejected, thus אֹמַר *I will say*. Cf. 2 S. xix. 14, xx. 9; Ps. cxxxix. 20.

The compound Shĕwa which verbs of this class take is found to vary, thus we have הֶאֱכַלְתִּי Ex. xvi. 32, and הַאֲכַלְתִּים Jer. xix. 9 &c.

In the future they have, like the regular verbs, *H*olem, *Z*erey or Pathah, thus יֹאמַר, יֶחֱזַק, יַעֲמֹד.

The infinitive of אמר with ל is always לֵאמֹר, but with ב and כ it is בֶּאֱמֹר, כֶּאֱמֹר.

3. In verbs (2) whose second letter is a guttural a compound Shĕwa is also substituted for a simple Shĕwa under the second letter, as יַעֲקֹף 3 plu. Fut.

The Dagesh which sometimes occurs in the second radical is of course omitted and compen-

sation required for it so that the preceding
Patha*h* becomes *Kamez* as יִמָאֵן. Fut. III.
short *Hirik* — *Zerey* as מֵאֵן. Past III.
Kibbuz — *Holem* as אֻכַּל. Past IV.

If however the second letter is ח the preceding vowel is seldom changed, as מְרַחֵף׃ so also with ה and ע sometimes, as תְּבַעֵת, יְבַהֵן &c.

Verbs whose second radical is ר always lengthen the previous vowel as שָׁרֵת, בָּרֵךְ &c.

4. In Verbs (3) whose third letter is ה, ח, or ע, the second pers. sing. of the Past takes two Patha*h*s to avoid the impossible combination of Shĕwa after compound Shĕwa as שָׁמַעְתְּ for שְׁמַעְתְּ. In other forms of the Past the simple Shĕwa remains, as שָׁמַחְנוּ, שָׁמַעְתִּי &c.

When the final vowel is long it is naturally followed by furtive Patha*h*, as נֹטֵעַ; for which however Patha*h* is sometimes substituted, as נֹטֵעַ; so יִשְׁבַּח or יָשֵׁב, הִשְׁבִּיחַ, הֶחְפֵּץ &c.

The future and imperative *K*al take *Kamez* before affixes, as שָׁלָחֵנִי &c.

In other cases simple Shĕwa is replaced by *Hatef* Patha*h*, as אֶשְׁלָחֲךָ.

Verbs in ה are inflected regularly נִבְהָה נָבַהּ הִנְבַּהְתִּי &c.

5. In verbs (4) beginning with Nun this letter is thrown out, when it has a silent Shĕwa, and its rejection is marked by the insertion of Dagesh in the next letter, as יִפֹּל for יִנְפֹּל.

But the Nun remains if the next letter does not take Dagesh, as תְּנַאֵף תְּנַהֵג &c.

The Nun is dropped in the Imperative *K*al and the construct infinitive. In the latter case ת is added and the word becomes Segolate in form, as נֶ֫שׁ, נֶ֫פַח.

Nun is sometimes retained when the Shĕwa is silent, as יִנְצֹר Jer. iii. 5, and sometimes when it is sonant, as נְטוֹשׁ Prov. xvii. 14.

The Verb לקח in Kal and Hofgal is conjugated like these verbs but it retains the ל in the past Nifgal and sometimes in Kal imperative, as 1 S. iv. 11, 17. Ezek. xxxvii. 16; 1 K. xvii. 10, 11.

6. Verbs whose first letter is י (5) are irregular only in I. II. V. and VI.

In I. the Future tense is sometimes — ־ יִ as יִישַׁן and sometimes — ־ יֵ as יֵשֵׁב, the Yod of the root being dropped. This latter class of verbs drops the Yod in the Imper. and forms the Const. Inf. like verbs in נ, as שֵׁב, שֶׁ֫בֶת.

The verbs which have Pathaḥ in the Future retain Yod in the Imp. and Inf. const. as יְטַב יְשַׁב &c.

Some verbs have both forms in the imp. as יְצֹק 2 K. iv. 41 and יְצָק Ezek. xxiv. 3 &c.

In II. Waw is substituted for Yod making the Past — ־ נו, as נוֹשַׁב, Fut. — ־ יִ, as יְיָשֵׁב, Imp. and Inf. — ־ הִי and Part. — ־ נו. The first pers. Sing. of Fut. II. takes *Hirik* instead of Segol, as אֲנַ֫חַר &c.

Six verbs beginning with Yod follow the analogy of verbs beginning with Nun. These are יצב *placed*, יצג *set*, יצע *spread out*, יצק *poured*, יצר *created*, יצת *kindled.* See the Table that follows the verbs.

In V. there are two forms as in Kal — י ־ ־ הִי which verbs whose future is Pathaḥ take, and — י ־ הו which those take whose future is in *Zerey*.

In VI. the Yod becomes Waw with Shurek as the first vowel, as הוּשַׁב &c.

7. The Hollow verbs (6) whose middle letter is Waw or Yod. A few of these are regular, as גָוַע *expired.*

In I. the Waw or Yod disappears from the past Tense.

In III. IV. and VII. the third letter is doubled.

In V. and VI. they assume these forms

	Past.	Fut.	Im.	In.	Part.
V.	—ִהֵ—י	וַ—ֶ—י	הָ—ֶ—	הָ—ִ—י	מֵ—ִי
VI.	—ַהוּ—	וִ—ֶ—		הוּ—ַ—	כוּ—ָ

In XI. and XII. the middle letter is omitted and the first and third are doubled thus

	Past. 3 1 3 1	Fut. 3 1 3 1	Im. 3 1 3 1	In. 3 1 3 1	Part. 3 1 3 1
XI.	—ֵ—ֵ—	—ֵ—ֵ—ְ		—ֵ—ֵ—	מְ—ֵ—ֵ
XII.	3 1 3 1 —ַ—ֵ—	3 1 3 1 —ַ—ֵ—ְ		3 1 3 1 —ַ—ֵ—	3 1 3 1 מְ—ַ—ֵ

8. Verbs with the second and third radicals alike (7).

In I. II. V. and VI. the second and third radicals coalesce and the coalition is marked by Dagesh.

But some verbs as בָּזַז *took spoil,* דָּמַם *meditated,* retain both letters. See the List of irregularities.

In III. IV. VII. XI. and XII. these verbs are like the hollow verbs in form, and these are the only two classes of verbs that have the XIth and XIIth conjugations.

But some verbs are regular in III. IV. and VII. as הִלֵּל מְהַלֵּל מִתְהַלֵּל.

9. Verbs whose third letter is ה (8).

When a termination is added the ה is either rejected or changed into ת, if ה follows, and into י before any other letter.

The ה is rejected in the apoc. Fut. and sometimes in III. Imp.

10. Verbs ending in א (9).

The chief irregularity arises form *Kamez*, *Zerey* or *Segol* being substituted for Pathah under the א and from the omission of soft Dagesh in those pronominal terminations that begin with ת.

In some verbs א is occasionally rejected Num. xi. 11; Job. xxxii. 18 &c. And sometimes ה takes the place of א Job. viii. 21 &c. Cf. Lam. iv. 1.

11. Verbs doubly irregular commonly unite the peculiarities of the respective classes to which they belong: but their changes will be best learnt by practice and by reference to the list of irregularities which follows the Paradigms.

(1) Paradigm of Verbs of the First Guttural.

gamad, *stood.*

The Past Tense.

	Sing.	I.	II.	III.	IV.	V.	VI.	VII.
	3. m.	עָמַד	¹עִמֵּד	עֳמַד	יֶעֱמַד	נֶעֱמַד	הֶעֱמִיד	הִתְעַמֵּד
	3. f.	עָמְדָה	עִמְּדָה	עֳמְדָה	יֶעֶמְדָה	נֶעֶמְדָה	הֶעֱמִידָה	הִתְעַמְּדָה
	2. m.	עָמַדְתָּ	עִמַּדְתָּ	עֳמַדְתָּ	יֶעֱמַדְתָּ	נֶעֱמַדְתָּ	הֶעֱמַדְתָּ	הִתְעַמַּדְתָּ
	2. f.	עָמַדְתְּ	עִמַּדְתְּ	עֳמַדְתְּ	יֶעֱמַדְתְּ	נֶעֱמַדְתְּ	הֶעֱמַדְתְּ	הִתְעַמַּדְתְּ
	1	עָמַדְתִּי	עִמַּדְתִּי	עֳמַדְתִּי	יֶעֱמַדְתִּי	נֶעֱמַדְתִּי	הֶעֱמַדְתִּי	הִתְעַמַּדְתִּי
Plur.	3	עָמְדוּ	עִמְּדוּ	עֳמְדוּ	יֶעֶמְדוּ	נֶעֶמְדוּ	הֶעֱמִידוּ	הִתְעַמְּדוּ
	2. m.	עֲמַדְתֶּם	עִמַּדְתֶּם	עֳמַדְתֶּם	יֶעֱמַדְתֶּם	נֶעֱמַדְתֶּם	הֶעֱמַדְתֶּם	הִתְעַמַּדְתֶּם
	2. f.	עֲמַדְתֶּן	עִמַּדְתֶּן	עֳמַדְתֶּן	יֶעֱמַדְתֶּן	נֶעֱמַדְתֶּן	הֶעֱמַדְתֶּן	הִתְעַמַּדְתֶּן
	1	עָמַדְנוּ	עִמַּדְנוּ	עֳמַדְנוּ	יֶעֱמַדְנוּ	נֶעֱמַדְנוּ	הֶעֱמַדְנוּ	הִתְעַמַּדְנוּ

IRREGULAR VERBS. [Chap. XI.

The Future Tense.

IRREGULAR VERBS.

	Abs. Consl.	Act. m. f.	Pass. m. f.
I.	עֲשֹׂה עֲשׂוֹת	עֹשֶׂה עֹשָׂה עֹשִׂים	עָשׂוּי עֲשׂוּיָה
II.	נַעֲשֹׂה נַעֲשׂוֹת		נַעֲשֶׂה
Infinitive. III.	עַשֵּׂה	מְעַשֶּׂה	
IV.	עֻשֵּׂה		מְעֻשֶּׂה
V.	הַעֲשׂוֹת הֲעֵשׂוֹת	מַעֲשֶׂה	מַעֲשֶׂה
VI.	הֻעֲשׂוֹת		מֻעֲשֶׂה
VII.	הִתְעַשּׂוֹת	מִתְעַשֶּׂה	

Participle.

Imperative.

	I.	II.	III.	IV.	V.	VI.	VII.
Sing.	קְטֹל	הִקָּטֵל	קַטֵּל	None	הִתְקַטֵּל	None	הַקְטֵל
	קִטְלִי	הִקָּטְלִי	קַטְּלִי		הִתְקַטְּלִי		הַקְטִילִי
	קְטֹל	הִקָּטֵל	קַטֵּל		הִתְקַטֵּל		הַקְטֵל
Plur.	קִטְלוּ	הִקָּטְלוּ	קַטְּלוּ		הִתְקַטְּלוּ		הַקְטִילוּ
	קְטֹלְנָה	הִקָּטֵלְנָה	קַטֵּלְנָה		הִתְקַטֵּלְנָה		הַקְטֵלְנָה

1. Some verbs are found with simple Shĕwa in the first syllable as יִקְּדוּ, יִקְּרוּ &c.
2. Also with Pathaḥ for Segol, Num. iii. 6 &c. Anom. forms are found Josh. vii. 7, Judg. ix. 9, 11. 13; Hab. I. 15; Nah. ii. 8.
3. In some verbs the future takes *Ḥateḟ Segol* as יַחֲזֹק יַעֲמֹד &c. and in some simple Shĕwa as יֶחֱזַק יֶחְדַּל. Anom. form Ezek. xxiii. 5.

IRREGULAR VERBS

(2) Paradigm of Verbs of the Second Guttural.

zagak, cried out   *barak*, blessed.

The Past Tense.

	I.	II.	III.	IV.	V.	VI.	VII.
Sing.							
3. m.	בֵּרַךְ	בֹּרַךְ	בֹּרַךְ	בֹּרַךְ	הִתְבָּרֵךְ	הִתְבָּרַךְ	הִתְבָּרֵךְ
3. f.	בֵּרְכָה	בֹּרְכָה	בֹּרְכָה	בֹּרְכָה	הִתְבָּרְכָה	הִתְבָּרְכָה	הִתְבָּרְכָה
2. m.	בֵּרַכְתָּ	בֹּרַכְתָּ	בֹּרַכְתָּ	בֹּרַכְתָּ	הִתְבָּרַכְתָּ	הִתְבָּרַכְתָּ	הִתְבָּרַכְתָּ
2. f.	בֵּרַכְתְּ	בֹּרַכְתְּ	בֹּרַכְתְּ	בֹּרַכְתְּ	הִתְבָּרַכְתְּ	הִתְבָּרַכְתְּ	הִתְבָּרַכְתְּ
1	בֵּרַכְתִּי	בֹּרַכְתִּי	בֹּרַכְתִּי	בֹּרַכְתִּי	הִתְבָּרַכְתִּי	הִתְבָּרַכְתִּי	הִתְבָּרַכְתִּי
Plur.							
3	בֵּרְכוּ	בֹּרְכוּ	בֹּרְכוּ	בֹּרְכוּ	הִתְבָּרְכוּ	הִתְבָּרְכוּ	הִתְבָּרְכוּ
2. m.	בֵּרַכְתֶּם	בֹּרַכְתֶּם	בֹּרַכְתֶּם	בֹּרַכְתֶּם	הִתְבָּרַכְתֶּם	הִתְבָּרַכְתֶּם	הִתְבָּרַכְתֶּם
2. f.	בֵּרַכְתֶּן	בֹּרַכְתֶּן	בֹּרַכְתֶּן	בֹּרַכְתֶּן	הִתְבָּרַכְתֶּן	הִתְבָּרַכְתֶּן	הִתְבָּרַכְתֶּן
1	בֵּרַכְנוּ	בֹּרַכְנוּ	בֹּרַכְנוּ	בֹּרַכְנוּ	הִתְבָּרַכְנוּ	הִתְבָּרַכְנוּ	הִתְבָּרַכְנוּ

The Future Tense.

	Sing. 3. m.	3. f.	2. m.	2. f.	1	Plur. 3. m.	3. f.	2. m.	2. f.	1
I.	יִפְעֹל	תִּפְעֹל	תִּפְעֹל	תִּפְעֲלִי	אֶפְעֹל	יִפְעֲלוּ	תִּפְעֹלְנָה	תִּפְעֲלוּ	תִּפְעֹלְנָה	נִפְעֹל
II.	יִפְעַל	תִּפְעַל	תִּפְעַל	תִּפְעֲלִי	אֶפְעַל	יִפְעֲלוּ	תִּפְעַלְנָה	תִּפְעֲלוּ	תִּפְעַלְנָה	נִפְעַל
III.	יִפָּעֵל	תִּפָּעֵל	תִּפָּעֵל	תִּפָּעֲלִי	אֶפָּעֵל	יִפָּעֲלוּ	תִּפָּעַלְנָה	תִּפָּעֲלוּ	תִּפָּעַלְנָה	נִפָּעֵל
IV.	יְפַעֵל	תְּפַעֵל	תְּפַעֵל	תְּפַעֲלִי	אֲפַעֵל	יְפַעֲלוּ	תְּפַעֵלְנָה	תְּפַעֲלוּ	תְּפַעֵלְנָה	נְפַעֵל
V.	יְפֻעַל	תְּפֻעַל	תְּפֻעַל	תְּפֻעֲלִי	אֲפֻעַל	יְפֻעֲלוּ	תְּפֻעַלְנָה	תְּפֻעֲלוּ	תְּפֻעַלְנָה	נְפֻעַל
VI.	יַפְעִיל	תַּפְעִיל	תַּפְעִיל	תַּפְעִילִי	אַפְעִיל	יַפְעִילוּ	תַּפְעֵלְנָה	תַּפְעִילוּ	תַּפְעֵלְנָה	נַפְעִיל
VII.	יֻפְעַל	תֻּפְעַל	תֻּפְעַל	תֻּפְעֲלִי	אֻפְעַל	יֻפְעֲלוּ	תֻּפְעַלְנָה	תֻּפְעֲלוּ	תֻּפְעַלְנָה	נֻפְעַל

IRREGULAR VERBS.

		Abs. Const.	Act. m. f.	Pass. m. f.
	I.	הָקֵם הָקֵים	מֵקִים מְקִימָה מְקִמֶת	מוּקָם מוּקָמָה
	II.	הָקֵים		הוּקַם הוּקְמָה הוּקָמֶת
Infinitive.	III.	קוּם	מֵקִים (Participle)	
	IV.	קוּם		נָקוֹם
	V.	הָקוֹם הָקוֹם	קָם	
	VI.	הָקוּם		קוּם
	VII.	הִתְקוֹמֵם	מִתְקוֹמֵם	

IRREGULAR VERBS. [Chap. XI.

Imperative.

	I.	II.	III.	IV.	V.	VI.	VII.
Sing.	קְטֹל	קִטֵּל	הִקָּטֵל	None.	קַטֵּל	None.	הִתְקַטֵּל
	קִטְלִי	קַטְּלִי	הִקָּטְלִי		קַטְּלִי		הִתְקַטְּלִי
Plur.	קִטְלוּ	קַטְּלוּ	הִקָּטְלוּ		קַטְּלוּ		הִתְקַטְּלוּ
	קְטֹלְנָה	קַטֵּלְנָה	הִקָּטֵלְנָה		קַטֵּלְנָה		הִתְקַטֵּלְנָה

Some verbs reject the compensation for Dagesh in III. and IV., as נְתַן Ex. x. 13, לְקַח Deut. iv. 27, יְרַשׁ Prov. xxx. 12 &c. Anomalous forms are found, Judg. v. 26, Ps. li. 7.

IRREGULAR VERBS.

(3) Paradigm of Verbs of the Third Guttural.

The Past Tense.

shāmag̱, heard.

	I.	II.	III.	IV.	V.	VI.	VII.
Sing. 1	שָׁמַעְתִּי	נִשְׁמַעְתִּי	שִׁמַּעְתִּי	שֻׁמַּעְתִּי	הִשְׁמַעְתִּי	הָשְׁמַעְתִּי	הִשְׁתַּמַּעְתִּי
3. m.	שָׁמַע	נִשְׁמַע	שִׁמַּע	שֻׁמַּע	הִשְׁמִיעַ	הָשְׁמַע	הִשְׁתַּמַּע
3. f.	שָׁמְעָה	נִשְׁמְעָה	שִׁמְּעָה	שֻׁמְּעָה	הִשְׁמִיעָה	הָשְׁמְעָה	הִשְׁתַּמְּעָה
2. m.	שָׁמַעְתָּ	נִשְׁמַעְתָּ	שִׁמַּעְתָּ	שֻׁמַּעְתָּ	הִשְׁמַעְתָּ	הָשְׁמַעְתָּ	הִשְׁתַּמַּעְתָּ
2. f.	שָׁמַעַתְּ	נִשְׁמַעַתְּ	שִׁמַּעַתְּ	שֻׁמַּעַתְּ	הִשְׁמַעַתְּ	הָשְׁמַעַתְּ	הִשְׁתַּמַּעַתְּ
Plur. 3	שָׁמְעוּ	נִשְׁמְעוּ	שִׁמְּעוּ	שֻׁמְּעוּ	הִשְׁמִיעוּ	הָשְׁמְעוּ	הִשְׁתַּמְּעוּ
2. m.	שְׁמַעְתֶּם	נִשְׁמַעְתֶּם	שִׁמַּעְתֶּם	שֻׁמַּעְתֶּם	הִשְׁמַעְתֶּם	הָשְׁמַעְתֶּם	הִשְׁתַּמַּעְתֶּם
2. f.	שְׁמַעְתֶּן	נִשְׁמַעְתֶּן	שִׁמַּעְתֶּן	שֻׁמַּעְתֶּן	הִשְׁמַעְתֶּן	הָשְׁמַעְתֶּן	הִשְׁתַּמַּעְתֶּן
1	שָׁמַעְנוּ	נִשְׁמַעְנוּ	שִׁמַּעְנוּ	שֻׁמַּעְנוּ	הִשְׁמַעְנוּ	הָשְׁמַעְנוּ	הִשְׁתַּמַּעְנוּ

IRREGULAR VERBS. [Chap. XI.

The Future Tense.

IRREGULAR VERBS.

	Abs.	Const.	Act. m.	Act. f.	Pass. m.	Pass. f.
I.	קָטוֹל	קְטֹל	קֹטֵל	קֹטֶלֶת	קָטוּל	קְטוּלָה
II.	נִקְטֹל				נִקְטָל	
III. (Infinitive)	קַטֵּל		מְקַטֵּל (Participle)			
IV. (Infinitive)	קַטֵּל		מְקֻטָּל			
V.	הִקְטִיל		מַקְטִיל			
VI.	הָקְטֵל				מָקְטָל	
VII.	הִתְקַטֵּל				מִתְקַטֵּל	

Imperative.

VII.	VI.	V.	IV.	III.	II.	I.	Sing.
הִשְׁתַּמַּע	None.	הַשְׁמַע	None.	שַׁמַּע	הִשָּׁמַע	שְׁמַע	
הִשְׁתַּמְּעִי		הַשְׁמִיעִי		שַׁמְּעִי	הִשָּׁמְעִי	שִׁמְעִי	
הִשְׁתַּמְּעוּ		הַשְׁמִיעוּ		שַׁמְּעוּ	הִשָּׁמְעוּ	שִׁמְעוּ	
הִשְׁתַּמַּעְנָה		הַשְׁמַעְנָה		שַׁמַּעְנָה	הִשָּׁמַעְנָה	שְׁמַעְנָה	

1. Irregular forms Gen. xxx. 15, 1 K. xiv. 3.

2. The furtive Pathah in these verbs which may be written in III. and VII. disappears in construction and apocopation, as שְׁלַח, שַׁלַּח, יִשְׁלַח, וַיִּשְׁלַח &c.

3. This Pathah becomes *Kamez* before the suffix, as יִשְׁמָעֵנִי Mic. vii. 7 &c.

(4) Paradigm of Verbs in Nun.

nagash, *came near.* The Past Tense.

In I, III, IV and VII it is regular.

Sing.	II.	V.	VI.
3. m.	נָגַשׁ	הִגִּישׁ	הֻגַּשׁ
3. f.	נָגְשָׁה	הִגִּישָׁה	הֻגְּשָׁה
2. m.	נָגַשְׁתָּ	הִגַּשְׁתָּ	הֻגַּשְׁתָּ
2. f.	נָגַשְׁתְּ	הִגַּשְׁתְּ	הֻגַּשְׁתְּ
1	נָגַשְׁתִּי	הִגַּשְׁתִּי	הֻגַּשְׁתִּי
Plur.			
3	נָגְשׁוּ	הִגִּישׁוּ	הֻגְּשׁוּ
2. m.	נְגַשְׁתֶּם	הִגַּשְׁתֶּם	הֻגַּשְׁתֶּם
2. f.	נְגַשְׁתֶּן	הִגַּשְׁתֶּן	הֻגַּשְׁתֶּן
1	נָגַשְׁנוּ	הִגַּשְׁנוּ	הֻגַּשְׁנוּ

Infinitive.

Abs.	נָגוֹשׁ	הִנָּגֵשׁ	הַגִּישׁ	הֻגַּשׁ
Const.	גֶּשֶׁת			

Participle.

Act.	נֹגֵשׁ	נִגָּשׁ	מַגִּישׁ	מֻגָּשׁ
Pass.	נָגוּשׁ			

1. When the last letter is a guttural, these Segols become Pathahs, as נָגַע from נגע, which makes also גַּע.

The Future Tense.

In II, III, IV, VII, it is regular.

VI.	V.	I.	Sing.
יַגֵּשׁ	יַגִּישׁ	יִשׁ	3. m.
תֻּגַּשׁ	תַּגִּישׁ	תִּגַּשׁ	3. f.
תֻּגַּשׁ	תַּגִּישׁ	תִּגַּשׁ	2. m.
תֻּגְּשִׁי	תַּגִּישִׁי	תִּגְּשִׁי	2. f.
אֻגַּשׁ	אַגִּישׁ	אֶגַּשׁ	1
			Plur.
יֻגְּשׁוּ	יַגִּישׁוּ	תִּשׁוּ	3
תֻּגַּשְׁנָה	תַּגֵּשְׁנָה	תִּגַּשְׁנָה	3. f.
תֻּגְּשׁוּ	תַּגִּישׁוּ	תִּגְּשׁוּ	2. m.
תֻּגַּשְׁנָה	תַּגֵּשְׁנָה	תִּגַּשְׁנָה	2. f.
נֻגַּשׁ	נַגִּישׁ	נִגַּשׁ	1

Imperative.

	V.	I.	Sing.
It is regular II, III, VII.	הַגֵּשׁ	גַּשׁ [1]	2. m.
There is none in IV, VI.	הַגִּישִׁי	גְּשִׁי	2. f.
			Plur.
	הַגִּישׁוּ	גְּשׁוּ	2. m.
	הַגֵּשְׁנָה	גַּשְׁנָה	2. f.

1. Also גְּשָׁה, גְּשִׁי and גְּשׁוּ.
2. The Nun is retained in V. and VI. Ezek. xxii. 20, Judg. xx. 31. Anom. II. In Ps. lxviii. 3, Jer. xxxii. 4.

(5) Paradigm of Verbs in Yod.

yalad, bore, begot. The Past Tense. *yanak, sucked.*

It is regular in I, III, IV, VII, but in VII. Yod sometimes becomes Waw throughout, as הִתְחַדֵּע.[1]

VI.	V.		II.	Sing.
הוֹלַד	הֵתִיק	הוֹלִיד	נוֹלַד	3. m.
הוֹלְדָה	הֵינִקָה	הוֹלִידָה	נוֹלְדָה	3. f.
חוֹלַדְתָּ	הֵינַקְתָּ	הוֹלַדְתָּ	נוֹלַדְתָּ	2. m.
הוֹלַדְתְּ	הֵינַקְתְּ	הוֹלַדְתְּ	נוֹלַדְתְּ	2. f.
הוֹלַחְתִּי	הֵינַקְתִּי	הוֹלַדְתִּי	נוֹלַ֫דְתִּי	1
				Plur.
הוּלְדוּ	הֵינִיקוּ	הוֹלִידוּ	נוֹלְדוּ	3
הוּלַדְתֶּם	הֵינַקְתֶּם	הוֹלַדְתֶּם	נוֹלַדְתֶּם	2. m.
הוּלַדְתֶּן	הֵינַקְתֶּן	הוֹלַדְתֶּן	נוֹלַדְתֶּן	2. f.
הוּלַ֫דְנוּ	הֵינַקְנוּ	הוֹלַ֫דְנוּ	נוֹלַ֫דְנוּ	1

Imperative.

V.		II.		I.	Sing.
הֵתֵק	הוֹלֵד	הִוָּלֵד	יְנַק	לֵד	2. m.
הֵתִיקִי	הוֹלִידִי	הִוָּלְדִי	יִנְקִי	לְדִי	2. f.
					Plur.
הֵינִיקוּ	הוֹלִידוּ	הִוָּלְדוּ	יִנְקוּ	לְדוּ	2. m.
הֵינַקְנָה	הוֹלַדְנָה	הִוָּלַדְנָה	יְנַקְנָה	לֵדְנָה	2. f.

1. We find however in *Kal* יְלִדְתִּיךָ Ps. ii. 7, and יִרָשָׁתָם Deut. iv. 1 &c.

The Future Tense.

It is regular in III, IV, VII.

VI.	V.		II.	I.		Sing.
יֹלֵד	יֵינַק[4]	יוֹלִיד[4]	יָלֵד[3]	יִינַק[2]	יֵלֵד[1]	3. m.
תּוֹלֵד	תֵּינִק[4]	תּוֹלִיד[4]	תָּלֵד	תִּינַק	תֵּלֵד[1]	3. f.
תּוֹלֵד	תֵּינִק[4]	תּוֹלִיד[4]	תָּלֵד	תִּינַק	תֵּלֵד[1]	2. m.
תּוֹלְדִי	תֵּינְקִי	תּוֹלִידִי	תָּלְדִי	תִּינְקִי	תֵּלְדִי	2. f.
אוֹלֵד	אֵינִק[4]	אוֹלִיד[4]	אָלֵד	אִינַק	אֵלֵד[1]	1
						Plur.
יוֹלְדוּ	יֵינְקוּ	יוֹלִידוּ	יָלְדוּ	יִינְקוּ	יֵלְדוּ	3. m.
תּוֹלַדְנָה	תֵּינַקְנָה	תּוֹלַדְנָה	תָּלֵדְנָה	תִּינַקְנָה	תֵּלַדְנָה	3. f.
תּוֹלְדוּ	תֵּינְקוּ	תּוֹלִידוּ	תָּלְדוּ	תִּינְקוּ	תֵּלְדוּ	2. m.
תּוֹלַדְנָה	תֵּינַקְנָה	תּוֹלַדְנָה	תָּלֵדְנָה	תִּינַקְנָה	תֵּלַדְנָה	2. f.
נוֹלֵד	נֵינִק	נוֹלִיד	נָלֵד	נִינַק	נֵלֵד	1

1 When apocopated *Zerey* becomes *Segol* here and *Pathah* when in pause.

2 After *Waw* conversive this *Pathah* is sometimes changed to *Segol*, Gen. ii. 7, ix. 24.

3 In one or two cases *Yod* is found in place of *Waw*, Gen. viii. 12, Ex. xix. 13.

4 When apocopated *Hirik* becomes *Zerey* or *Segol*.

Infinitive.

VI.	V.		II.	I.		
הוֹלֵד	הֵינִיק	הוֹלִיד	הִוָּלֵד	יָלֹד		Abs.
				לֶדֶת[1]		Const.

Participle.

	מֵינִיק	מוֹלִיד		יֹלֵד		Act.
סוּלָד			נוֹלָד	יָלוּד		Pass.

1 If the last radical is a guttural these *Segols* become *Pathahs*.

IRREGULAR VERBS.

(6) Paradigm of Verbs having Medial Waw, or Hollow Verbs.

kom, to arise.   The Past Tense.   *gîl, to rejoice.*

	I.	II.	III.	IV.	V.	VI.	VII.	Sing.
	גָּל	הֵגִיל	גֻּל	גֻּלַּל	הִתְגּוֹלֵל	נָגֹל	קוֹמֵם	3. m.
	גָּלָה	הֵגִילָה	גֻּלָּה	גֻּלְלָה	הִתְגּוֹלְלָה	נָגֹלָּה	קוֹמְמָה	3. f.
	גַּלְתָּ	הֱגִילוֹתָ	גֻּלֵּתָ	גֻּלַּלְתָּ	הִתְגּוֹלַלְתָּ	נְגֹלּוֹתָ	קוֹמַמְתָּ	2. m.
	גַּלְתְּ	הֱגִילוֹת	גֻּלֵּת	גֻּלַּלְתְּ	הִתְגּוֹלַלְתְּ	נְגֹלּוֹת	קוֹמַמְתְּ	2. f.
	גַּלְתִּי	הֱגִילוֹתִי	גֻּלֵּתִי	גֻּלַּלְתִּי	הִתְגּוֹלַלְתִּי	נְגֹלּוֹתִי	קוֹמַמְתִּי	1
								Plur.
	גָּלוּ	הֵגִילוּ	גֻּלּוּ	גֻּלְלוּ	הִתְגּוֹלְלוּ	נָגֹלּוּ	קוֹמְמוּ	3
	גַּלְתֶּם	הֱגִילוֹתֶם	גֻּלֵּתֶם	גֻּלַּלְתֶּם	הִתְגּוֹלַלְתֶּם	נְגֹלּוֹתֶם	קוֹמַמְתֶּם	2. m.
	גַּלְתֶּן	הֱגִילוֹתֶן	גֻּלֵּתֶן	גֻּלַּלְתֶּן	הִתְגּוֹלַלְתֶּן	נְגֹלּוֹתֶן	קוֹמַמְתֶּן	2. f.
	גַּלְנוּ	הֱגִילוֹנוּ	גֻּלֵּנוּ	גֻּלַּלְנוּ	הִתְגּוֹלַלְנוּ	נְגֹלּוֹנוּ	קוֹמַמְנוּ	1

The Future Tense.

	I.	II.	III.	IV.	V.	VI.	VII.
Sing. 3. m.	יָקוּם[5]	יָקוּם	יְקוֹמֵם	יְקוֹמַם	יָקִים[7]	יוּקַם	יִתְקוֹמֵם
3. f.	תָּקוּם[6]	תִּקּוֹם	תְּקוֹמֵם	תְּקוֹמַם	תָּקִים[7]	תּוּקַם	תִּתְקוֹמֵם
2. m.	תָּקוּם[5]	תִּקּוֹם	תְּקוֹמֵם	תְּקוֹמַם	תָּקִים[7]	תּוּקַם	תִּתְקוֹמֵם
2. f.	תָּקוּמִי	תִּקּוֹמִי	תְּקוֹמְמִי	תְּקוֹמְמִי	תָּקִימִי	תּוּקְמִי	תִּתְקוֹמְמִי
1	אָקוּם[1]	אֶקּוֹם	אֲקוֹמֵם	אֲקוֹמַם	אָקִים[8]	אוּקַם	אֶתְקוֹמֵם
Plur. 3. m.	יָקוּמוּ	יִקּוֹמוּ	יְקוֹמְמוּ	יְקוֹמְמוּ	יָקִימוּ	יוּקְמוּ	יִתְקוֹמְמוּ
3. f.	תְּקוּמֶינָה[6]	תִּקֹּמְנָה	תְּקוֹמֵמְנָה	תְּקוֹמַמְנָה	תָּקֵמְנָה	תּוּקַמְנָה	תִּתְקוֹמֵמְנָה
2. m.	תָּקוּמוּ	תִּקּוֹמוּ	תְּקוֹמְמוּ	תְּקוֹמְמוּ	תָּקִימוּ	תּוּקְמוּ	תִּתְקוֹמְמוּ
2. f.	תְּקוּמֶינָה	תִּקּוֹמְנָה	תְּקוֹמֵמְנָה	תְּקוֹמַמְנָה	תָּקֵמְנָה	תּוּקַמְנָה	תִּתְקוֹמֵמְנָה
1	נָקוּם	נִקּוֹם	נְקוֹמֵם	נְקוֹמַם	נָקִים	נוּקַם	נִתְקוֹמֵם

IRREGULAR VERBS.

Infinitive.

I.	II.	III.	IV.	V.	VI.	VII.
קֹם	הָקִים	הוּקַם	קוֹמֵם	קוֹמַם	הִתְקוֹמֵם	

	Abs.	Constr.
I.	קוֹם	קוּם
	הָקֵם	הָקִים

Participle.

	Act.	Pass.
I.	קָם	קוּם
III.	מוּקָם	
IV.	מְקוֹמֵם	מְקוֹמָם
V.		
VI.	מֵקִים	
VII.	מִתְקוֹמֵם	

Imperative.

	I.	II.	III.	V.	VII.
Sing. 2. m.	קוּם	הָקֵם	הוּקַם	קוֹמֵם	הִתְקוֹמֵם
2. f.	קוּמִי	הָקִימִי	הוּקְמִי	קוֹמְמִי	הִתְקוֹמְמִי
Plur. 2. m.	קוּמוּ	הָקִימוּ	הוּקְמוּ	קוֹמְמוּ	הִתְקוֹמְמוּ
2. f.	קֹמְנָה	הֲקֵמְנָה	הוּקַמְנָה	קוֹמֵמְנָה	הִתְקוֹמֵמְנָה

IRREGULAR VERBS [Chap. XI

1. מִשְׁפָּט Anom. form Mal. iii. 20.
2. A variation Ezek. xi. 17, xx. 43 &c.
3. We have also forms like קְטֶלְתָּ Lam. i. 8 &c.
4. Variations Ex. xx. 25, Num. xvii. 6 &c.
5. When apocopated Shurek becomes Holem or more commonly Komez here. Pathah is found Ruth iv. 1, and Anom. forms Job. xxxi. 5, 1 Sam. xv. 19, xxv. 14.
6. Variations Ezek. xvi. 55.
7. When shortened Hirik becomes Zerey or Segol here. We have also forms like קְטֵל Prov. iv. 21 &c.
8. A variation Is. xxv. 10.

The Future Tense.

Sing.	Plur.
יִקְטֹל	יִקְטְלוּ
תִּקְטֹל	תִּקְטֹלְנָה or תִּקְטַלְנָה
תִּקְטֹל	תִּקְטְלוּ
תִּקְטְלִי	תִּקְטֹלְנָה or תִּקְטַלְנָה
אֶקְטֹל	נִקְטֹל

[Chap XL] IRREGULAR VERBS. 95

(7) Paradigm of Verbs with Double Radical.

The Past Tense.

סוֹבֵב, *went round*.

	VI.	V.	II.	I.	Sing.
	הֵסֵב	סֹבֵב	יָסֹב	סַב	3. m.
	הֵסַבָּה	סֹבְבָה	יָסֹבִּי	סַבָּה	3. f.
	הֵסַבֹּתָ	סֹבַבְתָּ	יָסַבֹּתָ	סַבֹּתָ	2. m.
	הֵסַבֹּתְ	סֹבַבְתְּ	יָסַבֹּתְ	סַבֹּתְ	2. f.
	הֵסַבֹּתִי	סֹבַבְתִּי	יָסַבֹּתִי	סַבֹּתִי	1
					Plur.
	הֵסֵבּוּ	סֹבְבוּ	יָסֹבּוּ	סַבּוּ	3
	הֵסַבֹּתֶם	סֹבַבְתֶּם	יָסַבֹּתֶם	סַבֹּתֶם	2. m.
	הֵסַבֹּתֶן	סֹבַבְתֶּן	יָסַבֹּתֶן	סַבֹּתֶן	2. f.
	הֵסַבֹּנוּ	סֹבַבְנוּ	יָסַבֹּנוּ	סַבֹּנוּ	1

These verbs are inflected like the Hollow verbs in III., IV. and VII.

סָבַב, סָבֹב, הִסָּבֵב &c. &c. &c.

The Future Tense.

	I.			II.	V.	VI.
Sing.						
3 m.	יִקֹּם	יָקֹם	יֵקַל	יִסֹּב	יִסַּב	יוּסַב
3 f.	תָּקֹם	תָּקֹם	תֵּקַל	תִּסֹּב	תִּסַּב	תוּסַב
2 m.	תָּקֹם	תָּקֹם	תֵּקַל	תִּסֹּב	תִּסַּב	תוּסַב
2 f.	תָּקֹמִי	תָּקֹמִי	תֵּקַלִּי	תִּסֹּבִּי	תִּסַּבִּי	תוּסַבִּי
1	אָקֹם	אָקֹם	אֵקַל	אֶסֹּב	אֶסַּב	אוּסַב
Plur.						
3 m.	יָקֹמוּ	יָקֹמוּ	יֵקַלּוּ	יִסֹּבּוּ	יִסַּבּוּ	יוּסַבּוּ
3 f.	תְּקֹמֶינָה	תְּקֹמֶינָה	תֵּקַלֶּינָה	תִּסֻּבֶּינָה	תִּסַּבֶּינָה	תּוּסַבֶּינָה
2 m.	תָּקֹמוּ	תָּקֹמוּ	תֵּקַלּוּ	תִּסֹּבּוּ	תִּסַּבּוּ	תוּסַבּוּ
2 f.	תְּקֹמֶינָה	תְּקֹמֶינָה	תֵּקַלֶּינָה	תִּסֻּבֶּינָה	תִּסַּבֶּינָה	תּוּסַבֶּינָה
1	נָקֹם	נָקֹם	נֵקַל	נִסֹּב	נִסַּב	נוּסַב

Infinitive.

VI.	V.	II.	I.	
הוֹסֵב	הָסֵב	הָסֵב	סָבוֹב	Abs.
			סֹב	Const.

Participle.

	V.	II.	I.	
	מֵסֵב[5]		סֹבֵב	Act.
מוּסָב		נָסָב[3]	סָבוּב	Pass.

Imperative.

V.	II.	I.	Sing.
הָסֵב	הָסֵב	סֹב	2. m.
הָסֵבִּי	הִסֵּבִּי	סֹבִּי	2. f.
			Plur.
הָסֵבּוּ	חִסֵּבּוּ	סֹבּוּ	2. m.
הֲסִבֶּתָה	הִסֵּבֶּינָה	סֹבֶּינָה	2. f.

1. Anom. forms Ezek. xli. 7, Is. xix. 3.
2. Without Dagesh, Prov. vii. 13.
3. הֻסֵבּוּ 1 Sam. v. 9, 10.
4. Anomalous forms are found Gen. xi. 6, 7; Jer. viii. 14.
5. Feminine מְסִבָּה נְסִבָּה. These verbs and the hollow verbs have the additional forms Pilpel and Polpal, which are inflected regularly P. 1. s. סְחַרְתִּי. F. 3. a. סְכְסֵךְ. P. 3. pl. כִּלְכְּלוּ &c.

galah, revealed.

(8) Paradigm of Verbs ending in ה.

The Past Tense.

	Sing.	I.	II.	III.	IV.	V.	VI.	VII.
	3. m.	גָּלָה	גִּלָּה	גֻּלָּה	נִגְלָה	הִגְלָה	הָגְלָה	הִתְגַּלָּה
	3. f.	גָּלְתָה	גִּלְּתָה	גֻּלְּתָה	נִגְלְתָה	הִגְלְתָה	הָגְלְתָה	הִתְגַּלְּתָה
	2. m.	גָּלִיתָ	גִּלִּיתָ	גֻּלֵּיתָ	נִגְלֵיתָ	הִגְלֵיתָ	הָגְלֵיתָ	הִתְגַּלִּיתָ
	2. f.	גָּלִית	גִּלִּית	גֻּלֵּית	נִגְלֵית	הִגְלֵית	הָגְלֵית	הִתְגַּלִּית
	1	גָּלִיתִי	גִּלִּיתִי	גֻּלֵּיתִי	נִגְלֵיתִי	הִגְלֵיתִי	הָגְלֵיתִי	הִתְגַּלִּיתִי
	Plur.							
	3	גָּלוּ	גִּלּוּ	גֻּלּוּ	נִגְלוּ	הִגְלוּ	הָגְלוּ	הִתְגַּלּוּ
	2. m.	גְּלִיתֶם	גִּלִּיתֶם	גֻּלֵּיתֶם	נִגְלֵיתֶם	הִגְלֵיתֶם	הָגְלֵיתֶם	הִתְגַּלִּיתֶם
	2. f.	גְּלִיתֶן	גִּלִּיתֶן	גֻּלֵּיתֶן	נִגְלֵיתֶן	הִגְלֵיתֶן	הָגְלֵיתֶן	הִתְגַּלִּיתֶן
	1	גָּלִינוּ	גִּלִּינוּ	גֻּלֵּינוּ	נִגְלֵינוּ	הִגְלֵינוּ	הָגְלֵינוּ	הִתְגַּלִּינוּ

The Future Tense.

	Sing. 3. m.	3. f.	2. m.	2. f.	1	Plur. 3. m.	3. f.	2. m.	2. f.	1
I.	יִגְלֶה	תִּגְלֶה	תִּגְלֶה	תִּגְלִי	אֶגְלֶה	יִגְלוּ	תִּגְלֶינָה	תִּגְלוּ	תִּגְלֶינָה	נִגְלֶה
II.	יִגָּלֶה	תִּגָּלֶה	תִּגָּלֶה	תִּגָּלִי	אֶגָּלֶה	יִגָּלוּ	תִּגָּלֶינָה	תִּגָּלוּ	תִּגָּלֶינָה	נִגָּלֶה
III.	יְגַלֶּה	תְּגַלֶּה	תְּגַלֶּה	תְּגַלִּי	אֲגַלֶּה	יְגַלּוּ	תְּגַלֶּינָה	תְּגַלּוּ	תְּגַלֶּינָה	נְגַלֶּה
IV.	יְגֻלֶּה	תְּגֻלֶּה	תְּגֻלֶּה	תְּגֻלִּי	אֲגֻלֶּה	יְגֻלּוּ	תְּגֻלֶּינָה	תְּגֻלּוּ	תְּגֻלֶּינָה	נְגֻלֶּה
V.	יַגְלֶה	תַּגְלֶה	תַּגְלֶה	תַּגְלִי	אַגְלֶה	יַגְלוּ	תַּגְלֶינָה	תַּגְלוּ	תַּגְלֶינָה	נַגְלֶה
VI.	יָגְלֶה	תָּגְלֶה	תָּגְלֶה	תָּגְלִי	אָגְלֶה	יָגְלוּ	תָּגְלֶינָה	תָּגְלוּ	תָּגְלֶינָה	נָגְלֶה
VII.	יִתְגַּלֶּה	תִּתְגַּלֶּה	תִּתְגַּלֶּה	תִּתְגַּלִּי	אֶתְגַּלֶּה	יִתְגַּלּוּ	תִּתְגַּלֶּינָה	תִּתְגַּלּוּ	תִּתְגַּלֶּינָה	נִתְגַּלֶּה

		Abs.	Const.
I.		גָּלֹה[3]	גְּלֵה[³]
II.		הַגְלֵה	
III.		גְּלֹה	
IV.		גְּלֵה	
V.		הִגָּלֹה	
VI.		הִגָּלֵה	
VII.		הִתְגַּלֵּה	

Infinitive.

	Act.	Pass.
I.	גֹּלֶה[4]	גָּלוּי[5]
II.	מְגַלֶּה	
III.	מַגְלֶה	
IV.	מֻגְלֶה	
V.	נִגְלֶה	
VI.	מִתְגַּלֶּה	
VII.	מִתְגַּלֶּה	

Participle.

I.	יִגֶל[8]
II.	יְגַל[7]
III.	יַגֶל
V.	יִגָּל[8]
VII.	יִתְגַּל

Future apocopated.

Chap. XI.] IRREGULAR VERBS. 101

Imperative.

	VII.	VI.	V.	IV.	III.	II.	I.	Sing.
2. m.	הִקָּטֵל	None	קְטֹל	None	גְּלֵ֫ה	הֲקֵל	גְּלֵה	
2. f.	הִקָּטְלִי		קִטְלִי		גְּלִי	הָקֵ֫לִי	גְּלִי	
								Plur.
2. m.	הִקָּטְלוּ		קִטְלוּ		גְּלוּ	הָקֵ֫לוּ	גְּלוּ	2. m.
2. f.	הִקָּטֵ֫לְנָה		קְטֹ֫לְנָה		גְּלֶ֫ינָה	הָקֵ֫לְנָה	גְּלֶ֫ינָה	2. f.

1. Another rare form is found Lev. xxv. 21, xxvi. 34, Jer. xiii. 19.
2. The accent marks out these verbs from hollow verbs see ii. 20.
3. Written defectively Gen. xxvi. 28. Irregular forms of In. Const. Gen. xlviii 11, l. 20. In some cases Yod is found in place of ה Deut. xxxii 37, Is. xxi. 12, Deut. viii. 13, Ps. lxxviii. 44, Is. xl. 25, Ex. xv. 5, Job. xix. 2, Is. liii. 10, Jer. xviii. 23, Jos. xiv. 8.
4. A fem. part. פֹּרָה Gen. xlix. 22, other fem. forms Prov. xxxi. 27, Ps. cxxviii. 3, Is. xli. 23.
5. Without Yod, Job. xv. 22, xli. 25.
6. An anomalous form (ii. 10) יַחְתְּ is found twice Ex. xviii. 9, Job. iii. 6. In the case of a guttural the Segol becomes Pathah as יְדַע.
7. רְאֵה Ps. cix. 13.
8. Other forms Gen. ix. 27, Is. xli. 2.
9. Or apocopated גַּל.

(9) Paradigm of Verbs ending in א.

מצא, *found.*

The Past Tense.

	I.	II.	III.	IV.	V.	VI.	VII.
Sing.							
3. m.	מָצָא	מֻצָּא	הִמְצִיא	מִצֵּא	נִמְצָא	הֻמְצָא	הִתְמַצֵּא
3. f.	מָצְאָה	מֻצְּאָה	הִמְצִיאָה	מִצְּאָה	נִמְצְאָה	הֻמְצְאָה	הִתְמַצְּאָה
2. m.	מָצָאתָ	מֻצֵּאתָ	הִמְצֵאתָ	מִצֵּאתָ	נִמְצֵאתָ	הֻמְצֵאתָ	הִתְמַצֵּאתָ
2. f.	מָצָאת	מֻצֵּאת	הִמְצֵאת	מִצֵּאת	נִמְצֵאת	הֻמְצֵאת	הִתְמַצֵּאת
1	מָצָאתִי	מֻצֵּאתִי	הִמְצֵאתִי	מִצֵּאתִי	נִמְצֵאתִי	הֻמְצֵאתִי	הִתְמַצֵּאתִי
Plur.							
3	מָצְאוּ	מֻצְּאוּ	הִמְצִיאוּ	מִצְּאוּ	נִמְצְאוּ	הֻמְצְאוּ	הִתְמַצְּאוּ
2. m.	מְצָאתֶם	מֻצֵּאתֶם	הִמְצֵאתֶם	מִצֵּאתֶם	נִמְצֵאתֶם	הֻמְצֵאתֶם	הִתְמַצֵּאתֶם
2. f.	מְצָאתֶן	מֻצֵּאתֶן	הִמְצֵאתֶן	מִצֵּאתֶן	נִמְצֵאתֶן	הֻמְצֵאתֶן	הִתְמַצֵּאתֶן
1	מָצָאנוּ	מֻצֵּאנוּ	הִמְצֵאנוּ	מִצֵּאנוּ	נִמְצֵאנוּ	הֻמְצֵאנוּ	הִתְמַצֵּאנוּ

IRREGULAR VERBS.

The Future Tense.

	I.	II.	III.	IV.	V.	VI.	VII.
Sing. 3. m.	יִקְטֹל	יְקַטֵּל	יַקְטִיל	יִקָּטֵל	יִתְקַטֵּל	יֻקְטַל	יָקְטַל
3. f.	תִּקְטֹל	תְּקַטֵּל	תַּקְטִיל	תִּקָּטֵל	תִּתְקַטֵּל	תֻּקְטַל	תָּקְטַל
2. m.	תִּקְטֹל	תְּקַטֵּל	תַּקְטִיל	תִּקָּטֵל	תִּתְקַטֵּל	תֻּקְטַל	תָּקְטַל
2. f.	תִּקְטְלִי	תְּקַטְּלִי	תַּקְטִילִי	תִּקָּטְלִי	תִּתְקַטְּלִי	תֻּקְטְלִי	תָּקְטְלִי
1	אֶקְטֹל	אֲקַטֵּל	אַקְטִיל	אֶקָּטֵל	אֶתְקַטֵּל	אֻקְטַל	אָקְטַל
Plur. 3. m.	יִקְטְלוּ	יְקַטְּלוּ	יַקְטִילוּ	יִקָּטְלוּ	יִתְקַטְּלוּ	יֻקְטְלוּ	יָקְטְלוּ
3. f.	תִּקְטֹלְנָה	תְּקַטֵּלְנָה	תַּקְטֵלְנָה	תִּקָּטַלְנָה	תִּתְקַטֵּלְנָה	תֻּקְטַלְנָה	תָּקְטַלְנָה
2. m.	תִּקְטְלוּ	תְּקַטְּלוּ	תַּקְטִילוּ	תִּקָּטְלוּ	תִּתְקַטְּלוּ	תֻּקְטְלוּ	תָּקְטְלוּ
2. f.	תִּקְטֹלְנָה	תְּקַטֵּלְנָה	תַּקְטֵלְנָה	תִּקָּטַלְנָה	תִּתְקַטֵּלְנָה	תֻּקְטַלְנָה	תָּקְטַלְנָה
1	נִקְטֹל	נְקַטֵּל	נַקְטִיל	נִקָּטֵל	נִתְקַטֵּל	נֻקְטַל	נָקְטַל

IRREGULAR VERBS. [Chap. XI.

	I.	II.	III.	IV.	V.	VI.	VII.
Infinitive Abs.	נְסֹׁעַ	נָסוֹעַ	נָסֹעַ	נְסֹעַ	נִסּוֹעַ	נִסֹּעַ	הִנָּסֵעַ
Const.	נְסֹעַ						

	Act.	Pass.
Participle	נֹסֵעַ	נָסוּעַ
		נִסָּע
		נֻסָּע
		מֻסָּע
		הִנָּסֵעַ

	I.	II.	III.	V.	VII.
Imperative Sing. 2. m.	סַע	הִסָּעֵר	הַסַּע	הִתְסָעֵר	
2. f.	סְעִי	הִסָּעִי	הַסְּעִי	הִתְסָעִי	
Plur. 2. m.	סְעוּ	הִסָּעוּ	הַסְּעוּ	הִתְסָעוּ	
2. f.	סַעְנָה	הִסָּעְנָה	הַסַּעְנָה	הִתְסָעְנָה	

IRREGULAR VERBS.

1. Sometimes the א falls away in these verbs Num. xi. 11, Job. xxxii. 18, Lev. xi. 43, Jer. xxxii. 35.

2. Sometimes like 2. f. in form Gen. xxxiii. 11. Cf. Is. vii. 14, Deut. xxxi. 29.

3. Once מָצָאתִ Eccles. vii. 26. (Cf. מָצָא Eccles. viii. 12.) f. חָטְאָה 2 Sam. xviii. 22, So חָטָאתִֿי Gen. xxiv. 15.

Verbs ending in א and ה sometimes interchange their forms

a. Verbs in א are pointed like those in ה Ps. cxix. 101, Jer. li. 34, 2 K. ii. 21, Job. xxxix. 24.

b. Or write ה for א Ps. lx 4, 1 K. xxii. 25, Job. viii. 21.

c. Or resemble them in both ways Ruth ii. 9, Ezek. xxviii. 16, Gen. xx. 6, Job. v. 18, Eccles. x. 5, Ps. xxxii. 1, Jer. li. 9, 1 Sam. x. 6. 13.

d. Verbs in ה like those in א Lam. iv. 1, 2 K. xxv. 29, 2 Ch. xvi. 12, 1 K. xvii. 14, 2 Sam. xxi. 12.

(10) Verbs doubly irregular.

The Past Tense.

	yarah, shot.		nasah, lifted up.		natah, stretched out.			bo', to come.	
	VI.	V.	V.	L	V.	V.	II.	L	Sing.
	יָרָה	יָרָא	נָשָׂה	נָשָׂא	נָטָה	נָטָא	נָטָא	בָּא	3. m.
	יָרְתָה	יָרְאָה	נָשְׂתָה	נָשְׂאָה	נָטְתָה	נָטְאָה	נָטְאָה	בָּאָה	3. f.
	יָרִיתָ	יָרִאתָ	נָשִׂיתָ	נָשָׂאתָ	נָטִיתָ	נָטָאתָ	נָטָאתָ	בָּאתָ	2. m.
				נָשָׂאת	נָטִית	נָטָאת	נָטָאת	בָּאת	2. f.
			or, נָשְׂאתִי	נָשָׂאתִי	נָטִיתִי	נָטָאתִי	נָטָאתִי	בָּאתִי	1
									Plur.
			נָשְׂאוּ	נָשְׂאוּ	נָטוּ	נָטְאוּ	נָטְאוּ	בָּאוּ	3
		or, נְשָׂאתֶם	נָשְׂאתֶם	נְשָׂאתֶם	נְטִיתֶם	נְטָאתֶם	נְטָאתֶם	בָּאתֶם	2. m.
	יָרִיאֶן		נָשִׂיאֶן	נָשָׂאתֶן	נְטִיתֶן	נְטָאתֶן	נְטָאתֶן	בָּאתֶן	2. f.
			נָשִׂינוּ	נָשָׂאנוּ	נָטִינוּ	נָטָאנוּ	נָטָאנוּ	בָּאנוּ	1

IRREGULAR VERBS.

The Future Tense.

	Sing. 3. m.	3. f.	2. m.	2. f.	1	Plur. 3. m.	3. f.	2. m.	2. f.	1
L.	יִתֵּן	תִּתֵּן	תִּתֵּן	תִּתְּנִי	אֶתֵּן	יִתְּנוּ	תִּתֵּנָּה	תִּתְּנוּ	תִּתֵּנָּה	נִתֵּן
V.	יִתֵּן	תִּתֵּן	תִּתֵּן	תִּתְּנִי	אֶתֵּן	יִתְּנוּ	תִּתֵּנָּה	תִּתְּנוּ	תִּתֵּנָּה	נִתֵּן
L.	יִגַּשׁ	תִּגַּשׁ	תִּגַּשׁ	תִּגְּשִׁי	אֶגַּשׁ	יִגְּשׁוּ	תִּגַּשְׁנָה	תִּגְּשׁוּ	תִּגַּשְׁנָה	נִגַּשׁ
L.	יִטַּע	תִּטַּע	תִּטַּע	תִּטְּעִי	אֶטַּע	יִטְּעוּ	תִּטַּעְנָה	תִּטְּעוּ	תִּטַּעְנָה	נִטַּע
V.	יִטַּע	תִּטַּע	תִּטַּע	תִּטְּעִי	אֶטַּע	יִטְּעוּ	תִּטַּעְנָה	תִּטְּעוּ	תִּטַּעְנָה	נִטַּע
L.	יִשָּׂא	תִּשָּׂא	תִּשָּׂא	תִּשְּׂאִי	אֶשָּׂא	יִשְּׂאוּ	תִּשֶּׂאנָה	תִּשְּׂאוּ	תִּשֶּׂאנָה	נִשָּׂא
V.	יִשָּׂא	תִּשָּׂא	תִּשָּׂא	תִּשְּׂאִי	אֶשָּׂא	יִשְּׂאוּ	תִּשֶּׂאנָה	תִּשְּׂאוּ	תִּשֶּׂאנָה	נִשָּׂא
VI.	אֶקַּח					נִקַּח				

	I.	V.	I.	V.	I.	V.	I.	V.
Infinitive.	Abs. יָדֹעַ	הֵרֹשׁ	אָסֹף	הֵאָסֵף	סֹב	הִסּוֹב	קֹם	הִקּוֹם
	Const. דַּעַת		אֲסֹף		סֹב			
Participle.	Act. יֹדֵעַ	נוֹדָע	אֹסֵף	נֶאֱסָף	סֹבֵב	נָסֹב	קָם	נָקוֹם
	Pass. יָדוּעַ		אָסוּף					נָקוֹם

VI.

IRREGULAR VERBS.

	Sing. 2. m.	2. f.	Plur. 2. m.	2. f.
I.	תֵּן	תְּנִי	תְּנוּ	תִּתֵּנָּה
V. תִּתֵּן	תִּתֵּן	תִּתְּנִי	תִּתְּנוּ	תִּתֵּנָּה

Future apocopated
I. I.

Imperative.

אֶתֵּן	נִתֵּן	תִּתְּנוּ

1. With affix 3. m. pl. כְּתֵם Num. xxi. 30.

(11) Paradigm of a Regular

Us.	You. m.	You. f.	Them. m.	Them. f.
שְׁמָרַנִי	שְׁמָרְכֶם	שְׁמָרְכֶן	שְׁמָרָם	שְׁמָרָן
שְׁמָרָתְנִי	שְׁמָרָתְכֶם	שְׁמָרָתְכֶן	שְׁמָרָתַם	שְׁמָרָתַן
שְׁמַרְתָּנוּ	שְׁמַרְתָּם		שְׁמַרְתָּם	שְׁמַרְתָּן
שְׁמַרְתִּיו	שְׁמַרְתִּיכֶם	שְׁמַרְתִּיכֶן	שְׁמַרְתִּים Id.	שְׁמַרְתִּין Id.
שְׁמָרוּנוּ	שְׁמָרוּכֶם	שְׁמָרוּכֶן	שְׁמָרוּם	שְׁמָרוּן
שְׁמַרְתּוּנוּ			שְׁמַרְתּוּם	שְׁמַרְתּוּן
	שְׁמַרְנוּכֶם	שְׁמַרְנוּכֶן	שְׁמַרְנוּם	שְׁמַרְנוּן
שָׁמְרֵנִי	שָׁמְרְכֶם	שָׁמְרְכֶן	שָׁמְרֵם 2Ch.xvii.1 בְּקָצְ֯ם Am.i.13.	שָׁמְרֵן
	שָׁמְרְכֶם	שָׁמְרְכֶן		
יִשְׁמְרֵנוּ	יִשְׁמְרֵכֶם	יִשְׁמְרֵכֶן	יִשְׁמְרֵם, ־הֶם	יִשְׁמְרֵן, ־הֶן
יִשְׁמְרוּנוּ	יִשְׁמְרוּכֶם	יִשְׁמְרוּכֶן	יִשְׁמְרוּם	יִשְׁמְרוּן
שָׁמְרֵנוּ			שָׁמְרֵם	
שְׁמָעוּנִי			וּבְצַעַם Am.ix.1	
שָׁמְרֵנוּ	אָשָׁרְכָ֯ם	שָׁפְרְכָן	שָׁמְרָם Hos. בִּקְשָׁתַם ii.9.	שְׁפְרָן
נָשְׁמִירֵנוּ	לְשָׁמְרְכֶם	לְשָׁמְרְכֶן	לְשָׁמְרֵם	לָשָׁמְרָן

1. Anomalous form אֱגָרֵם Zech. vii. 14. *esagarem*.

Verb with Affixes.

Her.	Him.	Thee. f.	Thee. m.	Me.	
שְׁמָרָהּ	שְׁמָרוֹ, ־הוּ	שְׁמָרֵךְ	שְׁמָרְךָ	שְׁמָרַנִי	3. m. Past.
שְׁמָרַתָּה	שְׁמָרַתְהוּ, ־תּוּ	שְׁמָרָתַךְ	שְׁמָרַתְךָ	שְׁמָרַתְנִי	3. f.
שְׁמַרְתָּהּ	שְׁמַרְתָּיו, ־תּוֹ	שְׁמַרְתָּךְ		שְׁמַרְתַּנִי in p. ־תָּנִי	2. m.
שְׁמַרְתִּיהָ	שְׁמַרְתִּיו, ־יהוּ	Id.	שְׁמַרְתִּיךְ	שְׁמַרְתִּינִי	2. f.
Id.	Id.				1
שְׁמָרוּהָ	שְׁמָרוּהוּ	שְׁמָרוּךְ	שְׁמָרוּךָ	שְׁמָרוּנִי	Plu. 3.
שְׁמַרְתּוּהָ	שְׁמַרְתּוּהוּ			שְׁמַרְתּוּנִי	2. m. f.
שְׁמַרְנוּהָ	שְׁמַרְנוּהוּ	שְׁמַרְנוּךְ	שְׁמַרְנוּךָ		1
שָׁמְרָהּ, ־הָ	שָׁמְרוֹ, ־הוּ	שָׁמְרֵךְ	שָׁמְרְךָ Prov. vii.5&c. לְשָׁמְרִי?	שָׁמְרִי ־נִי Ezek. xxxiv.27. בְּשָׁמְרִי	Inf.
יִשְׁמְרָהּ	יִשְׁמְרֵהוּ	יִשְׁמְרֵךְ	יִשְׁמָרְךָ	יִשְׁמְרֵנִי	Fut. 3. m.
יִשְׁמְרֶנָּה	יִשְׁמְרֵנוּ		יִשְׁמָרֶךָּ	יִשְׁמְרֵנִי	With epenth.
יִשְׁמְרוּהָ	יִשְׁמְרוּהוּ Prov. v. 22. יִלְכְּדֻנוֹ	יִשְׁמְרוּךְ	יִשְׁמְרוּךָ	יִשְׁמְרוּנִי Prov. i. 29. יִקְרָאֻנְנִי	3. pl.
שָׁמְרָהּ	שָׁמְרֵהוּ Prov. iii.6. וְיַשֵּׁרֻ	שָׁמְרֵךְ	שָׁמְרֵךָ	שָׁמְרֵנִי שְׁמָעֵנִי	Imp.
שְׁמָרָהּ	שָׁמְרוּ	שָׁמְרֵךְ	שָׁמְרְךָ Deut. xxviii.8. וּבֵרַכְךָ	יִשָּׂרְחִיךָ Is. lx. 7,11.	שְׁמַרְתִּי Joh. xix. 2. הִדְבָּאֻנִי	III. P.
יַשְׁמִירָהּ	יַשְׁמִירֵהוּ	יַשְׁמִירֵךְ	יַשְׁמִירְךָ	יַשְׁמִירֵנִי	V. F.

(12) List of irregular Verbal forms.

א

אבר V. F. אֹבִירָה Jer. xlvi. 8.

אבל הַאֲכִיל V. יָאֲכַל F. אבל

אגר F. יָאֱגֹר.

אדם IV. Part. מְאָדָּם.

אהב אֲהָבָה In. יֶאֱהַב F.

אור P. אוֹרוּ Im. אִירִי.

אול P. אָלַת Deut. xxxii. 36. F. חֵילִי Jer. ii. 36.

און V. הָאֲוֵין and הַאֲזִין F. אָוֶן Job. xxxii. 11. part. מֵזִין Prov. xvii. 4.

אזר F. תֶּאֱזֹר II. Part. נֶאְזָר.

אח F. יֵאָחוּ and הַאֲחוֹ II. P. נאחזו Josh. xxii. 9.

אחר F. אֶחָרֵי ,אַחַר V. וָיֹּאחַר III. אֶחַר יָחַר 2 S. xx. 5.

אטר F. תֶּאָטֵר Ps. lxix. 16.

אבל F. יֹאכַל in p. 'כְ In. cr. אֱכֹל and אֲכֹל II. In. הֵאָכֵל Lev. vii. 18. xix. 7. V. F. אוֹכִיל Hos. xi. 4. In. הָכִיל. Ezek. xxi. 33.

אלה V. F. ap. וַיֹּאֶל 1 S. xiv. 24.

אלף F. תְּאַלֵּף III. Part. מְאַלֵּף Job. xxxv. 11. Cf. xxxiii. 33.

אמץ F. יֶאֱמָץ.

אמר F. יֹאמַר in p. 'מֵ. ap. 'מָ. אָחַר א dropped Ps. cxxxix. 20.

אנף F. יֶאֱנַף.

אנק F. יֶאֱנֹק.

אסף F. יֶאֱסֹף and יַאַ' 'אָסֹף Mic. ii. 12. and אֹסְפָה iv. 6. וַיֶּאֱסֹף 2 S. vi. 1. Cf. Ps. civ. 29. II. In. הֵאָסֵף 2 S. xvii. 11.

אסר F. יֶאְסֹר and יַאְסָ׳ In. cr. לֶאְסֹר Ps. cv. 22. cxxxix. 8.

אפד F. יֶאְפֹּד Lev. viii. 7.

אפה F. יֹאפֶה יאפו Im. אֵפוּ Ex. xvi. 23.

אצל V. F. וַיָּאצֶל Num. xi. 25.

ארב F. יֶאֱרֹב V. F. וַיֶּאֱרֹב 1 S. xv. 5.

ארג F. הָאַרְגִּי Jud. xvi. 13. יֶאֱרֹגוּ Is. lix. 5.

ארר II. Part. מְאָרֵר III. part. אֹרֵר נֶאֱרִים

אשם F. יֶאְשָׁם Hos. iv. 15 &c.

אהה P. אָתָנוּ F. יֶאֱתָה ap. יַאת, יֵתָא aff. תֶאָתָה אֲתָיָנִי V. Im. אֵתָיוּ part. fem. pl. אֵתָיוֹת Im. יַאֲתָיוּ הֵתָיוּ.

ב

בא P. בָּא בָּאָה בָּאתָ בָּאת בָּאתִי בָּאוּ and בָּאִי בָּאנוּ בָּאתֶם. Im. בֹּא בֹּאִי בֹּאוּ and תָּבֹאנָה F. יָבֹא V. הֲבִיאָה, הָבִיא and הַבֵּאתְ, תָּבֹאתָ, הֲבֵאתֶם F. אָבִי Mic. i. 15. Im. בֹּאִי Ruth iii. 15. VI. P. 3 f. הֻבָאָה 2. הֻבֵאת.

בש P. בּוֹשָׁה, בֹּשְׁתְּ, בֹּשְׁתִּי, בֹּשׁוּ, בֹּשְׁנוּ F. יֵבוֹשׁ יַבְלוּשׁוּ Im. בּוֹשׁ בּוֹשִׁי בּוֹשׁוּ part. pl. בּוֹשִׁים V. הוֹבִישָׁה הֻבַשְׁתִּי F. הֲבִישׁוֹת הֲבִישׁ P. הֱבִישׁ הֲבִישׁוּ and הֲבִישׁוּ.

בזה II. anom. part. נִמְבְזָה 1 Sam. xv. 9.

בו P. בָּז Zach. iv. 10. Cf. Is. xxxiii. 23. בַּז Ezek. xxix. 19. בָּזֹז בָּזַז Deut. ii. 35. and בּוֹזּוּ Deut. iii. 7. F. נָבוֹז 1 Sam. xiv. 36. II. In. הָבֵז.

בכה F. ap. וַיֵּבְךְּ, יִבְכָּיוּן part. f. בֹּכִיָּה

בלל F. ap. יָבֶל, נָבְלָה Gen. xi. 7.

בנה II. F. אֶבְנֶה.

בער III. P. בֵּעֵר F. יְבַעֵר.

בעת III. P. בִּעֵת F. יְבַעֵת.

IRREGULAR VERBS [Chap. XI.

בקק P. aff. בְּקָקִים Nah. ii. 3. II. P. נָבְקָה In. תָּבוֹק
כרך III. P. כָּרֵךְ and רָ'.
ברר P. בָּרוּתִי in. cr. בּוֹר aff. בָּרָם Eccles. iii. 18. II.
    Im. הִבָּרוּ Is. lii. 11. V. Im. הָבֵרוּ Jer. li. 11.
    In. הָבַר iv. 11. VII. F. תִּתְבָּרָר Ps. xviii. 27.
    2 S. xxii. 27. יִתְבָּרֲרוּ Dan. xii. 10.

נ

נדד F. יָנוּד, יָנֹד Ps. xciv. 21.
נלה V. P. הִגְלָה and הָ VL part. pl. מְגֻלִּים Jer. xl. 1.
נלל P. נַלּוּ Gen. xxix. 3, 8. Im. גַּל Ps. cxix. 22.
    II. P. נָלּוּ Is. xxxiv. 4. V. F. יָגֵל Gen.
    xxix. 10.
נעש VII. P. הִתְנַעֵשׁ and הִתְנַגֵּשׁ.

ר

רגה F. ap. יֵרֶא Ps. xviii. 11.
דבק VL part. סְרָבָק.
דבר III. P. דִּבֶּר and כָּ VII מְדַבֵּר Num. vii. 89. &c.
דדה VII. F. אֶדַּדֶּה.
דרש II. In. cr. הִדּוֹרֵשׁ.
דחה IV. P. דֹּחוּ Ps. xxxvi. 13.
דבא VII. F. יִדַּבְּאוּ.
דלה Im.? דַּלְיוּ Prov. xxvi. 7.
דלל דַּלּוּ and דָּלְלוּ.
רמה VII. F. אֶדַּמֶּה.
דמם F. דֹּמִּי יוֹם Jer. xlviii. 2. יִדְּמוּ אָדָם and יִדַּמּוּ.
דקק V. P. הֵדַק 2 K. xxiii. 15. In. הָדֵק and הָדֵק
    Ex. xxx. 36. 2 Ch. xxxiv. 7.

| IRREGULAR VERBS. |

דרך V. F. יַדְרְכוּ Jer. ix. 2.
דרש II. F. אֶדְרָשׁ.
דשן VIII. P. הֻדַּשְׁנָה Is. xxxiv. 6.

ה

הבל F. יֶהְבָּלוּ p.
הגה F. יֶהְגֶּה IV. In. הֲגוֹ Is. lix. 13.
הדף F. יֶהְדֹּף.
הדר F. יֶהְדַּר.
הוה F. יְהוּא Eccles. xi. 3. הֱוֵה Gen. xxvii. 29, and הֹוֵא Job. xxxvii. 6.
היה F. יִהְיֶה p. יָהִי, תְּהִי תְּהִי תִּהְיֶה אָהֱיָה אֱהִי יִהְיוּ in im. הֱיֵה הֱיִי and 'נ תִּהְיֶינָה נְהִי part. נִהְיָה Mic. ii. 4. נִהְיָתָה נִהְיֵית נִהְיָה II. Prov. xiii. 19.
הלך P. הֵלִיכָא Josh. x. 24. F. יַהֲלֹךְ and תַּהֲלַךְ.
הלל part. הוֹלֵל and הִלֵּל III. הֵלוּ In. aff. הֵילַל and לְהוֹלֵל VII. הֵלֵל IV. הִתְחֹלֵל and הִתְהוֹלֵל.
המה F. אֶהֱמֶה, תֶּהֱמִי, יֶהֱמוּ and אֶהֱסָיָה, תְּהָמִי and נֶהֱמָה part. הָמוֹת in. cr. יֶהֱסָיוּן and חָמִיָה.
הסה V. F. ap. יַהַס Num. xiii. 30.
הפך II. In. נַהֲפֹךְ Est. ix. 1.
הרה F. ap. תַּהַר part. f. הָרָה and הֹרָה.
הרס F. יֶהֶרְסוּ יַהֲרֹס aff. יֶהֶרְסֵם.
החל III. P. הוּחַל F. יִתַּל תְּתַחֵל Job. xiii. 9.

ז

זמם p. Ps. xxxi. 14. זָמֹתִי, זַמּוֹתִי and זַמֹּתִי וְזָמָה וזם F. יָזְמוּ Gen. xi. 6.

ונה IV. P. וַיָּנָה Ez. xvi. 34.
ורם III. וְרָמִי Ps. lxxvii. 18.

ח

הבא II. הֶחְבִּאָתָה V. P. נֶחְבְּאוּ נֶחְבָּא.
דבש F. יַחֲבֹשׁ and יַחְבָּשׁ.
חדה F. ap. יָחַדְּ.
חדל F. יֶחְדַּל.
חוב III. P. חָיָב.
חוה Im. הֲוֵה ap. חֱוֵה and יָחֲוֻוּ נְחַוֶּיִן יְחַוֶּה F. אֶחֱוֶה.
      In. cr. חַוּוֹת.
חוק F. יָחֻק.
הטא F. יֶחֱטָא Part. f. חֹטֵאת Ezek. xviii. 4. 20.
חיה F. אֶחְיֶה תִּחְיֶה הִחְיָה ap. יְהִי in p. יְהִי חָיוּ cr.
      חָיֹה and תְּחִי חֲיֵה in. חֲיִי im. נְחְיֶה תְּחִיוּ תְחֶיֶינָה
      וְהַחֲיִתֶם הֶחֱיֵיתִי הֶחֱיָה V. חָיוֹת.
חכם F. יֶחְכַּם V. הֶחְכִּים.
חלה II. Part. f. נַחְלָה II. חָלוֹת in. cr. יַחַל ap. יֶחֱלֶא F. נֶחְלָה.
חלל II. P. נְחַל Ezek. xxv. 3. F. יָחֵל in. הָחֵל III. חִלֵּל
      and חָלַל IV. חַלּוֹתִי aff. in. הִלֵּל, and
      V. הַחִלּוֹתִי הָחֵל ap. יָחֵל F.
חלש F. יַחֲלֹשׁ and יֶחֱלַשׁ.
חמץ F. יֶחְמָץ.
חמר F. יֶחְמַר XVII. חֳמַרְמָרוּ Lam. ii. 11.
חנן F. יָחֹן Am. v. 15. III. P. חֻנַּן and חֹן VI. F. יֻחַן
      VII. הִתְחַנֵּן.
חנף F. תֶּחֱנָף.
תחה P. הָסָיָה Ps. lvii. 2. חָסָיוּ Deut. xxxii. 37. F.
      חָסוּ im. חֲסָיִין and יֶחֱסוּ יֶחֱסֶה, אֶחֱסֶה, תֶּחֱסֶה
      in. cr. הֲסוֹת.

IRREGULAR VERBS.

חבר F. יַחְסַר and יַ׳ חֶחְסַר.
חפץ F. חֶפֶץ תֶּחְפָּץ אֶחְפָּץ and יַחְפֹּץ תֶּחְפֹּץ אָחְפַּץ.
חצה II. F. ap. יַחַץ ap. יֶחֱצֶה F. חצה
חקק IV. Part. מְחֹקֵק VI. F. יָחְקוּ Job. xix. 23.
חרב V. הֶחֱרַבְתִּי and הַחֵם.
חרד P. חָ׳ V חָ׳ and יָחְרְדוּ F. חרד
חרה V. F. ap. יַחַר ap. יֶחֱרֶה F. חרה
חרם V. P. הַחֲרַמְתִּי and הַחֵ׳.
חרר II. P. נִחַר Ps. lxix. 4, cii. 4. נָחַר Jer. vi. 29.
חשף Im. חֶשְׂפִי Is. xlvii. 2.
חשה F. יֶחֱשֶׁה יֶחֱשׁוּ V. Im. הֶחֱשׁוּ.
חשך V. יָחְשְׁכוּ תֶּחְשַׁךְ F. הֶחְשִׁיךְ הֶחְשַׁכְתִּי.
חתם II. In. נַחְתּוֹם Est. viii. 8.
חתת II. P. נָחַת III. חִתַּת V. הֵחִתֹּתָ Is. ix. 3. הַחִתַּתִּי Jer. xlix. 37. aff. אֲחִתְּךָ Jer. i. 17. יְחִיתַן Hab. ii. 17.

ט

טהר 'טָהַ׳ in p. הִטֶּהָרוּ VII. P. יִטְהַר F. טִהַר III. P. הִטָּהֲרוּ im. יִטָּהֲרוּ F. הִטַּהַרְנוּ.
טמא הִטַּמָּא VII. F. יִטַּמָּא VIII. P. הֻטַּמָּא.

י

יבש F. יִיבַשׁ and יָבוֹשׁ Hos. xiii. 15. In. cr. יְבֹשׁ and יְבֹשֶׁת Gen. viii. 7. III. F. יַבֵּשׁ Nah. i. 4.
ינה II. Part נוֹנִים Zeph. iii. 18. Lam. i. 4.
ידה הִתְוַדָּה VII. P. הוֹרָה V. P. יָדוּ Joel iv. 3. III. F. יָדִי Lev. v. 5.
ידע F. יֵדַע יָדַע Ps. cxxxviii. 6. im. דַּע in. cr. דַּעַת הִתְוַדַּע VII. P. הוֹדַע VI. P.
יהב only in im. הַב and הָבָה, הָבִי הָבוּ.

יחד F. חֵתַר III. im. יָחַד Ps. lxxxvi. 11.

יטב V. F. יֵיטִיב Job. xxiv. 21.

יכח VII. P. הִתְוַכַּח.

יכל in. cr. יְכָלָה.

ילד F. חֶלֶד and חֶלַדְנָה aff. יְלָדְתִּיךָ Ps. ii. 7. in. יֵלֵד, and לֵדָה 2 K. xix. 3, and לָח 1 Sam. iv. 19. V. הוֹלִיד.

ילך Mic. i. 8. אֵילְכָה.

ילל V. P. הֵילִיל F. יְלִיל יְלִילוּ and יְהֵילִלוּ Is. lii. 5.

ימן V. F. הַאֲמִינוּ אֵימִין im. הֵמִינִי in. הָמֵן part. מַאֲמִינִים.

יסר III. In. יַסֵּר V. F. aff. אֲיַסְּרֵם Hos. vii. 12.

יפה F. ap. וַיִּיף Ez. xxxi. 7. תּוֹפִי Ez. xvi. 13

יצא F. יָצָא im. צֵא in cr. צֵאת V. P. הוֹצִיא.

יצב II. הִתְיַצַּב VII. P. הֵצַב VI. P. יַצִּיב F. הַצִּיג V. נְצַב.

יצג V. P. הִצִּיג F. יַצִּג VI. F. יָצֵג.

יצע V. F. יַצֵּעַ VI. F. יָצֻע.

יצק F. יָצֹק and יָצַק im. צַק and צֹק V. F. יַצִּיק part. מוּצָק.

יצר F. ap. יִיצֶר, אֵצוּר.

יצת F. יָצַת V. P. הִצִּית.

יקר F. יַקָּר Is. x. 16, and יִיקַר Deut. xxxii. 22, in. cr. יְקָר.

יקע F. יַקַּע V. P. הוֹקַע.

יקץ F. יִיקַץ ap. קֻ׳ and יָקַץ 1 K. iii. 15.

יקר F. יַקָּר V. יִיקַר and יַקָּר הוֹקִיר.

ירא F. וַיִּירָא im. יְרָא in. cr. יְרֹא, and יִרְאָה with pref. לְרֹא 1 Sam. xviii. 29.

ירד F. יֵרֵד im. רַד and רְדָה in. רֶדֶת and יָרֹד V. הוֹרִיד.

ירה F. יִרְאָה im. יָרָה in. cr. יְרוֹח II. F. יִירֶה Ex. xix. 13. V. P. הוֹרָה F. יוֹרֶה once יוֹרָא Prov. xi. 25.

ירש P. יִרְשָׁתֶּם Deut. iv. 1. Cf. ילד im. יָרְשָׁה Deut. xxxiii. 23, and רַשׁ 1 K. xxi. 15, and רָשׁ in p. Deut. ii. 24.

ישב in. יָשֹׁב and שׁוֹב.

ישם F. תֵּשַׁם.

ישן in. cr. יִשַׁן.

ישר V. F. יְשָׁרוּ Prov. iv. 25.

יתר V. F. ap. תֹּחַר Ruth ii. 14.

כ

בבס VIII. הָכַבַּס Lev. xiii. 55, 56.

כהה F. יִכְהֶה ap. חֲכָה Job. xvii. 7. III. P. כָּהָה.

כהן III. P. כִּהֵן F. יְכַהֵן.

כון VII. הַכּוֹנֵן and הִתְכּוֹנֵן.

כלה F. יִכְלוּ. F. Ps. lxxii. 20. P. IV. כָּלוּ and יִכְלוּ F. יִכְלָיוּן בָּלְלוּ כלל.

כסה IV. P. כָּסוּ F. יְכַסֶּה.

כסף II. In. נִכְסֹף.

כפת II. F. אֶכְפַּת Mic. vi. 6.

כפר IX. נְכַפַּר.

כרח IV. כָּרֹחַ Ezek. xvi. 4.

כשל VI. part. מָכְשָׁלִים Jer. xviii. 23.

כתת III. כִּתַּת IV. כַּתֵּת V. F. יִכַּתּוּ Deut. i. 44. VI. F. יְכָתּוּ יֻכַּת.

ל

לאה הָלְאָה F. תִּלְאֶה Job. iv. 2. ap. חֲלָא Job. iv. 5. V. הֶלְאָה
    3. f. הֶלְאֵת Ezek. xxiv. 12.

להה F. ap. חָלָה Gen. xlvii. 13.

להט יְלַהֵט. F. לְהֵט III. P. לֹהֵט

לח V. F. לֵחוֹ Prov. iv. 21.

לון part. לָנֶה for לָנָה Zech. v. 4. Cf. Is. lix. 5.
    pl. לֵנִים for לָנִים Neh. xiii. 21. V. P. הֵלִין
    and הָלִין F. יָלִין and יָלַן.

ליץ part. לֵץ.

להם II. in. הִלָּחֵם and נִלְחַם.

לקח VI. קָחַח in. cr. לְקַח and קַח im. יִקַּח F. לָקַח

לקק P. לָקְקוּ III. part. מְלַקְקִים.

מ

מדר יִמֹדּד and יִמַדּד F. מֹדַד III. מָדֹתָם מָדְדוּ מַדֹּתִי

מות מוּת and יָמוּת F. מָתִנוּ מֵתוּ מַתִּי סָקָה מֵתָה מֵת
    הֵמִתָּם הֵסֵתָה V. מֵתִים pl. כֵּח part.

מחה V. F. ap. תֶּמַח II. F. יִמַּח.

מלא Lev. מָלֹאת In. מָלוּ מָלְחִי and מָלְאוּ מָלֵאתִי and מָלֵא
    xii. 4. part. מָלֵא.

מלח VI. הִמְלִיחַ.

מלט II. F. אִמָּלֵט.

מלל III. מְלַל F. יְמַלֵל.

מסס נָמֵס part. הֵמֵס in. cr. II. מְסֹס in. cr. מְסֹס 1 S.
    xv. 9.

מרר תֵּמַר F. הֵמֵר V. P. יְחָרֵר III. F. יָמַר F.

משש III. מִשֵׁשׁ F. יְמַשֵׁשׁ

נ

נאה נָאֲוָה נָאווּ.
נאף סָאַף part. הַנֲאָפָנָה יִנְאֲפוּ F. נִאֵף III. נאף
נאץ מְנֹאָץ Part. VIII. נִאֵץ In. נִאֵץ III. נאץ
נאר גֵאֵר נֵאַרְתָה III. נאר
נבא הִתְנַבֵּית and 'הִנַּ and הִתְנַבֵּא VII. נִבֵּאתָ and נִבֵּא II. 1 Sam. x. 6.
נבל נָבֵל in. cr.
נגד יַגֵּד F. הַגֵּד VI. P.
נגע נָגַע and נְגֹעַ in. cr. נַע im.
נגף נָגֹף in. cr.
נגר מֻגָּרִים VI. part.
נשׁ נִשָּׂא נְשִׂי נְשָׂא or נְשֵׂה Im. or with Holem נְשִׂי, נְשׂוּ VI. תִּשָּׂא.
נדד יָדַד VI. F. הֵנֵד V. P. יָדַד and יִדֹּד F. נָדְדוּ נָדְדָה
נדח מֻדָּח VI. Part. נִדֹּחַ in cr.
נדף הִנָּדֹף Ps. lxviii. 3. II. In. תִּנְדֹּף and הִדֹּף F.
Ps. lxviii. 3.
נדר נָדֹר in. cr.
נהג יִנְהַג F. נִהַג III. P.
נהל אֶתְנַהֲלָה VII. F. יְנַהֵל F. נִהֵל III. P.
נוא יָנִי V. F. Ps. cxli. 5.
נוח הָנַח and הִנִּיחַ V. P. יָנִיחַ F. הִנִּיחַ P. יָנִיחַ F. הוּנַח VI.
נזה חָז ap. חַ Is. lxiii. 3. and ץַ 2 K. ix. 33. V. P. יַזֶּה F. הִזָּה ap. חַ.
נחת יַחַת F. and יִנְחַת.
נטה יַט ap. יַטֶּה F. הִטָּה V. נָטוּי II. יֵט ap. יִטֶּה F.
im. הַטֵּה and הַט.

נטע in. cr. נְטַע and הַעַט.
נטר F. תִּטֹּר Jer. iii. 5.
נטש in. cr. נְטֹשׁ.
נכה הַכֵּה im. הַךְ ap. יַכֶּה F. הִכָּה V. נֻכָּה IV. נִכָּה II. and הִכָּה VI הַךְ F. יְטוּ.
נלה V. in. cr. הַגְלֵה Is. xxxiii. 1.
נסג VI. הִסֵּג.
נסה III. im. נַס.
נסך VI. הִסֵּךְ.
נסע in. cr. נְסֹעַ.
נער II. F. אֶנָּעֵר.
נפל im. נְפֹלוּ in. cr. נְפֹל XIV. נָפָל Ezek. xxviii. 23.
נצה II. F. תִּצֶּינָה Jer. iv. 7.
נצל II. F. אֶנָּצֵל VI. Part. מֻצָּל.
נצר F. יִצֹּר and יְצוֹר im. נְצֹר.
נקב F. יָקֹב and תִּקֹּב im. נָקְבָה Gen. xxx. 28.
נקם in. cr. נְקֹם VI. F. יִקֹּם.
נקף F. תְּקֹף.
נקר In. cr. נְקוֹר 1 S. xi. 2.
נשא F. יִשָּׂא im. שָׂא in. cr. שְׂאֵת and שֵׂאת.
נשק in. cr. נְשֹׁק.
נחך VI. הִתֵּךְ.
נתן נָתַתִּי נָתַתָּ סַתָּה and נָתַתָּה and נָתַנּוּ in. cr. תְּנָה im. תְּנָה חֵן F. יִתֵּן im. נְתֻנוּ Ps. viii. 2. Cf. Gen. xlvi. 3. נְתֹן and תַּת aff. תִּתּוֹ VI. F. יִתֵּן.
נתץ in. cr. נְתֹץ VI. יֻתַּץ.
נתק VI. הִנָּתֵק.
נתש in. cr. נְתוֹשׁ VI. F. יִתֵּשׁ.

ס

סבב II. F. סָבַב and סֹב in. cr. סַבּוּ and סָבְכוּ
Ex. וַיָּסַב V. F. סָבַב in. וְסֹבֵב III. F. יָסֵבּוּ
xiii. 18.

סוג F. נָבוֹג Ps. lxxx. 19.

סוך F. יָסוּךְ and יִיסַךְ Ex. xxx. 32.

סוח F. יָסִיחַ P. הֵסִיחַ F. יָסִיחַ P. הֵסִיחַ סוח

סכך V. F. יָסֵךְ Ps. xci. 4. VI. F. יֻסָּךְ.

ע

עבט V. הַעֲבֵט.

עבר V. הַעֲבֵר 'הַעֲ' and 'הֵעֲ' הַעֲבַרְתָּ Josh. vii. 7.

עדה F. תַּעֲדֶה ap. תַּעְדִּי im. עֲדֵה.

עוד III. עוֹדֵד and עוֹרֵר.

עוה IL part. נַעֲוֵיתִי נַעֲוָה.

עול III. עוֹלֵל.

עור part. עֵר II. F. יֵעוֹר III. F. עוֹרֵר and יְעֹרְרוּ
Is. xv. 5.

עוח III. עָוַח IV. עָוֹחַ VII. הִתְעַוֵּחַ.

עזז II. part. נוֹעַז.

עטה F. עֹטְיָה Cant. i. 7. part. f. עֹטַה ap. עַט 'עִי' F. עטה

עלה F. עָלָה II. נַעֲלָה ap. יַעַל אֶעֱלֶה ap. יַעַל חֵעָלוּ
Ezek. xxxvi. 3 V. הֶעֱלִית 'לְ' הַעֲלִית F. יַעֲלֶה
הַעֲלָה הֶעֱלָה im. הַעַל V. אַעַל ap. אַעֲלֶה יַעַל
Hab. i. 15. VI. הָעֳלָה Judg. vi. 28. VII. F.
יִתְעַל ap.

עלל VII. הִתְעוֹלֵל and הִתְעַלֵּל.

עלם II. P. נֶעֱלָם 3. f. נֶעֶלְמָה Job. xxviii. 21. Part.
f. נֶעֶלְמָה Nah. iii. 11.

| | IRREGULAR VERBS. | [Chap. XL |

עמד V. P. הָעֳמַדְתָּ and 'הָעֳ.

עמם P. עֲמָמוּ.

ענה עָנִי im. אֱעָן ap. אֱעֶנֶה and אֶעֱנֶה ap. יַעַן תַּעֲנֶה F. תַּעֲנֶה ap. אֶעֱנֶה Job. xix. 7. II. P. נַעֲנֵיתִי F. אֱעָנֶה and עֲנוּ

עשה נַעֲשָׂה II. P. אֵעַשׂ ap. אֶעֱשֶׂה תַּעַשׂ ap. יַעֲשֶׂה F. נֶעֶשְׂתָה part. נַעֲשָׂה.

עשש P. עָשְׁשׁוּ עָשֵׁשָׁה.

עתק F. יַעְתַּק V. P. הָעְתִּיק.

עתר F. יָעְתַּר II. in. נַעְתּוֹר 1 Ch. v. 20, and הֶעְתַּר part. נַעְתָּרוֹת Prov. xxvii. 6. V. P. הֶעְתַּרְתִּי.

פ

פלא II P. נִפְלְאַתָה 2 S. i. 26.

פלל III. P. פִּלֵּל VII. הִתְפַּלַּל.

פקד הִתְפָּקְדוּ VII. 2 Ch. xxxiv. 12. part. מִפְקָד VI. הָפָקַד VIII. הָתְפָּקְדוּ F. יִתְפָּקֵד.

פרה part. f. פֹּרִיָּה and פֹּרָת Gen. xlix. 22.

פרר VI. F. יָפֵר.

פתה F. ap. יָפְתְּ Job. xxxi. 27. V. F. ap. יַפְתְּ Gen. ix. 27.

צ

צבע VII. F. יִצְטַבַּע.

צהב VI. מָצְהָב.

צוה III. צַו ap. צַוֶּה im. צִיָּה and צִיָּהָ.

צוח II. נָצַח V. הִצִּיחַ F. יַצִּיחַ and יֵצִיחַ.

צלל מֵצַל V. part. הַצְּלָנָה and הִצְלֶינָה F. צַלְלוּ P. צָלְלוּ Ez. xxxi. 3.

צמא צָמֵתִי Jud. iv. 19. צָמְאָה and צָמָת Ruth ii. 9. P. צמא.

IRREGULAR VERBS.

צמח II. P. נִצְמַתִּי XIV. aff. צִמַּתּוּתִי Ps. lxxxviii. 17.
צעק III. part. מִצְעָק.
צרר P. צַר and צָרַר Prov. xxx. 4, Hos. iv. 19. צְררוּ F. יָצַר ap. יֵצַר and צֹר Is. xi. 13. V. part. מְצֵרָה Jer. xlviii. 41, xlix. 22.

ק

קדד F. יָקֹד, אָקֹד, יִקְּדוּ.
נקט Ezek. נָקְטוּ Job. x. 1. II. נְקֹטָה and י׳ F. אָקוּט קוט vi. 9.
קום III. קִים and קִימֵם.
קטר VI. F. יָקְטָר part. מְקֻטָּר.
קלל IV. יָקֵל F. קָלַל III. יֵקַל F. קלל
קנן III. קִנֵּן IV. קִנֵּן.
קצע VI. part. מְהֻקְצָעוֹת Ezek. xlvi. 22.
קצץ III. קִצֵּץ IV. קֻצַּץ.
קרח VI. part. מָקְרָח Ezek. xxix. 18.

ר

ראה ה׳ and הִרְאָה V. אֵרָא תֵּרָא, יֵרָא and תֵּרָא F. ap. יֵרָא 2 K. xi. 4.
רבב רְבוּ and רַבּוּ Gen. xlix. 23.
רדד in. cr. רַד Is. xlv. 1.
רדה F. ap. יֵרְדְּ III. F. ap. יָרַד Jud. v. 13. V. F. ap. יֵרְדְּ Is. xli. 2.
רדף VI. Part. מְרֻדָּף Is. xiv. 6.
רוה F. יִרְוְיֻן Ps. xxxvi. 9. III. F. aff. אֲרַיֶּךָ Is. xvi. 9.
רוח F. יָרְוַח IV. part. מְרֻוָּחִים Jer. xxii. 14.
רכך F. יֵרַךְ V. P. הֻרַךְ.

126　　　　IRREGULAR VERBS.　　　[Chap XI.

רמם　P. רֹמוּ Job. xxiv. 24. im. הָרֹמוּ Num. xvii. 10.
רנן　F. יָרֹן Prov. xxix. 6. im. רָנִּי and רֹנִּי Is. xii. 6.
　　　V. F. יָרְנִין.
רעע　F. ap. יָרַע.
רצץ　III. and רִצֵּץ and רֹצֵץ.

ש

שדד　III. F. יְשֹׁדֵד.
שטה　F. ap. יָשְׂטְ Prov. vii. 25.

ש

שאל　P. with aff. שְׁאֵלָתָם: שְׁאָלוּנוּ, שְׁאֵלְתִּיהוּ.
שאר　II. P. נֶאְשַׁאר Ezek. ix. 8.
שבת　F. ap. יָשְׁבְּ Num. xxi. 1.
שדד　III. שֻׁדַּד and 'ד F. יָשׁוּר and שָׁדוּ and שָׁדְרוּ IV. שֹׁדֵד.
שטע　III. P. שָׁטַעְתִּי.
שחה　VII. F. יִשְׁתַּחֲוֶה הִשְׁתַּחֲוֵיתִי, הִשְׁתַּחֲוִיתָ, הִשְׁתַּחֲוָה ap. יִשְׁתַּחוּ.
שחח　F. יָשׁחַ and שׁחוּ and שָׁחָחוּ שְׁחִ.
שבב　VI. הֻשַׁב and 'הֻ in. cr. שְׁכָב.
שכך　in. cr. שֹׁךְ Jer. v. 26.
שלו　שְׁלוּ שְׁלוּתִי Lam. i. 5. F. ap. יֶשֶׁל Job. xxvii. 8. יִשְׁלָיוּ Job. xii. 6.
שלך　VI. הָשְׁלַךְ and 'הֻ.
שמם　P. שָׁמְמוּ F. יִשֹּׁם and יָשֵׁם V. F. יָשֵׁם and יָשִׁים part. שֹׁמֵמִים Ezek. iii. 15. VI. in. הִשַּׁמָּה הָשַׁמּוּ Lev. xxvi. 34. הֻשַּׁמּוּ Job. xxi. 5.
שנן　III. שָׁנַּן and P. שִׁנַּנְתִּי.
שקה　V. F. ap. יָשְׁקְ.

שתה F. ap. יֵשְׁתְּ.

שתת II. נִשְׁתָּה Jerem. li. 30. in. p. נָשְׁתָה Is. xli. 17. נִשְּׁתוּ Is. xix. 5.

ת

תמך part. תוֹמֵךְ and תוֹמִיךְ Ps. xvi. 5.

תמם F. יִתֹּם and יִתַּם יִתֹּמוּ and יִתַּמּוּ in. p. יִתֹּמִי. V. P. הֻתַּמּוּ F. יַתֵּם VII. F. תִּתַּמָּם Ps. xviii. 26.

תעב III. P. הִעֵב F. יְתָעֵב and 'תָּ.

תעה F. ap. תַּתַע Prov. vii. 25. V. F. ap. יַתַע 2 Ch. xxxiii. 9.

CHAPTER XII.

THE PARTICLES.

1. The Hebrew Particles are separable or inseparable. The inseparable Particles are used as prefixes, and are comprised in the words מֹשֶׁה וּכֲלֵב.

2. The particles לְ, כְּ, בְּ, are prefixed with Shěw*a*, which before another Shěwa becomes short *Hirik*, and before a compound Shěwa the vowel of the compound, as לְאֹהָלִים, לִנְבִיאִים. Sometimes a contraction takes place, as לֵאלֹהִים, לַאדֹנָי, instead of Patha*h* and *Ha*(*l*ef Patha*h*, Segol and *Ha*(*l*ef Segol. So in the case of infinitives beginning with ה servile, as לְהַשְׁמִיעַ for לַשְׁמִיעַ, Ps. xxvi. 7 &c. Before a tone syllable, i. e. a monosyllable or a dissyllable accented on the penult. the vowel is often *k*′*a*mez, as כָּהֶם, לָלֶדֶת לָחֵת &c. Cf. Gen. i. 6, viii. 22, Deut. xvii. 8, Lam. i. 1, Prov. iv. 1, but not before a noun in constr., as Is. xxxiv. 10. Before Yod with Shěwa the vowel is long *Hirik*, as לִיהוּדָה.

3. When לְ, כְּ, בְּ, precede the definite article they displace the ה and take its vowel, as הָאָרֶץ *the earth*, בָּאָרֶץ *in the earth*, &c. following the conditions expressed iii. 9, 10, 11, 12. Sometimes, but rarely, the elision of the article does not take place.

Deut. vi. 24; Ps. xxxvi. 6 &c. If these particles precede a Shĕw*a*, Dagesh is not inserted in a following aspirate, because that Shĕw*a* is not supposed to be silent, as לִנְבוֹל, נְבוֹל. Before an infinitive construct however they commonly, but not always, cause the insertion of Dagesh, under such circumstances. (iii. 4. 3.) Before an infinitive with an affix they take Shĕw*a*, Deut. vi. 7; Lev. xxiii. 39, but in the case of the 2. pers. sing. m. and 2. pers. pl. m. f. there is an alternative form used when the sense is strictly objective, as לְשָׁמְרָךְ *to keep thee*, Prov. vii. 5 &c.

4. The significations of בְּ are as follows: *In, into, among, on, unto, against, by, with, for, in the place of, as.* With an infinitive *at the time of, when*, &c. see the Lexicons. The preposition בְּ is also used to express the superlative degree, see e. g. Cant. i. 8. *oh fair one among women,* i. e. *thou fairest among women.*

a. Sometimes it merely denotes the object as Prov. ix. 5.

5. The significations of כְּ are: *as, like, according to, about;* when repeated, *as — so;* with an infinitive, *as soon as.* כְּ is not used before a tense, but כַּאֲשֶׁר. It often takes *Kamez* (2) as כָּזֹאת, כָּאֵלֶּה.

6. The significations of לְ are: *To, for, in order to, for the purpose of, on account of, by, towards, until, at, with respect to, as to, according to, in the place of, as.* Frequently used with an infinitive constr. הָיָה followed by לְ, prefixed to a substantive, often means *became,* Gen. xviii. 18, and before a pronoun or a proper name denotes *possession,* as הָיָה לִי, *there was to me, I had.* So לְ also means

belonging to, בֶּן לְיִשַׁי, *a son belonging to Jesse*, 1 Sam. xvi. 18. לְבֹעַז, *belonging to Boaz*, Ruth ii. 3.

a. לְ sometimes merely denotes the object as 2 Sam. iii. 30. *they slew Abner*, Ps. cxxxv. 11, and cxxxvi. 19, 20. Analogous with this usage is that of אֶל as if for אֵת, Ps. ii. 7, Jer. x. 2, xxv. 9.

7. The particle ו is prefixed commonly with Shĕwa, which before a labial or another Shĕwa becomes Shurek as also before an anomalous compound Shĕwa, as Gen. ii. 12. Deut. v. 24.

a. ו is also prefixed with Kamez (sometimes even before a labial, as Ezek. xxviii. 8) when it joins together two words closely connected in sense the latter of which is a monosyllable or a dissyllable with the accent on the penult. Gen. i. 2, vii. 13, viii. 22.

b. ו before compound Shĕwa takes the vowel of the compound as וַאֲנִי, וַאֲמֶת, but with א sometimes a contraction takes place, as וַאדֹנָי, וֵאלֹהִים. Before ה or ח with compound Shĕwa followed by י, the Shĕwa of ו is changed to short *Hirik* or *Segol* and the compound Shĕwa becomes simple, as וְחָיוּ Gen. xlii. 18. וְהָיָה Gen. xii. 2. Before י coalition takes place as וַיְהִי.

c. Before the future tense ו prefixed with Pathaḣ followed by Dagesh marks it as a past, or the ordinary historic tense of narration. This Dagesh is omitted if the verb begins with י, as וַיְדַבֵּר. If the first letter is a guttural the Pathaḣ becomes *Kamez*, וָאֹמַר Ezek. xxi. 5.

8. The significations of ו are manifold. It is by far the most common conjunction and answers to many others used in English, e. g. *and, also, even,*

moreover, but, yet, nevertheless, then, therefore, in that case, that, so, so that &c. *Seeing that*, Gen. xxvi. 27, *that is to say*, 1 Sam. xvii. 40, xxviii. 3.

9. The prefix ה is used as the definite article and also as the particle of interrogation. For the method of prefixing it as the article see iii. 14: as the particle of interrogation iii. 13.

10. The article is used not only before nouns but also before adjectives and participles, anomalously also before verbs as Josh. x. 24. Ezra viii. 25, x. 14, 17, 2 Ch. i. 4, xxix. 36. Cf. perhaps Jer. v. 13, and even before a preposition with an affix, as 1 Sam. ix. 24. In these cases it may be regarded as standing for the relative.

a. A legitimate use of the article is that which it has when prefixed to a participle governing a noun or pronoun, as Job. xl. 19, Deut. viii. 16, Ps. xviii. 33 &c.

b. The article is often used to express the Vocative as in Lam. ii. 13, Jer. ii. 31, Ps. ix. 7, cxiv. 5, Zech. iii. 8.

c. Compound proper names may be resolved into two words of which the second takes the article, as בֶּן־הַיְמִינִי *the Benjamite*, Judges iii. 15 &c.

11. The article is often prefixed to the pronouns זֶה, זֹאת, הוּא, הִיא, הֵם, הֵן &c. which are then put after the nouns to which they refer, as הָאִישׁ הַזֶּה *this man*, הָאִשָּׁה הַהִיא *that woman*.

12. Nouns with pronominal affixes do not take the article because they are considered to be definite. There are however a few exceptions which

are highly anomalous. Josh. vii. 21, viii. 33, Lev. xxvii. 23, 2 K. xv. 16, Mic. ii. 12. Cf. Prov. xvi. 4, and Job. xl. 19, where the affix is objective. If an adjective or participle qualifies a noun with an affix the adjective or participle must have the definite article prefixed.

13. Any sentence is made interrogative by prefixing הֲ to the first word of it. In some cases however this particle is understood 1 Sam. xxi. 16, Job. xxxix. 2, xl. 25, especially with לֹא as 1 Sam. xiv. 30. So also Prov. vi. 30, may be much better rendered "Do not men despise a thief though he steal &c.?" So also Ezek. xxxii. 27. הֲ is sometimes followed by אִם. Cf. Jer. viii. 22 and Ps. xxx. 10.

14. The prefix מ stands for מִן. It is therefore commonly prefixed with short *Hirik* followed by *Dagesh*, but if the next letter does not admit *Dagesh* the *Hirik* becomes *Zerey*, as מֵעַל for מִן עַל iii. 9. So מֵהָעִיר, מֵאֵת, מֵעִם and even מֵיְהוָה: but before ח the *Hirik* remains, as מִחוּץ. The meanings of מִן are *from, out of, by reason of, by, more than, without* &c. It is used after adjectives to express the comparative degree, as Gen. iii. 1, "more subtle than any beast of the field" מִכֹּל: So also before infinitives, as Gen. iv. 13. "Is my iniquity too great to be forgiven?" מִנְּשֹׂא. It is sometimes *privative*, as Job. xi. 15. "Thou shalt lift up they face without spot" מִמּוּם. Cf. Ps. lxxxiii. 5, Gen. xxvii. 1, Deut. xxxiii. 11. Sometimes *partitive*, as Gen. iii. 6, Job. xxvii. 6, and sometimes *causative* or *instrumental* as Deut. vii. 8. Job. vii. 14, Gen. xlix. 12.

15. The prefix שׁ is shortened from אֲשֶׁר (see the following List). It is commonly prefixed with Segol

followed by Dagesh, if the letter takes Dagesh, Cant. i. 6, Eccles. i. 9, 10, 14 &c. 1 Ch. xxvii. 27, Ps. cxxiv. 6, otherwise with Segol alone Judg. vii. 12, Lam. iv. 9, Eccles. ii. 11, but in Eccles. iii. 18 it is prefixed with Shĕwa. In Gen. vi. 3, Judg. v. 7, bis. and Job. xix. 29, it is prefixed with Pathah followed by Dagesh. In Judg. vi. 17 it is prefixed with *Kamez*.

This prefix can itself take a prefix as Jon. i. 7, 12 &c. כְּשֶׁלִּי for בַּאֲשֶׁר לִי where it stands before a preposition and its affix. In Eccles. viii. 17 we find it before בַּאֲשֶׁר in the form בְּשֶׁל אֲשֶׁר which stands for בַּאֲשֶׁר לַאֲשֶׁר. See Preston *in loco*.

This abbreviation of the relative is most common in Cant. and Eccles. where it is very frequent.

---

16. The following are separable Particles used as adverbs conjunctions or prepositions and not susceptible of pronominal affixes

 אוֹ   *Or*.

  אוּלַי   *Peradventure, perchance, if by chance*, Num. xxii. 33. See Mason and Bernard's Grammar, i. 539.

  אָז or אֲזַי (Ps. cxxiv.) *Then*. Sometimes gives the force of a past to a future in prose, Ex. xv. 1, Josh. x. 12, not always in poetry, Ps. ii. 5, Is. xxxv. 6. Cf. Ps. lxix. 5.

 אַחַר   *After*.

 אֵיךְ   *How?*

 אַךְ   *Only, except*.

 אָכֵן   *Surely, truly*.

 אֵיפֹה and אֵיפוֹא *Where? How?*

אַל *Not.*

אֵלֶּה and אֵל *These.* The latter only with def. art. Lev. xviii. 27.

אֵלֶה, is found with a singular 1 Ch. xi. 11.

אִלּוּ *Otherwise, unless.*

אִם *If, whether; whether — or; when?* Is. iv. 4. Am. vii. 2 &c.

אִם כִּי *unless, except.*

אִם is used in oaths as a negative Ps. xcv. 11, Ezek. xx. 3 &c. &c.

אִם־לֹא is used in oaths as an affirmative Ezek. xx. 33 &c. &c. but אִם־לֹא is negative in Ex. xxii. 10, it must be rendered separately, *surely not*, Job. xxii. 20, interrogatively Job. xxxi. 31. It is simply *if not*, Jer. xvii. 27, Judg. iv. 8. In Jer. xxxiii. 25, it is used as an oath, but is equivalent to *if not*. In Jer. li. 14,

אִם־לֹא — כִּי־אִם as an oath in affirmation.

אָנָה *Whither.*

אַף *Also, moreover, yea, indeed.*

אָז and אָזַי *Now then, in that case.*

אֲשֶׁר *Who, which; he who, she who, that which, what;* as a conjunction, *that* Est. iii. 4, thus it = כִּי 1 K. xv. 5, Ex. xi. 7. So שׁ Cant. i. 7. אַחַר א׳ *after that*, בַּעֲבוּר א׳, עַד א׳, תַּחַת א׳, עַל א׳, יַעַן א׳, *because.* עַד א׳ *until;* בַּאֲשֶׁר *In which, where, because;* כַּאֲשֶׁר *As, as if, as soon as, when.* אֲשֶׁר sometimes means *because*, Deut. iii. 24, Ezek. xxix. 20, xxxix. 29, Gen. xxxi. 49, xxxiv. 27; sometimes *in order that*, Deut. iv. 10. It is equivalent to *if*, Lev. iv. 22, and to *when*, Ps. cxxxix. 15.

As the relative pronoun it has no distinction of number, gender, or case, and thus, not admitting of inflexion, requires the repetition of the personal pronoun after it, e. g. *in whom*, אֲשֶׁר בּוֹ, אֲשֶׁר בָּם; *to whom* אֲשֶׁר לוֹ, אֲשֶׁר לָהֶם &c.

בַּל *Not.*

בְּמוֹ used for בְּ poetically.

גַּם *Also, even;* גַּם — גַּם, *Both — and;* גַּם כִּי *Although.*

הֲלָזֶה Gen. xxiv. 65; הֲלָז Judg. vi. 20, 2 K. iv. 25. Once הַלָּזוּ Ezek. xxxvi. 35. *This.*

הֵן *Beho'd.*

זֶה m. זֹאת f. *This. Such as this*, Cant. v. 16. Is found with a plural Job. xix. 19, often stands for אֲשֶׁר or must have אֲשֶׁר understood after it, e. g. Prov. xxiii. 22, Ps. lxxiv. 2.

זוֹ, ‖ Ps. cxxxii. 12. ‖ Ps. lxviii. 29, cxlii. 4, cxliii. 8. *This; who, which.*

טֶרֶם *Not yet, before.* בְּטֶרֶם *Before.* לִפְנֵי is construed with an Infinitive mood, טֶרֶם with a tense, generally the future rather than the past, 1 Sam. iii. 3, 7.

כֹּה *Thus; here, hither.* עַד־כֹּה *Thus far.*

כִּי *For, because, when, if; that* before a statement. Sometimes stands for אֲשֶׁר, e. g. in Gen. iv. 25 (according to Bril) *whom Cain slew:* So Ps. v. 11, *who have rebelled against thee.* It also asks a question, as Gen. iii. 1, Job. xxxvii. 20.

כָּכָה *Thus.*

כֵּן *Thus, so;* אַחֲרֵי כ *Afterwards;* לָכֵן, (1) עַל־כֵּן, *therefore* (2) כִּי־עַל־כֵּן *Seeing that, since, because*, Gen. xxxiii. 10; (1) is sometimes put for (2) Gen. xviii. 5, Ps. xlii. 7, xlv. 3. עַד־כֵּן *Thus far*.

לָכֵן *Therefore*.

לֹא *No, not.* אַל and לֹא are never used with an imperative, only with a future or a future apocopated; אַל *apocopates*, but לֹא *does not*, except very rarely, e. g. Job. xxiii. 9, 11.

לוּ *If, O that*, with a future or a past.

לוּלֵי and לוּלֵא *If not, unless*.

לָמוֹ poetically for לְ.

מַדּוּעַ *Why? why*.

מָה and מַה־ מָה *What? what, somewhat, anything.* כַּמָּה *according to what, how much, how many* &c. Gen. xlvii. 8, לָמָה, לְמָה and עַל־מָה, עַל־מָה *Why?*

מָה is used before הָ, חָ, or עָ and sometimes before nongutturals also, as Is. i. 5, Jer. xvi. 10, 1 Sam. i. 8, Ex. xxii. 26. מָה is used before א and ר, and at the end of a sentence, e. g. Prov. ix. 13. מֶה is used before ה and ע having another vowel than *Kamez*, and always before הִיא and הוּא. מַה־ followed by Ma*kk*af frequently takes euphonic D*a*gesh in the next letter.

מִי *Who?* sometimes probably not interrogative, as Ex. xxiv. 14, Joel ii. 14. "He who is wise will return and repent &c." Eccles. iii. 21, according to Mendelssohn. Cf. Ex. xxxii 33, Judg. vii. 3, Jonah iii. 9. "He who is wise will return, and God will repent."

מָתַי *When? when.* אַחֲרֵי מ' *after how long?* לְכָתַי
and עַד־מָתַי *How long?*

נָא *I pray thee, pray, now.*

עִמָּדִי *With me.*

פֹּה, פֹּו, פֹּא, *Here, hither.*

פֶּן *Lest.* Equivalent to *take care lest, beware lest*, or the like, in Gen. iii. 22, and Is. xxxvi. 18. Cf. 1 Sam. xiii. 19, Jer. li. 46, Ps. xxxviii. 17.

פִּתְאֹם *Suddenly.*

שָׁם *There, thither.* שָׁמָּה *Thither, there.* מִשָּׁם *Thence.* אֲשֶׁר־שָׁם *Where.* אֲשֶׁר־מִשָּׁם *Whence.*

---

17. The following particles receive pronominal affixes.

אַחֲרֵי *After.*

אַשְׁרֵי *Oh how happy!*

אַיֵּה and אֵי *Where? where.*

אֵין cr. אֵין *None, not; is not, was not.* The cr. form is used when it stands before the noun, the abs. when the noun stands first; but אֵין follows the noun Gen. xlvii. 13, 1 Sam. xvii. 50, Prov. xxx. 27; it is used with לְ Ps. cxxxv. 17, and becomes אִי 1 Sam. iv. 21, Prov. xxxi. 4.

אֶל אֱל־ *To, unto.* See עַל.

אֶפֶס *Without, nothing more, none besides.* אֲפָסִי *none besides me.*

אֵצֶל *Near, close to, by the side of.*

אֵת אֶת־ *mark of the objective case.* As a preposition, *In reference to, as to, with.*

בִּגְלַל *Because of.*

בֵּין *Among, between.* Repeated before each noun or affix, if definite; if indefinite לְ sometimes stands before the second noun. Gen. i. 6, Deut. xvii. 8.

בִּלְתִּי *Except, unless, besides; not, without.* בְּ אִם *except, unless.* בִּלְתָּךְ, בִּלְתִּי p.

בִּלְעֲדֵי *Not as far as; except, without.* בִּלְעָדֶיךָ p. בִּלְעָדַי, בִּלְעָדָיו.

בַּעֲבוּר *Because of, in return for, in order that, because, while.*

בְּעַד *On account of, in behalf of, for, in exchange for, instead of, through, over, up, upon, about, around.* מִבַּעַד לְ *Through.*

הֵן *Behold; if, whether.*

הִנֵּה *Behold! here is, here was, there is, there was.*

זוּלַת (and וּלְתִי Deut. i. 36, iv. 12 &c.) *Besides, except.* זוּלָתְךָ, זוּלָתִי.

יֵשׁ *There is, there was.*

כֹּל כָּל־ *All, every one, any, the whole of.*

כְּמוֹ used for כְּ.

לְאַט *Slowly.* לְאִטִּי *at my slow pace, at my ease.* Gen. xxxiii. 14.

לְבַד *Alone, by self.*

לְמַעַן *For the purpose that; in order that, because, because of.*

לְעֻמַּת *Near, at, over against, accordingly.* לְעֻמָּתָם, לְעֻמָּתוֹ.

לִפְנֵי *Before.*

לִקְרַאת *To meet, opposite to.*

מוּל *Near, over against, opposite.* מִמֻּלִי Num. xxii. 5.

נֶגֶד *Before, in the presence of, in front of, opposite to, in comparison with, in the mind of.*

נֹכַח *Before, opposite, over against, in sight of, straight forwards.* נִכְחוֹ Ezek. xlvi. 9.

עַד *As far as, unto, until, before, during, still;* has the force of *while*, Judg. iii. 26, Jon. iii. 2, perhaps for עוֹד 2 K. iii. 25. עָדֶן and עַדְנָה

for עַד הֲנֵה are once met with Eccles. iv. 2, 3.

עוֹד *Again, besides, still, any longer;* has the force of *a good deal,* Gen. xlvi. 29.

עַל *Upon, on, over, above, near, besides, concerning, in reference to, towards, against, on account of, in behalf of:* sometimes means *as well as, together with, along with.* Gen. xxxii. 11, Hos. x. 14, Ex. xxv. 22, Job. xxxviii. 32.

אֶל and עַל are sometimes interchanged. Cf. Jer. xi. 10 and 23, Jer. xviii. 11, xix. 15, xxvii. 19. Even לְ corresponds to עַל Jer. xlvi. 2. עַל is put for אֶל 2 Sam. xv. 4, 2 K. xxv. 20, Is. xvii. 7. They are interchanged 1 Sam. xiv. 33, 34. Cf. 1 Sam. iv. 21. "Because the ark of God was taken and because of her father-in-law (אֵל)" 2 Sam. xxi. 1.

עִם *With, in company with, among.*

תַּחַת *Under, instead of, in the place of, in return for, on account of,* תַּחְתָּי *In his own place,* מִתַּחַת *From under, under.* מִתַּחַת לְ Id. תּ׳ אֲשֶׁר *because of, instead of.* תּ׳ כִּי *Because.*

a. The Particles מִפְּנֵי, לִפְנֵי, בִּלְעֲדֵי, אַ׳עֲרֵי, אֶל, אַחֲרֵי, סָבִיב, עַד, עַל, תַּחַת take the plural affixes, and the others the singular, as will be seen of the following Tables.

				Particles with
Them. f.	Them. m.	You. m.	Us.	Her.
אַחֲרֵיהֶן	אַחֲרֵיהֶם	אַחֲרֵיכֶם	אַחֲרֵינוּ	אַחֲרֶיהָ
	אֵים			
	אֵינָם[1]			אֵינֶנָּה
אֲלֵיהֶן ,'לָה'	אֲלֵיהֶם ,'לֵה'[2]	אֲלֵיכֶם ,'לֵכ'	אֵלֵינוּ	אֵלֶיהָ
	אֶצְלָם			אֶצְלָהּ
אִתְהָן,אִתָּן,אִתָּנָה[7]	אִתָּהֶם ,אִתָּם[6]	אִתְּכֶם[5]	אִתָּנוּ	אִתָּהּ
	אִתָּם	אִתְּכֶם	אִתָּנוּ	אִתָּהּ
בָּהֵן בָּהֶן	בָּם ,בָּהֶם ,בָּהֵמָּה	בָּכֶם	בָּנוּ	בָּהּ
		בְּגַלְלְכֶם		
	בֵּינֵיהֶם ,בֵּינֹתָם	בֵּינֵיכֶם	בֵּינֵינוּ ,בֵּינוֹתֵינוּ	
	בַּעֲדָם	בַּעַדְכֶם	בַּעֲדֵנוּ	בַּעֲדָהּ
	הֵנָּם		הִנֶּנּוּ,הִנְנוּ,הִנֵּנוּ	
		יֶשְׁכֶם ,לֶשׁ[9]		
	כְּהֶם ,כָּהֶם	כָּכֶם		

1. Poetically נֵמוֹ ,אֵינֵימוֹ. 2. or אֶל. Poet. אֱלֵי. commonly appropriated to the sign of the objective case, in the later books, the preposition takes the form of the xxiv. 24, Is. lix. 21, Jer. x. 5, 2 K. i. 15. both forms occur 8. Once הֵנָּה Gen. xix. 2. 9. Or יֵשׁ.

Pronominal Affixes.

	Me.	Thee. m.	Thee. f.	Him.
אַחֲרֵי	אַחֲרַי, רָי p.	אַחֲרֶיךָ	אַחֲרַיִךְ	אַחֲרָיו
אַיֵּה		אַיֶּכָּה		אַיּוֹ
אֵי	אֵינֶנִּי	אֵינְךָ	אֵינֵךְ	אֵינֶנּוּ
אֶל [2]	אֵלַי, לַי p.	אֵלֶיךָ	אֵלַיִךְ	אֵלָיו
אֵצֶל	אֶצְלִי			אֶצְלוֹ
אֵת [4]	אִתִּי	אִתְּךָ, תָּה, אִתָּכָה, אִתָךְ p.	אִתָּךְ	אִתּוֹ
אֶת [4]	אֹתִי	אֹתְךָ	אֹתָךְ	אֹתוֹ
בְּ	בִּי	בְּךָ, בְּכָה	בָּךְ	בּוֹ
בִּגְלַל		בִּגְלָלֶךָ p.	בִּגְלָלֵךְ	
בֵּין	בֵּינִי	בֵּינְךָ, בֵּינֶ׳ p., צְךָ	בֵּינֵךְ	בֵּינוֹ, בֵּינָיו
כְּעֲדֵי	כְּעָדַי, דַי p.			
בַּעֲבִיר	בַּעֲבוּרִי	בַּעֲבִירְךָ p.		
בְּעַד	בַּעֲדִי, דֵנִי	בַּעַדְךָ, בַּעֲדֶךָ p.	בַּעֲדֵךְ	בַּעֲדוֹ
הִנֵּה [8]	הִנְנִי, הִנֶּנִּי, הִנֵּנִי	הִנְּךָ, הִנֶּךָ, הִנְּכָה	הִנָּךְ	הִנֵּהוּ, הִנּוֹ
יֵשׁ [9]		יֶשְׁךָ		יֶשְׁנוֹ
כְּ				

3. Poet. אֱלֵימוֹ.   4. or אֶת־. The first of these forms is the second to the preposition; but in some places, especially first, Josh. xiv. 12, 2 K. iii. 12, viii. 8, Lev. xv. 18. 24, 2 Sam. 2 K. vi. 16.   5. Once אִתְכֶם.   6. Once אוֹתְהֶם.   7. Once אוֹתְהָן.

Particles with Pro

Them. f.	Them. m.	you. m.	us.	Her.
כְּנָה[3]	כְּלָם[2]	כְּלְכֶם	כְּלָנוּ	כְּלָה
	כְּמוֹהָם	כְּמוֹכֶם		כָּמוֹהָ
לָהֶן	לָהֶם[4]	לָכֶם	לָנוּ	לָהּ
לְבַדְּהָן, לְבַדְּנָה	לְבַדָּם	לְבַדְּכֶם		לְבַדָּהּ
		לְמַעַנְכֶם		
	לִפְנֵיהֶם	לִפְנֵיכֶם		לְפָנֶיהָ
	לִקְרָאתָם	לִקְרָאתְכֶם	לִקְרָאתֵנוּ	לִקְרָאתָהּ
מֵהֶן Ezek. xvi. 47, 52.	מֵהֶם[8]	מִכֶּם		מִמֶּנָּה
	נֶגְדָּם	נֶגְדְּכֶם		נֶגְדָּהּ
		עֲדֵיכֶם		עָדֶיהָ
	עֵדָם			עוֹדֶנָּה
עֲלֵיהֶן, לְהֵי[12]	עֲלֵיהֶם, לָבֵי[11]	עֲלֵיכֶם, לָכֵי	עָלֵינוּ	עָלֶיהָ
	עִמָּם, עִמְּרָם	עִמָּכֶם	עִמָּנִי	עִמָּהּ
	תַּחְתָּם, תַּחְתֵּיהֶם		תַּחְתֵּינוּ	תַּחְתֶּיהָ[13]

1. Or בָּל־.   2. Once כְּלָהֶם 2 Sam. xxiii. 6.
6. Twice, Ps. xviii. 23, Job. xxi. 16.   7. Once מֶנֵּהוּ Ps.
9. Poet. עָרֵי.   10. Poet. עָלֵי.   11. You. f. עֲלֵיכֶן. The other
12. Poet. עָלֵימוֹ.   13. Once תַּחְתֶּנָּה Gen. ii. 21.

THE PARTICLES. 143

nominal Affixes cont.

Me.	Thee. m.	Thee. f.	Him.
כָּל ¹			כֻּלֹּה, כֻּלּוֹ
כָּמֹו	כָּמֹנִי	כָּמוֹךָ, כָּמֹכָה		כָּמֹהוּ
לְ	לִי	לְךָ, לְכָה, לָךְ ·p	לָךְ	לוֹ
לְבַד	לְבַדִּי	לְבַדְּךָ, דָּ' ·p		לְבַדּוֹ
לְמַעַן	לְמַעֲנִי	לְמַעַנְךָ		לְמַעֲנוֹ
לִפְנֵי	לְפָנַי	לְפָנֶיךָ		לְפָנָיו
לִקְרַאת	לִקְרָאתִי	לִקְרָאתְךָ, תָ' ·p		לִקְרָאתוֹ
מִן ⁵	מִמֶּנִּי, מִנִּי, מֶנִּי	מִמְּךָ, מִמֶּךָּ	מִמֵּךְ	מִמֶּנּוּ ⁷
נֶגֶד	נֶגְדִּי	נֶגְדְּךָ, דָּ' ·p		נֶגְדּוֹ
עַד ⁹	עָדַי	עָדֶיךָ		עָדָיו
עוֹד	עוֹדֶנִּי	עוֹדְךָ	עוֹדָךְ	עוֹדֶנּוּ
עַל ¹⁰	עָלַי, לָי ·p	עָלֶיךָ	עָלַךְ, לְ ·p	עָלָיו
עִם	עִמִּי, עִמָּדִי	עִמְּךָ, מָךְ ·p עִמָּכָה		עִמּוֹ
תַּחַת	תַּחְתַּי, תַּחְתֵּנִי	תַּחְתֶּיךָ		תַּחְתָּיו

3. Once בִּלְהֵנָה.   4. Poet. לָמוֹ.   5. Poet. מִנִּי, מֵנִי Is. xxx. 11. lxviii. 24; מִנְּהוּ Job. iv. 12.   8. Once מִנְּהֶם Job. xi. 20. forms in 2 f. pl, if met with, would be analogous to this.

18. The letters א ה ו י ן are occasionally added on to the end of words and so are called *Paragogic* letters.

א In such cases is mostly pleonastic as Ezek. xli. 15, Josh. x. 24, Is. xxviii. 12, Jer. x. 5, Eccles. xi. 3.

ה Is either (1) what is called the ה *of motion*, when it is added on to nouns to express motion to a place, as צָפוֹן *north*, צָפֹנָה *northwards*; נֶגֶב *south*, נֶגְבָּה *southwards*; בֵּיתָה יוֹסֵף *to the house of Joseph*, Gen. xliii. 24. In 1 Sam. xxi. 2, we find it added with Segol נֹבֶה *to Nob*; or (2) the ה *paragogic*, expressing emphasis and the like, as אֲסַפְּרָה Ps. ii. 7, for אֲסַפֵּר, שָׁמְרָה Ps. xxv. 20. for שְׁמֹר. Ezek. xxiii. 48, 49. In Ps. xx. 4 and Zech. v. 4 we find it added with Segol and in Amos i. 11 we have the unusual from שֶׁמְרָה.

ו Paragogic occurs in the phrases בְּנוֹ בְעֹר *son of Beor*, Num. xxiv. 3, 15 for 'בְּן, חַיְתוֹ־אֶרֶץ Gen. i. 24, Is. lvi. 9, Ps. lxxix. 2 &c. for 'חַיַּת, לְמַעְיְנוֹ־מָיִם Ps. cxiv. 8 for לְמַעְיַן &c.

י Paragogic is chiefly found in poetry, as אֹסְרִי "*binding* the foal of his ass" Gen. xlix. 11 bis. Cf. Lam. i. 1, Deut. xxxiii. 16, Ps. ciii. 3. 6, cx. 4, cxiii. 5. 6. 7, cxiv. 8, cxvi. 12. In prose cf. Gen. xxxi. 39. In some cases י paragogic changes a previous ה into ת as Lam. i. 1, Cant. i. 9, and in some cases the י seems to be dropped from a form so changed, as פּוֹרָת Gen. xlix. 22. זִמְרָת Ex. xv. 2, Is. xii. 2, Ps. cxviii. 14; or these forms may be variations of the feminine. Cf. Ps. cxviii. 23, 2 Sam. i. 26, Deut. xxx. 11, Is. vii. 14. Paragogic י often takes the accent as Gen. xlix. 11.

ן Paragogic marks intensity, emphasis and the like, as תְּחִילִין for תְּחִילִי Is. xlv. 10. Cf. Ruth ii. 8. 1 Sam. ii. 22, Ps. xxxvi. 9 &c. Some consider this ן to be latent in the affixes ךָ־, ו־ and the like, when they term it the Nun Epenthetic. Nun Paragogic makes the accent ultimate; Nun Epenthetic, penultimate.

CHAPTER XIII.

THE CONSTRUCTION OF SENTENCES.

1. If the adjective qualifies the noun it is put last, as בֵּן חָכָם *a wise son*, Prov. x. i. In like manner the demonstrative pronouns and the ordinal numbers are preceeded by the noun to which they refer, as יוֹם שֵׁנִי *a second day*, הַדְּבָרִים הָאֵלֶּה *these words* &c.

2. But if the adjective is used as a predicate it commonly stands first, as טוֹב דְּבַר יְהוָֹה *good is the word of the Lord*, 2 K. xx. 19; though its position is really determined by the requirements of the emphasis, the more emphatic word standing first, as תּוֹרַת יְהוָֹה תְּמִימָה *the Law of the Lord is perfect*, Ps. xix. 8 &c.

3. When two nouns stand together as subject and predicate, the predicate may stand first and the substantive take the article, as לֵץ הַיַּיִן Prov. xx. 1, but to this there are many exceptions, see e. g. the remainder of the verse. The predicate does not generally take the article unless for special emphasis, as אַתָּה הָאִישׁ *Thou art the man*, cf. Jer. xix. 13, and this marks the difference between an adjective so used and one which qualifies the noun, as הָעִיר גְּדוֹלָה *the city is great*, but הָעִיר הַגְּדוֹלָה *the great city*, so הַמִּזְבֵּחַ עֵץ Ezek. xli. 22

In such a sentence, as דָּוִד הוּא הַקָּטֹן, 1 Sam. xvii. 4, it is plain that the predicate must take the article.

4. Emphasis is often expressed by repetition, as *the vale of Siddim was pits, pits;* i. e. *full of pits*, Gen. xiv. 10 &c. and superlative greatness by the use of one of the divine names, as Jonah iii. 3, *an exceeding great city*, lit. *a city great to God*, 1 Sam. xiv. 15, xxvi. 12, Ps. xxxvi. 7, lxxx. 11, Cant. viii. 6, Gen. xxx. 8. Cf. ἀστεῖος τῷ Θεῷ, Acts vii. 20.

5. The verb commonly precedes its subject and of course must do so if constructed with Waw conversive (xiii. 61). If however the subject is emphatic it will precede the verb, see Gen. xxxvii. 4, Job. xxviii. 14. Hence also the position of the nominative in Gen. i. 2. *And as for the earth—it was waste and desolate* &c.

6. The verb commonly precedes its object, as in Gen. i. 1; unless for the sake of emphasis, as in Gen. xl. 22.

7. In like manner for the sake of emphasis the principal noun is sometimes isolated and brought forward, as *Your land—strangers devour it in your presence*, Is. i. 7. *As for the wise man, his eyes are in his head*, Eccles. ii. 14. If the chief stress lies on an affix, the corresponding absolute pronoun is added likewise, as *thy blood, even thine*, גַּם אַתָּה 1 K. xxi. 19, *but me hath he not called*, וְלִי אָנִי 1 K. i. 26. Cf. Gen. iv. 26. *And to Seth, to him also was there born a son* גַּם־הוּא and Num. xiv. 32, 2 Sam. xvii. 5, Ps. ix. 7, Jer. xxv. 14, xxvii. 7, Prov. xi. 25, xxii. 19, xxiii. 15, 1 Sam. xix. 23, 2 Sam. xix. 1, Zech. vii. 5, Dan. viii. 1, 15, Gen. xxiv. 27, xxvii. 34.

8. The subject and the object thus being often brought into juxta-position, the particle אֵת is used to distinguish the object and has then no prepositional force, Gen. xl. 23, but the object sometimes stands without אֵת when no ambiguity can arise, or takes a preposition בְּ or לְ instead of it, as Prov. ix. 5, 2 Sam. iii. 30.

9. אֵת in this case may be used before proper names, or nouns with the article, or nouns with an affix, or nouns in construction; but אֵת is anomalously found in a few places before nouns not made definite by the article, or by an affix, or by being in the construct state, as 1 Sam. xxiv. 6, Lev. xx. 14, 2 Sam. iv. 11, xviii. 18, Ex. xxi. 28, Prov. xiii. 21. אֵת is occasionally found before כֹּל, זֹאת, &c. without the article. אֵת as a preposition may of course stand without the article, as Ezek. xxxii. 27.

10. Sometimes the subject is thrown into greater prominence by means of the particle אֵת, as 2 K. vi. 5, *as for the iron it fell into the water.* 2 K. x. 15, *as for thy heart is it right?* Cf. 2 K. ix. 25, Is. liii. 8. So also Judg. xx. 44. 46, 2 Sam. xi. 25, Ezek. xliii. 7, Neh. ix. 19. 32. 34, Dan. ix. 13, Josh. xxii. 17.

11. But especially is a similar use of אֵת with passive verbs to be remarked, as *his flesh shall not be eaten* אֶת־בְּשָׂרוֹ Ex. xxi. 28. So Num. xi. 22, xxvi. 55, xxxii. 5, Lev. x. 18, Deut. xii. 22, xvi. 16, 1 K. xviii. 13, Prov. xvi. 33, Jer. xxxv. 14, Ps. lxxii. 19, Josh. vii. 15, Gen. xxvii. 42.

12. The pronoun which is really inherent in the verb is for the sake of emphasis expressed, as

הֵמָּה יֹאבֵדוּ וְאַתָּה תַעֲמֹד Ps. cii. 27. *They shall perish but thou shalt endure.*

13. The objective pronouns are expressed by the verbal affixes or in the case of emphasis by את with an affix. If the verb has two accusatives the affix marks the nearer object and את the more remote, as 2 Sam. xv. 25.

14. Sometimes the objective pronoun though implied is not expressed in Hebrew, as Gen. ii. 19, Judg. vi. 19, Ex. ii. 3.

15. Sometimes on the other hand the pronoun in Hebrew is pleonastic, as *she saw him — the child* for *she saw the child*. Ex. ii. 6, xxxv. 5. Cf. Job. xxix. 3, xxxiii. 20, Prov. v. 22, Ezek. x. 3, Jer. ix. 14, 1 K. xix. 21, 1 Sam. xxi. 14, 2 Sam. xiv. 6, Ps. lxxxiii. 12. This is a construction common in the Talmud and in Syriac.

16. Sometimes the pronominal affix has a pregnant and condensed meaning as though a preposition were implied, as Jer. x. 20, *my children are gone forth of me*, יְצָאֻנִי. Cf. Ps. v. 5, Ezek. xxix. 3, Zech. vii. 5, Is. xliv. 21, Jer. viii. 13, and Job. xxxi. 18, where see Bernard's Commentary by Chance.

17. The pronominal affixes when joined to nouns have the possessive and objective significations, as *thou art my king o God*, i. e. whom I obey Ps. xliv. 5. *Yet have I set my king upon my holy hill*, i. e. whom I have appointed Ps. ii. 6, זִכְרְךָ Ps. vi. 6, *Thy memory*, i. e. of which Thou art the object, Job. iii. 10, *my womb*, i. e. my mother's, in which I lay, אֵידָם *Their calamity*, i. e. which they inflict, Job. xxx. 12, which they suffer, Prov. xxiv. 22. Cf. vi. 15.

18. The adjective which qualifies a definite noun must itself be definite, as הַמָּאוֹר הַגָּדֹל *the great light*, Gen. i. 16. שִׁמְךָ הַגָּדֹל *Thy great name*, 2 Ch. vi. 32. מַעֲשֵׂה יְהוָה הַגָּדֹל *the great work of the Lord*, Deut. xi. 7.

Sometimes the article is anomalously omitted before the adjective, as 2 Sam. vi. 3. Cf. Gen. xxix. 2; and sometimes before the noun, as Gen. i. 31, 1 Sam. xix. 22, Jer. xxxviii. 14, xlvi. 16, Ps. lxii. 4 &c. In some of these cases the article may possibly stand for the relative (xii. 10).

In lofty or poetical diction the use of the article is often times uncertain and arbitrary.

19. The adjective ought properly to agree with the noun it qualifies, but it very often does not either in gender or number, e. g. אֲדֹנִים קָשֶׁה Is. xix. 4. אֱלֹהִים קְדֹשִׁים Josh. xxiv. 19. צֹאן אֲבָדוֹת Jer. l. 6. רוּחַ גְּדוֹלָה וְחָזָק 1 K. xix. 11. Cf. 1 Sam. xv. 9 &c. Adjectives used as predicates frequently do not agree with the noun to which they refer, e. g. קָרַח אֱלֹהִים לִי טוֹב Ps. lxxiii. 28 &c.

20. The word אלהים is generally construed with a singular verb, but in a very few cases it takes a plural verb adjective or participle, e. g. Gen. xx. 13, xxxi. 53, xxxv. 7, Ex. xxxii. 1. 4. 8, Josh. xxiv. 19, 2 Sam. vii. 23 (pl. verb, s. pron.) Ps. lviii. 12. Some other verbs though plural are occasionally used to denote a singular, as אֲדֹנִים Is. xix. 4, בְּעָלָיו Ex. xxi. 29, xxii. 10, Prov. xxv. 13. Cf. עֹשָׂי Job. xxxv. 10, Ps. cxlix. 2.

21. Dual nouns take plural adjectives and verbs, as יָדַיִם רָפוֹת Job. ix. 3, שֹׁפְטֵי תַרְבֵּרְנָה Job. xxvii. 4. Anomalies, Ex. xvii. 12, 1 Sam. iv. 15.

22. Adjectives and verbs referring to one noun in construction with another ought to agree with the antecedent, e. g. Ps. i. 6, Eccles. viii. 1, but in some cases they do not, e. g. *The bows* (sing.) *of the mighty men are broken* חַתִּים 1 Sam. ii. 4, 2 Sam. xix. 9. *The voice of thy brother's blood* (pl.) *crieth*, צֹעֲקִים Gen. iv. 10. Cf. Job. xxix. 10, xxxviii. 21, Is. ii. 11. xxii. 7, xxv. 3, &c.

23. Nouns of multitude commonly take the sing. verb, as Gen. i. 22, Job. v. 23, but sometimes the plural, as Ezek. xxxi. 6, Job. xl. 20. *People* may take the sing. or plu. Ex. xxxii. 9, Num. xiii. 18 (sing.), Ex. xiv. 31 (plu.), Deut. vi. 1, 2 (both), xxviii. 68 (both). Cf. Ex. xiv. 9, 10 (both), Jer. ii. 31. Sometimes they take a feminine verb, Ex. v. 16, Ps. cxiv. 2, but as a fact.

24. The principles of concord in Hebrew admit of considerable variety; sometimes the grammatical form is sacrificed to the logical idea, Judg. xi. 39, 1 Sam. ii. 33, Zeph. ii. 9, Jer. xlviii. 15, Num. xx. 11, and sometimes the logical idea to the grammatical form, Job. xxii. 7, Eccles. vii. 27, but see Preston; and the examples in 22.

25. If a verb has two or more subjects it may stand regularly in the plural, as Gen. viii. 22. Cf. Ps. lxxxv. 11, or irregularly in the sing., as Gen. xxi. 32, Ex. xxi. 4, agreeing with the nearest 2 Sam. iii. 22, Jer. vii. 20, or with the most worthy Ex. ix. 19, xxi. 4, Ps. lv. 6, Prov. xxvii. 9.

When a verb put impersonally refers to rational agents it may stand in 3 pers. sing. mas. or 3 pers. pl. mas. or 2 pers. sing. mas. But if it refers to things it may stand either in 3 pers. sing. mas. or 3 pers. sing. fem.

26. Plural nominatives fem. referring not to persons often take a sing. verb, as Joel i. 20, Gen. xlix. 22 &c. on the other hand the plural fem. verb is sometimes used where we should expect the sing., as Ex. i. 10, Judg. v. 26, Is. xxviii. 3. Cf. Ob. 13.

27. Sometimes a plural nom. has a sing. verb preceding, as 1 Sam. i. 2, Is. xiii. 22 &c., or following, as Eccles. ii. 7, Gen. xlvi. 22, Is. lxiv. 10 &c. Sometimes the construction varies in the same sentence Gen. i. 14, Num. ix. 6, Ezek. xiv. 1.

28. Anomalous violations of gender are met with, e. g. a mas. pron. refers to a fem. noun Ex. i. 21, xi. 6, Judg. xix. 24. The reverse occurs Deut. v. 27, 2 Sam. iv. 6. The genders are confounded or disregarded in Gen. xxxii. 9, Josh. ii. 17, Jer. xliv. 19, Prov. ii. 10, 15, xiv. 3, Lev. vi. 8, Lam. ii. 20, Hab. iii. 17, Hos. xiv. 1, Is. iii. 16. Much confusion of genders is found in the book of Ruth, e. g. fem. pron. refers to mas. noun i. 13 &c. Cf. Jer. iii. 5, Ezek. xxiii. 49.

29. When the verb precedes its subject it is often found disagreeing with it in gender and number, e. g. Gen. v. 23, sing. verb with m. pl. noun. Ex. xvii. 12, s. v. with dual n. Ex. i. 10, f. pl. v. with f. s. n. 1 Sam. xxv. 27, m. s. v. with f. s. n. Job. xlii. 15, Mic. vi. 16, m. s. v. with f. pl. n. Job. xiv. 19, f. s. v. with m. pl. n. Ezek. xix. 12, pl. m. v. with m. s. n. Ps. lvii. 2, lxxiii. 7, m. s. v. with f. pl. n. 1 Ch. ii. 48. f. n. with m. v. Cf. Hag. ii. 7, *The desire of all nations shall come*, pl. v. with f. s. n. Cf. Judg.

xxi. 10. 13. 21, Num. xxxii. 25, 2 Ch. xi. 12, Is. xxiv. 4, xxviii. 3, xxxiv. 13, xliv. 26, Jer. iv. 14, xii. 4, xiii. 16. 18, xlvi. 15, li. 29. 48, Job. xxvii. 20, 2 Sam. xix. 9 &c.

30. Sometimes the singular is used, where the plural might be expected, to express the individual relation of the predicate to all the members of the subject, as Prov. iii. 18 (*every one of*) *those who lay hold on her* (*is*) *blessed*, part. sing. Job. vi. 20 (*all*) *were ashamed for* (*each*) *trusted.* Cf. Gen. xxvii. 29, xlix. 22, Prov. xx. 18, xxvii. 16, Ex. xxxi. 14, Job. xii. 7.

31. The relation expressed by the constructive state in Hebrew is susceptible of many meanings, but they chiefly divide themselves into two classes (1) the subjective and (2) the objective, e. g.

1) חֲמַת יְהֹוָה *The wrath of the Lord*, i. e. which He feels, of which He is the subject.

2) יִרְאַת יְהֹוָה *The fear of the Lord*, i. e. which is felt towards Him, of which He is the object.

3) It expresess *possession*, as יַד יְהֹוָה *the hand of the Lord*, which belongs to Him. דְּבַר יְהֹוָה *the word of the Lord*, which comes from Him, is spoken by Him, of which He is the author. בֵּית יְהֹוָה *the house of the Lord*, which is dedicated to Him, and devoted to his service.

4) It expresses the relation of *cause*, as עֵץ הַחַיִּים *the tree of life*, i. e. causing life, Gen. ii. 9. *The cup of trembling*, i. e. which causes trembling Is. li. 22.

5) It expresses the relation of *consequence*, as זַעֲקַת־דָּל *the cry of the poor*, which is the consequence of his oppression as being poor Prov. xxi. 13, *the heritage of those that fear Thy name*, which

is the reward of those that fear Thy name, the consequence of fearing it Ps. lxi. 6.

6) It expresses family relationship, as אֵשֶׁת אַבְרָם *the wife of Abram,* בֶּן־דָּוִד *the son of David.*

7) It expresses *direction,* as *the path of life,* i. e. leading to life, Ps. xvi. 11, *the way of the plain,* i. e. toward the plain 2 K. xxv. 4, *the way of the wilderness,* Josh. viii. 15, *the way to Beth-horon,* 1 Sam. xiii. 18; *the way of Beth-shemesh,* 1 Sam. vi. 12 &c.

8) It expresses the *purpose, object,* or *intention,* as מוּסַר שְׁלוֹמֵנוּ *the chastisement of our peace,* i. e. to procure our peace Is. liii. 5, *corn* for *the famine of your houses,* i. e. intended to satisfy the hunger, avert the famine, of your houses, Gen. xlii. 19.

9) It expresses the *end* or *destiny,* as *sheep* for *the slaughter,* destined to be slain, Ps. xliv. 23. בַּדֵּי שְׁאֹל *limbs destined to the grave,* Job. xvii. 16. See Bernard. בְּכוֹר מָוֶת *first born destined to die,* xviii. 13.

10) It expresses the relation of *quality,* in the consequent, where in many cases we should use an adjective, as אִמְרֵי בִינָה *the words of intelligence,* for, intelligent words &c. So likewise the *substance* of which a thing is made, as כְּלִי כֶסֶף *vessels of silver,* i. e. silver vessels &c.

11) Sometimes it implies the action of a verb or particle understood, as לֶחֶם סְתָרִים *the bread of secrets,* i. e. bread *eaten in secret,* Prov. ix. 17.

12) It is used before the proper names of rivers, countries, &c., as נְהַר פְּרָת *the river Euphrates.* אֶרֶץ מִצְרַיִם *the land of Egypt,* &c.

32. Adjectives and participles are used in the constructive state with the sense of *with, of, as to,* &c., e. g. קְרֻעֵי בְגָדִים *torn* as to *the garments*, Is. xxxvi. 22. חֲגוּרַת־שָׂק *girded* with *sackcloth*, Joel i. 8. נְשׂוּי־פֶּשַׁע *forgiven* as to *sin*, Ps. xxxii. 1. קְשֵׁה־עֹרֶף *hard* of *neck, stiffnecked* Deut. ix. 6 &c.

33. Sometimes a noun stands in construction with an adjective, as חַיִל כָּבֵד Is. xxxvi. 2, Prov. ii. 9, Ps. lxxviii. 49, Cant. 7. 10, Lev. xxiv. 22, Is. xvii. 10. Cf. אַנְשֵׁי הַתָּרִים (a rare use) *the merchant-men* 1 K. x. 15. But much more common is an adjective in construction with a following noun.

34. When the consequent has the force of a qualifying adjective (31.10) it is the consequent that takes the affix, as in Ps. ii. 6, *the mountain of my holiness,* for *my holy mountain,* Job. viii. 6, or the noun is repeated, as in Gen. xliv. 2.

35. Sometimes it is the antecedent which has the force of the qualifying adjective, as *greenness of herb* for *green herb,* Gen. i. 30, in such cases also the consequent takes the affix, as *the willingness of her hands* for *her willing hands,* Prov. xxxi. 13; *the greatness of his strength* for *his great strength,* Is. lxiii. 1.

36. Generally the consequent serves as a qualifying adjective to the antecedent, but sometimes the antecedent to the consequent as in 35; e. g. מְרוֹם הָרִים *the hight of mountains* for *high mountains* 2 K. xix. 23, particularly when the consequent has a pronominal affix, as *thy choice valleys,* Is. xxii. 7. Cf. xxxvii. 24. Jer. xxii. 7, Zeph. iii. 11. So כָּל־הָאָרֶץ *all the earth.*

37. In some cases, especially after כְּ, the antecedent is understood, as *their sin is like* (*the sin of*)

Sodom Is. iii. 9. *He maketh my feet like (those of) hinds* 2 Sam. xxii. 34. *Roaring like (the roaring of) the lion,* Prov. xix. 12 &c.

38. In like manner, after a noun with a pron. affix, the noun itself must sometimes be supplied as the antecedent of the following word, thus מַחֲסִי־עֹז *my refuge (the refuge of) strength,* i. e. *my strong refuge,* Ps. lxxi. 7; מַרְכְּבֹתֶיךָ יְשׁוּעָה *Thy chariots (the chariots of) salvation,* Hab. iii. 8. This is an exceptional usage not to be imitated in composition.

39. When two nouns are connected by the state of construction the consequent ought properly to bear the pronominal affix, as בֵּית־תְּפִלָּתִי *my house of prayer,* but in a few cases (38) we find the affix joined to the antecedent, as Lam. iv. 17, Ezek. xvi. 27 &c.

40. Two nouns in construction cannot have the same consequent in common, thus we are obliged to say *the chariot of Israel and the horsemen thereof,* instead of *the chariot and horsemen of Israel.* This is called by some the *mediate* state of construction.

41. A noun in the construct state is sometimes separated by a preposition from its consequent, as שִׂמְחַת בַּקָּצִיר *the joy of harvest,* Ps. ii. 12. חוֹסֵי בוֹ Is. ix. 2. מַשְׁכִּימֵי בַבֹּקֶר *who rise early in the morning,* Is. v. 11. אַחֲרֵי לָנוּם Is. lvi. 10. יוֹרְדַי אֶל־אַבְנֵי־בוֹר Is. xiv. 19, Ezek. xxi. 17, מְשָׁרְתַי אוֹתִי *who serve Me,* Jer. xxxiii. 22. מָשׁוֹשׂ אָח־רִצִּין Is. viii. 6. אֱלֹהֵי מִקָּרוֹב *a God near at hand,* Jer. xxiii. 23. הֹלְכֵי עַל־דָּרֶךְ Judg. v. 10, or by וְ, Is. xxxiii. 6, xxxv. 2, &c. Cf. li. 21, or by אֲשֶׁר, Gen. xxxix. 20, xl. 3, Lev. vi. 18, vii. 2, Num. ix. 17, 1 Sam. iii. 13, Deut. xxii. 24, Eccles. i. 7, xi. 3, or by זֶה Ps. civ. 8.

42. Sometimes the antecedent is divided from its consequent by other words, Is. v. 24, xiv. 6, xx. 1, Jer. xxii. 23, Ezek. xxxix. 11, or has a sentence for its consequent, as 1 Sam. xxv. 15, Lam. i. 14, Ps. lxxxi. 6, Is. xxix. 1, xxx. 29, Hos. i. 2, Lev. iv. 24, xiv. 46, Ex. vi. 28, Gen. xl. 3, 1 Sam. iii. 13, 2 Sam. iii. 13, Job. xviii. 21, xxvi. 2, Ps. cxxix. 6.

43. Sometimes the constructive seems to be put for the absolute, as Jer. xlviii. 5, 36, Is. xxxiii. 6, xxxv. 2, li. 21, 2 K. ix. 17, Ps. xvi. 3, lxxiv. 19.

44. Sometimes the absolute is put for the constructive, as 1 K. xxii. 27, Prov. xxii. 21, Deut. xvi. 21, xxxiii. 11, Judg. v. 13, vii. 8, Jer. x. 10, Ps. lix. 6, lx. 5, Ezek. xlvii. 4, 2 Ch. xv. 8, Is. xxii. 17, xxiv. 22, Ps. cxx. 2. 3, Lev. vi. 13.

45. Two nouns are sometimes found in apposition with each other, as אֲנָשִׁים מְאָט *a few men*, Neh. ii. 12. Cf. Deut. xxvi. 5, though here מְאָט is more properly an adverb. בְּבָרִים כָּסֶף *two talents of silver*, 2 K. v. 23. הַבָּקָר הַנְּחֹשֶׁת *the brazen oxen*, 2 K. xvi. 17. טוּרִים אֶבֶן Ex. xxviii. 17. שְׁנָתַיִם יָמִים Gen. xli. 1. So Dan. x. 3, Ruth ii. 17, 2 K. vii. 1. It is a question whether in some of these cases the abs. form does not stand for the constr.

a. In like manner the noun is often put absolutely to denote *the place where* or *whether, time when* or *how long*, as Gen. xviii. 1, xxvii. 44, *the material of which a thing is made*, Gen. ii. 7 *the measure of a thing*, Gen. vii. 20, *the Greek construction of κατά*, Ps. iii. 8, and a certain Adverbial use Deut. xxiii. 24.

46. An Infinitive in construction with a noun may be followed by one or more nouns in the objective, that is, the accusative case, as Gen. ii. 4, *in the day of the Lord God's making earth and heaven*, Gen. xli. 39 &c. In such cases the subject commonly precedes the object and immediately follows the verb, as in the last two passages, but not always, as e.g. Gen. iv. 15, Is. v. 24, xx. 1.

The affixes to an inf. construct. or part. sometimes denote the *subject* and sometimes the *object* of the verb. The ambiguity is sometimes removed by the *object* taking אֵת, but the affix ־ְנִי always denotes the *object*.

47. The substantive verb is frequently omitted in Hebrew Gen. iii. 10, xlii. 11 &c. &c. Sometimes it is expressed by an idiomatic use of the personal pronouns, Gen. xxv. 16, 2 Sam. vii. 28, 1 K. xviii. 39, Ps. xxiv. 10, Is. li. 12, lii. 6, Jer. li. 19, Zech. i. 9, but in all these cases we may rather consider the substantive verb to be understood and the subject as made more emphatic in consequence.

48. There is an impersonal use of the Tenses in Hebrew corresponding to our "*one* did so and so", or "it was done &c.", as *one called the well* &c. Gen. xvi. 14. Cf. xxvii. 36, xlviii. 1, 1 Sam. xix. 22. 24, 2 Sam. iii. 6. 7, xi. 3, xv. 31, xxiv. 1 with which cf. 1 Ch. xxi. 1, where another subject is given; 1 K. xviii. 26, 2 K. vi. 32.

49. Some verbs are followed by an accusative of a like signification, as רָאָשׁ, יָרַע, שָׂרַע, &c. Gen. i. 11, 20 &c.

50. Causative Verbs take two accusatives, one of the person and another of the thing, as Eccles. xii. 9, Ps. cxliii. 8, 1 K. xxii. 27, Gen. xli. 42 &c.

The same construction is found with verbs in *K*al sometimes, as Gen. ii. 7 &c.

51. Verbs in Hebrew govern their object either mediately or immediately, that is, with or without a preposition before it, and some are susceptible of both constructions, occasionally the sense varies according to the preposition used and as it is omitted or expressed. All this must be learnt from the Lexicon.

52. The Infinitive absolute is sometimes used as a kind of gerund Is. xxii. 13, or noun of action Hosea iv. 2, or for a finite tense 1 K. xxii. 30, 2 K. iv. 43, Ezek. xi. 7, e. g. for a past tense Jer. xiv. 5, Job. xv. 35, Dan. ix. 5, or an imperative Deut. v. 12, xvi. 1, Num. xxv. 17, Jer. ii. 2, or a future Deut. xiv. 21, Is. v. 5, Ezek. xi. 7, Jer. xxxii. 44. As a verbal noun Is. vii. 15, xlii. 24, Jer. ix. 4.

53. But more commonly it is used to add force and emphasis to a finite tense which it *precedes*, as מוֹת תָּמוּת *to die thou shalt die*, i. e. *thou shalt surely die*, Gen. xxxvii. 8, 1 Sam. xx. 6 &c. Sometimes it comes *after* the tense, when it denotes continued action, as 2 Sam. xv. 30, Gen. viii. 7, xix. 9, xlvi. 4. It is found with an Imperative Is. vi. 9, Judg. v. 23, Num. xi. 15.

54. Thus used it is commonly of the same conjugation as the Tense, but not always, as Job. vi. 2 (*K*al and Nif*g*al), Ezek. xvi. 4 (Hof*g*al and Pu*g*al), Ex. xix. 12. 13, Gen. xxxvii. 33, Is. xxiv. 19.

1) Sometimes the Infinitive is from a kindred verb, as Is. xxviii. 28, Jer. viii. 13, xlii. 10, xlviii. 9.

2) Sometimes the infinitive absolute is used adverbially, as 1 Sam. iii. 12.

3) And in some few cases, the Infinitive constructive seems perhaps to be put for the Infinitive absolute, Is. lx. 14, Hab. ii. 10, Num. xxiii. 25, Ruth ii. 16, Ps. l. 21, Judg. iv. 20.

55. The particles בכלם are prefixed not to the absolute but to the constructive form of the Infinitive. In such cases the Infinitive is frequently in construction with a following noun. An Infinitive with an affix may be the consequent to a noun in construction.

56. Passive participles are found in construction with the noun (32) and also in the absolute form with the noun put absolutely, as לְבֻשׁ בַּדִּים Ezek. ix. 2, 1 Sam. ii. 18, but לְבוּשׁ הַבַּדִּים Ezek. ix. 11.

57. Two verbs are often used in Hebrew when we should express the first by an adverb, as *he returned and dug* for *he dug again*, Gen. xxvi. 18. Sometimes the second verb is an infinitive, as Gen. xxvii. 20.

58. Adverbial particles are repeated to mark intensity, as מְאֹד מְאֹד *very much*, &c. As in English they are sometimes used to qualify nouns &c., as בְּלִי שֵׁם *of no name*, Job. xxx. 8. Two negative adverbs strengthen the negation, as 1 K. x. 21, Ex. xiv. 11, Zeph. ii. 2, but not always, according to Mendelssohn, as Eccles. iii. 11, *so that a man cannot but find* &c.

59. *Use of the Tenses.* As there are but two tenses in Hebrew it is obvious that they must be used to express the various shades of distinction in time which other languages express by additional moods and tenses, e. g. the Past Tense may express

1) A pluperfect, as Gen. ii. 2, 5 &c.

2) A complete past, as Job. i. 1.

3) A past continuing to the present time, as יָדַעְתִּי *I know.* Cf. 1 Sam. xv. 2, Prov. i. 7, *have despised and yet despise.*

4) The prophetic future, as Gen. xv. 18.

5) The imperative mood, after an imperative and with ו prefixed, as Gen. vi. 21, or without the preceding imperative, as Gen. xxxiii. 10, but for this see 62.

6) The subjunctive, as Num. xxii. 33, *I would have slain thee and saved her alive,* Judg. viii. 19, *I would not slay you.*

7) The optative, as Num. xiv. 2, *Would God we had died in the land of Egypt.*

8) The future perfect, as Gen. xxviii. 15, *until I shall have done that which I have spoken to thee of.*

60. The Future expresses

1) The actual future, as *I will never leave thee nor forsake thee,* Josh. i. 5.

2) The future perfect, as Num. xxiii. 24, *he shall not lie down till he shall have eaten of the prey and drunk the blood of the slain.*

3) The present, as Ps. ii. 1. *Why do the people imagine a vain thing?*

4) The present of habitual action, as *he meditates in His law day and night,* Ps. i. 2.

5) The past of habitual action, as *righteousness lodged in it but now murderers,* Is. i. 21. Cf. Job. i. 5.

6) The imperfect, as Job. iii. 3. *The day in which I was born,* Gen. ii. 10. The particles אָז and

שָׁם, especially in prose, have a tendency to give this meaning to the Future, Gen. ii. 5, Deut. iv. 41.

7) Continuous or contemporaneous action and so following a past, as Ex. xv. 12, Is. xli. 5.

8) The conditional or subjunctive, as Ps. xxiii. 4, *even though I were to walk through the valley of the shadow of death I would fear no evil.*

9) The optative, as Job. iii. 4, *may no light shine upon it.*

10) The imperative, especially with negatives, as Jer. ix. 22, *let not the rich man glory in his riches.*

11) The English *may, must, ought,* &c., as *which thing ought not to be done,* Gen. xxxiv. 7.

61. But in addition to this flexibility of use, each of the tenses is liable to be modified by the operation of the *Waw conversive* which has the effect, with comparatively few exceptions, of changing the past to a future and the future to a past, with most of the meanings in either case which have already been assigned to those tenses.

62. A past therefore with וְ prefixed must be construed regularly as a future with some one of the significations given above that may best suit the context, e. g. Gen. i. 15. וְהָיוּ *and they shall be,* or, as the context demands *and let them be.* A past with וְ frequently follows an imperative, as Lev. i. 2. דַּבֵּר—וְאָמַרְתָּ *speak and say.*

Waw conversive retains its power as a conjunction in all cases, *and, so, then* &c. as the sense requires. Ruth i. 1, and Esther i. 1. can scarcely be called exceptions.

Chap. XIII.] THE CONSTRUCTION OF SENTENCES. 163

In some instances, however, Waw prefixed to a past does not change it to a future, e. g. when it immediately follows another past, as וַיַּעַל 2 Sam. xiii. 18. Cf. Gen. xxxviii. 5. 9, Ex. xxxvi. 1. 29, Judg. xvi. 18, xix. 30, 1 Sam. xvii. 35, 1 K. iii. 11, xiii. 3, xix. 18, xxi. 12, 2 K. xiv. 7. 14, xviii. 36, xxiii. 5, Jer. vi. 17, xx. 9, Ezek. ix. 7, xvii. 18, xxxvii. 7, 1 Ch. v. 20, 2 Ch. xxv. 19, Ezra viii. 30. 36, Neh. ix. 7, seq. x. 33, Dan. x. 14, &c. As many of these passages refer to single acts they cannot be explained by attributing to them the frequentative meaning of the future. They are sufficient to prove that Waw does not act *universally* on the past so as to convert it to a future though such is its normal use. The past therefore with ן is almost always to be rendered as if it were a future.

The Waw conversive in the past tense commonly shifts the accent from the penultimate to the ultimate syllable. Cf. Gen. xxxii. 13, xliv. 4 &c. (When the accent falls on the last syllable but one it is termed milge͞yl *from above*, on the last milrag *from below*). The exceptions to this rule are 1) Verbs in א or ה *generally*. 2) The first person plural *always*. 3) Verbs with the pause on the penult. 4) When a tone syllable immediately follows. In these cases the accent remains *milgeyl*, and is not affected by Waw conversive. Ex. וְאָמַרְתִּי, וְאָמַרְתִּי, וְאָמַרְנוּ.

63. On the other hand the Future with ן prefixed (subject to the regular variations in the points) retains its proper meaning as to time, e. g. Gen. i. 6, remaining a simple future with the significations given above.

64. But if the Waw is prefixed with Pathah followed by Dagesh it changes the future to a past.

11*

And the future so modified becomes the ordinary historical tense used in narration. This Pathaḥ is subject to the changes specified above xii. 7 &c.

The exceptions in this case are not so numerous as before, but there are a few instances in which a future with Waw conversive appears to remain a future still, e. g. Jer. xv. 6, 7, though this may be taken as a predictive past, 2 Sam. xix. 2, 1 K. xxi. 6. In some cases the tense with Waw conversive refers to time anterior to that of the previous tense, e. g. Judg. iv. 21, "*he was fast asleep for he had been tired*". Cf. Bernard on Job. xiv. 10. This is really the figure known in Greek as ὕστερον πρότερον.

The Waw conversive in the future commonly shifts the accent from the last syllable to the last but one except, 1) In the first person singular *always*. 2) Verbs ending in א. 3) When the pause comes on the final syllable. 4) When more than a single vowel intervenes between the accent and the ו and when Shěwa is expressed or implied, as וַיֵּשְׁתְּ, וַיֵּפֶן, וַיִּפְקֹד, וַיִּסְחַר. In these cases the accent remains *milrag*, Ex. וַיֹּאמֶר, וַיֹּאמֶר, וַיֹּאמַר. Rather than rest on a slight vowel substituted for Shěwa the accent is even found at times on the antepenult, e. g. Is. l. 8.
See Mason and Bernards Hebrew Grammar Vol. i. 304.

65. In a general way then

The past tense with ו֥ = *and* with the future,
and the future with וַ֫ = „ „ the past,
thus וְדִבֵּר = „ „ יְדַבֵּר
and וַיְדַבֵּר = „ „ דִּבֵּר

So וִידַבֵּר is Future *and he will speak*,
but וַיְדַבֵּר is Past *and he spake.*

66. There can however be no doubt that the tenses are occasionally used in a somewhat loose way, more especially in the poetical portions of the Bible, and the sequence of them is a matter not always admitting very readily or certainly of explanation. See e. g. the following passages where they seem to be used indifferently, Deut. ii. 12, Dan. x. 17, Ezra ix. 3, 4, 5 &c. Nevertheless the construction of the tenses is a point more likely to perplex the advanced student than the beginner lying as it does in the genius of the language and among its more critical niceties. The general bearing and regimen of them is sufficiently clear and intelligible. Not seldom the tense first used in a sentence appears to exercise a certain modifying influence with regard to time upon those which follow it, e. g. Gen. ii. 25, Ex. xv. 12, Is. viii. 2, 3. xli. 5, 1 K. xxi. 6 &c.

67. The Imperative mood is used to express

1) a simple imperative with the ordinary modifications of exhortation, entreaty, permission, &c.

2) a future, often when immediately preceded by an imperative, as *Do this and live*, i. e. do this and you shall live Gen. xlii. 18, Prov. iii. 3, 4, 7 &c. So likewise when it is connected with a future which precedes Gen. xlv. 18, or follows Is. xlv. 11, &c. Cf. Gen. xx. 7, Is. liv. 14, Ruth i. 9.

68. The optative is expressed by the future with ה paragogic, and the particle נא, or by the particles אם, לו, Gen. xvii. 18, xxiii. 13, Num. xx. 3, Ps. lxxxi. 14, or the phrase מי יתן followed by a tense, an infinitive mood, or a noun 2 Sam. xv. 4, Deut. v. 26, xxviii. 67, Ex. xvi. 3.

69. Not only is the pronoun sometimes pleonastic in Hebrew (15). Cf. Cant. i. 6, ii. 11. 17, Job. xii. 11, xix. 29, Ps. cxliv. 2, but also the prepositions בְּ Ex. xxxii. 22, Hos. xiii. 9, לְ Judg. xix. 30. Cf. Job. v. 5, and מִן Deut. xv. 7.

70. On the other hand Ellipses in Hebrew are of very frequent occurrence: each of the particles בכלם has occasionally to be supplied, e. g.

1) We find ellipses of בְּ in Num. xxx. 11, וְאִם בֵּית for וְאִם בְּבֵית, so also 2 K. xi. 3, Ps. xviii. 35. Cf. 2 K. xxv. 10, Prov. ii. 16, Job. xl. 22, Is. v. 12, Jer. xxix. 26, Mic. vi. 10 &c.

2) Ellipses of כְּ Ps. lxxiii. 22, Jer. xlviii. 34, perhaps. Cf. Cant. v. 10—16, where the particle כ is alternately inserted and omitted, Lam. iv. 14, Job. xxiv. 5.

3) Ellipses of לְ Prov. xiv. 35, Ezek. xii. 10, Ps. xlvii. 7, 2 Sam. iv. 2.

4) Ellipses of מִן Jer. xviii. 15, so the A. V. takes it. 1 K. xiii. 33, perhaps, *he became* (one of) *the priests of* (the) *high places.* Is. xl. 21, where it must be supplied from the former member. Cf. Mic. vii. 12, 2 Sam. xx. 19, a clear instance. Gen. xlix. 25.

5) So Ellipses of וְ Hab. iii. 11, Judg. xix. 2, v. 27, Is. lxiii. 11. Cf. 2 K. ix. 32, 1 Sam. xx. 12. Is. xvii. 6 &c.

6) Ellipses of אֲשֶׁר are very frequent and it is important to observe them Gen. xlii. 28, Ex. iv. 13, Prov. vii. 5, xii. 17, Ps. lxv. 5, lxix. 23, Is. vi. 6, lvii. 16, Jer. ii. 8. 11, viii. 13, xii. 5, Job. xiii. 28, Lam. i. 21, iii. 1 &c. &c.

7) Sometimes we find an ellipse of שָׁם after

אֲשֶׁר Is. lxiv. 10, or of אֲשֶׁר שָׁם Job. xii. 24, xxxviii. 26. Cf. xxvi. 5, and Bernard's commentary *in locis.*

8) An occasional ellipse of אִישׁ or אֲנָשִׁי is also to be observed, as *harvest* for *harvest-man,* Is. xvii. 5, *bow* for *bowmen,* xxi. 17, *righteousness* for *righteous men,* xli. 2. Cf. Dan. ix. 23, cfd. with x. 11, 19. Obad. 7. לְחָמְךָ for אֲישׁ לְ. Job. xxxi. 32, *way* for *way faring man,* Mic. vi. 9, Zech. x. 2, possibly Prov. xiii. 6, xvii. 4, xxiii. 28, 2 Sam. xii. 4, or some of these may be cases of the abstract for the concrete.

9) Sometimes it is necessary to supply לֵאמֹר or some such word, as Jer. vi. 17, xxxi. 3. Cf. xl. 5, Hos. xiv. 9, Is. xlv. 14, &c. Eccles. viii. 2 and a very curious ellipse Judg. xvi, 2. Other ellipses to be supplied by the sense of the context are to be seen in Ps. vi. 4, xcii. 12, cxviii. 7, cxxxvii. 5, Prov. xviii. 19.

71. In many cases it is requisite to supply in one member of a sentence some word or words expressed in another whether it be the first or second, e. g. in Prov. xiii. 1, יִשְׁמַע in the first member must be supplied from שָׁמַע in the second. So in Ex. vi. 3. שֵׁם must be supplied from the second member בְּ from the first. Ps. ix. 19, Jer. xii. 5, Prov. xiv. 25; Hosea i. 9, supply "God" in second member from "people" in the first; Am. iii. 12, Obad. 7. supply אֲשֶׁר, Is. xxxviii. 18, xl. 21. Cf. a remarkable instance in 1 Chr. xvii. 5, Ezek. xi. 11, xxiv. 17.

72. It is often necessary to transpose the order of the words in Hebrew before translating them into English, e. g. the predicate is interposed between the

adjective and its noun in the latter part of Prov. xii. 27. Cf. Am. v. 16, Hos. xiv. 3, Mic. v. 4, Ps. xlvi. 6, lxix. 27. 33, so Job. iv. 6, see Bernard's commentary. Gen. ii. 19, Prov. vii. 23, *as the bird hastens to a snare and knows not that it is for his life till a dart strikes through his liver* &c.

73. Changes of construction must be familiar to every student of the Old Testament, such e. g. as the following Gen. xxxix. 18, *when I lifted up my voice and cried* for *when I lifted up my voice then I cried*, Prov. xix. 26, Is. i. 29, *they shall be ashamed of the oaks which ye have desired*, Gen. xlix. 4, Prov. viii. 17, Mic. i. 2. These are very common in Isaiah e. g. xxii. 19, xlii. 24, xliv. 26.

74. *The Accents.* The complex system of Accentuation which is followed in the Hebrew Bible is a study for the advanced student alone and also one of considerable obscurity. What has already been said in ii. 20, 21, xiii. 62, 64 is sufficient for ordinary purposes, but it may be desirable to give a table of all the accents, with a few additional remarks by way of explanation.

75. The Accents serve three purposes

1) They mark the *tone-syllable*.

2) They indicate the logical connection and relation of the words in a sentence, thus forming an elaborate system of *punctuation*.

3) They regulate the *chanting* of the scriptures, which last is a matter of Music and not of Grammar.

76. They are called moshĕlim, *rulers*, or mĕsharĕthím, *servants*.

The moshĕlim are *disjunctive*, that is indicate greater or less separation between the word they accompany and the following word: the mĕshŏrēthím are *conjunctive*, that is, they serve to link the word which bears them to the following word.

77. The moshēlím are divided into four classes according to their power 1. Kisrím, *Cæsars* or *Emperors;* 2. mĕlakím, *Kings;* 3. sarim, *Princes;* 4. pĕkídim, *Officers.*

The consecution of the accents is liable to great variety and uncertainty every where, but in the Psalms, Proverbs and Job this variety is acknowledged to amount to confusion and disorder. Certain accents moreover are found exclusively in these three books. Where the accents are most regular the following was noted as their usual sequence by the late Mr. Bernard of Cambridge but a reference to the Hebrew Bible will show that it is open to numerous exceptions.

For the first clause, according to length;
Tip*h*a, Ethna*h*.
Merka, Tip*h*a, Ethna*h*; or, Tip*h*a, Muna*h*, Ethna*h*.
Merka, Tip*h*a, Muna*h*, Ethna*h*; or, Revia*g* (Zakef Gadol, T'ev*i*r or Pashta), Merka, Tip*h*a, Ethna*h*.

For the second clause, according to length;
Tip*h*a, Sillu*k*.
Merka, Tip*h*a, Sillu*k*; or, Tip*h*a, Merka, Sillu*k*.
Merka, Tip*h*a, Merka, Sillu*k*; or Revia*g* (Zakef Gadol, T'ev*i*r or Pashta) Merka, Tip*h*a, Sillu*k*.

When either clause has more than four words the additional accents may be as follows:
Zarka, Segol,
Zarka, Muna*h*, Segol,
Pashta, Zakef,
Muhpak, Pashta, Muna*h*, Zakef,

Munah, Revia*g*,
Kadma, Azlah, Revia*g*,
* Darga, Tevir.

It is not within the plan of this little book to treat further on the subject of the accents. A Table of them is subjoined.

76. Disjunctives.

1. כָּלוּק or סוֹף פָּסוּק ־ֽ   } Emperors.
2. אֶתְנָח ־ָ

3. סְגֹלְתָּא ־֓
   זָקֵף קָטֹן ־ֵ
   זָקֵף גָּדֹל ־ֵ
   טִפְחָא ־ָ   } Kings.

   רְבִיעַ ־ִ
   זַרְקָא ־ָ
4. פַּשְׁטָא ־ָ
   תְּבִיר ־ִ
5. יְתִיב ־ִ
   שַׁלְשֶׁלֶת ־ֶ   } Princes.

   פָּזֵר ־ֵ
   קַרְנֵי פָרָה ־ָ
   תְּלִישָׁא גְדֹלָה ־ֹ
   גֶּרֶשׁ or אַזְלָא ־ָ   } Officers.
   גֵּרְשַׁיִם ־ַ
6. פָּסִיק ׀

---

* See Mason and Bernard's Hebrew Grammar Vol. II. 236 seq.

Conjunctives.

מֵיָרַח —
מַהְפָּךְ —
קַדְמָא ־
דַּרְגָּא ־
תְּלִישָׁא קְטַנָּה ־
מֵרְכָא ־
מֵרְכָא כְפוּלָה ־
יָרַח ־

1. Found at the end of every verse — *stop*.
2. Marks the chief division of the verse — *breathing*.
3. Always over the last letter independently of the tone.
4. Kadma stands over a letter bearing an accented vowel. Pashta always on the last letter. When the accent is penultimate a second is used over the accented vowel.
5. Yethiv stands to the right of the vowel in the first letter, Mahpak to the left of the accented vowel.
6. Stands between two words.
7. Always stands on the first letter of a word.
8. Sometimes a disjunctive of the fourth class. Metheg found with Shĕwa, as at Job. xix. 6, is called Gahya.

APPENDIX.

GENESIS. Chs. i—vi.

1.

בְּרֵאשִׁית בָּרָא אֱלֹהִים אֵת הַשָּׁמַיִם וְאֵת הָאָֽרֶץ: א
וְהָאָרֶץ הָיְתָה תֹהוּ וָבֹהוּ וְחֹשֶׁךְ עַל־פְּנֵי תְהוֹם וְרוּחַ אֱלֹהִים 2
מְרַחֶפֶת עַל־פְּנֵי הַמָּֽיִם: וַיֹּאמֶר אֱלֹהִים יְהִי אוֹר וַיְהִי־אֽוֹר: 3
וַיַּרְא אֱלֹהִים אֶת־הָאוֹר כִּי־טוֹב וַיַּבְדֵּל אֱלֹהִים בֵּין הָאוֹר 4
וּבֵין הַחֹֽשֶׁךְ: וַיִּקְרָא אֱלֹהִים לָאוֹר יוֹם וְלַחֹשֶׁךְ קָרָא לָיְלָה ה
וַיְהִי־עֶרֶב וַיְהִי־בֹקֶר יוֹם אֶחָֽד: וַיֹּאמֶר אֱלֹהִים יְהִי רָקִיעַ 6
בְּתוֹךְ הַמָּיִם וִיהִי מַבְדִּיל בֵּין מַיִם לָמָֽיִם: וַיַּעַשׂ אֱלֹהִים 7
אֶת־הָרָקִיעַ וַיַּבְדֵּל בֵּין הַמַּיִם אֲשֶׁר מִתַּחַת לָרָקִיעַ וּבֵין הַמַּיִם
אֲשֶׁר מֵעַל לָרָקִיעַ וַֽיְהִי־כֵֽן: וַיִּקְרָא אֱלֹהִים לָרָקִיעַ שָׁמָיִם 8
וַיְהִי־עֶרֶב וַיְהִי־בֹקֶר יוֹם שֵׁנִֽי: וַיֹּאמֶר אֱלֹהִים יִקָּווּ הַמַּיִם 9
מִתַּחַת הַשָּׁמַיִם אֶל־מָקוֹם אֶחָד וְתֵרָאֶה הַיַּבָּשָׁה וַֽיְהִי־כֵֽן:
וַיִּקְרָא אֱלֹהִים לַיַּבָּשָׁה אֶרֶץ וּלְמִקְוֵה הַמַּיִם קָרָא יַמִּים י
וַיַּרְא אֱלֹהִים כִּי־טֽוֹב: וַיֹּאמֶר אֱלֹהִים תַּֽדְשֵׁא הָאָרֶץ דֶּשֶׁא 11
עֵשֶׂב מַזְרִיעַ זֶרַע עֵץ פְּרִי עֹשֶׂה פְּרִי לְמִינוֹ אֲשֶׁר זַרְעוֹ־בוֹ
עַל־הָאָרֶץ וַֽיְהִי־כֵֽן: וַתּוֹצֵא הָאָרֶץ דֶּשֶׁא עֵשֶׂב מַזְרִיעַ זֶרַע 12
לְמִינֵהוּ וְעֵץ עֹשֶׂה־פְּרִי אֲשֶׁר זַרְעוֹ־בוֹ לְמִינֵהוּ וַיַּרְא אֱלֹהִים
כִּי־טֽוֹב: וַיְהִי־עֶרֶב וַיְהִי־בֹקֶר יוֹם שְׁלִישִֽׁי: וַיֹּאמֶר אֱלֹהִים 13 14
יְהִי מְאֹרֹת בִּרְקִיעַ הַשָּׁמַיִם לְהַבְדִּיל בֵּין הַיּוֹם וּבֵין הַלָּיְלָה
וְהָיוּ לְאֹתֹת וּלְמוֹעֲדִים וּלְיָמִים וְשָׁנִֽים: וְהָיוּ לִמְאוֹרֹת בִּרְקִיעַ טו

10 הַשָּׁמַיִם לְהָאִיר עַל־הָאָרֶץ וַיְהִי־כֵן: וַיַּעַשׂ אֱלֹהִים אֶת־שְׁנֵי הַמְּאֹרֹת הַגְּדֹלִים אֶת־הַמָּאוֹר הַגָּדֹל לְמֶמְשֶׁלֶת הַיּוֹם וְאֶת־
17 הַמָּאוֹר הַקָּטֹן לְמֶמְשֶׁלֶת הַלַּיְלָה וְאֵת הַכּוֹכָבִים: וַיִּתֵּן אֹתָם
18 אֱלֹהִים בִּרְקִיעַ הַשָּׁמָיִם לְהָאִיר עַל־הָאָרֶץ: וְלִמְשֹׁל בַּיּוֹם וּבַלַּיְלָה וּלְהַבְדִּיל בֵּין הָאוֹר וּבֵין הַחֹשֶׁךְ וַיַּרְא אֱלֹהִים כִּי־
19 טוֹב: וַיְהִי־עֶרֶב וַיְהִי־בֹקֶר יוֹם רְבִיעִי: וַיֹּאמֶר אֱלֹהִים יִשְׁרְצוּ הַמַּיִם שֶׁרֶץ נֶפֶשׁ חַיָּה וְעוֹף יְעוֹפֵף עַל־הָאָרֶץ עַל־פְּנֵי רְקִיעַ
21 הַשָּׁמָיִם: וַיִּבְרָא אֱלֹהִים אֶת־הַתַּנִּינִם הַגְּדֹלִים וְאֵת כָּל־נֶפֶשׁ הַחַיָּה הָרֹמֶשֶׂת אֲשֶׁר שָׁרְצוּ הַמַּיִם לְמִינֵהֶם וְאֵת כָּל־עוֹף
22 כָּנָף לְמִינֵהוּ וַיַּרְא אֱלֹהִים כִּי־טוֹב: וַיְבָרֶךְ אֹתָם אֱלֹהִים לֵאמֹר פְּרוּ וּרְבוּ וּמִלְאוּ אֶת־הַמַּיִם בַּיַּמִּים וְהָעוֹף יִרֶב בָּאָרֶץ:
23 וַיְהִי־עֶרֶב וַיְהִי־בֹקֶר יוֹם חֲמִישִׁי: וַיֹּאמֶר אֱלֹהִים תּוֹצֵא
24 הָאָרֶץ נֶפֶשׁ חַיָּה לְמִינָהּ בְּהֵמָה וָרֶמֶשׂ וְחַיְתוֹ־אֶרֶץ לְמִינָהּ
25 וַיְהִי־כֵן: וַיַּעַשׂ אֱלֹהִים אֶת־חַיַּת הָאָרֶץ לְמִינָהּ וְאֶת־הַבְּהֵמָה לְמִינָהּ וְאֵת כָּל־רֶמֶשׂ הָאֲדָמָה לְמִינֵהוּ וַיַּרְא אֱלֹהִים כִּי־
26 טוֹב: וַיֹּאמֶר אֱלֹהִים נַעֲשֶׂה אָדָם בְּצַלְמֵנוּ כִּדְמוּתֵנוּ וְיִרְדּוּ בִדְגַת הַיָּם וּבְעוֹף הַשָּׁמַיִם וּבַבְּהֵמָה וּבְכָל־הָאָרֶץ וּבְכָל־
27 הָרֶמֶשׂ הָרֹמֵשׂ עַל־הָאָרֶץ: וַיִּבְרָא אֱלֹהִים אֶת־הָאָדָם בְּצַלְמוֹ בְּצֶלֶם אֱלֹהִים בָּרָא אֹתוֹ זָכָר וּנְקֵבָה בָּרָא אֹתָם:
28 וַיְבָרֶךְ אֹתָם אֱלֹהִים וַיֹּאמֶר לָהֶם אֱלֹהִים פְּרוּ וּרְבוּ וּמִלְאוּ אֶת־הָאָרֶץ וְכִבְשֻׁהָ וּרְדוּ בִּדְגַת הַיָּם וּבְעוֹף הַשָּׁמַיִם וּבְכָל־
29 חַיָּה הָרֹמֶשֶׂת עַל־הָאָרֶץ: וַיֹּאמֶר אֱלֹהִים הִנֵּה נָתַתִּי לָכֶם אֶת־כָּל־עֵשֶׂב זֹרֵעַ זֶרַע אֲשֶׁר עַל־פְּנֵי כָל־הָאָרֶץ וְאֶת־כָּל־
ל הָעֵץ אֲשֶׁר־בּוֹ פְרִי־עֵץ זֹרֵעַ זָרַע לָכֶם יִהְיֶה לְאָכְלָה: וּלְכָל־ חַיַּת הָאָרֶץ וּלְכָל־עוֹף הַשָּׁמַיִם וּלְכֹל רוֹמֵשׂ עַל־הָאָרֶץ אֲשֶׁר־בּוֹ נֶפֶשׁ חַיָּה אֶת־כָּל־יֶרֶק עֵשֶׂב לְאָכְלָה וַיְהִי־כֵן:
31 וַיַּרְא אֱלֹהִים אֶת־כָּל־אֲשֶׁר עָשָׂה וְהִנֵּה־טוֹב מְאֹד וַיְהִי־עֶרֶב וַיְהִי־בֹקֶר יוֹם הַשִּׁשִּׁי:

2.

וַיְכֻלּוּ הַשָּׁמַיִם וְהָאָרֶץ וְכָל־צְבָאָם: וַיְכַל אֱלֹהִים בַּיּוֹם ² הַשְּׁבִיעִי מְלַאכְתּוֹ אֲשֶׁר עָשָׂה וַיִּשְׁבֹּת בַּיּוֹם הַשְּׁבִיעִי מִכָּל־מְלַאכְתּוֹ אֲשֶׁר עָשָׂה: וַיְבָרֶךְ אֱלֹהִים אֶת־יוֹם הַשְּׁבִיעִי ³ וַיְקַדֵּשׁ אֹתוֹ כִּי בוֹ שָׁבַת מִכָּל־מְלַאכְתּוֹ אֲשֶׁר־בָּרָא אֱלֹהִים לַעֲשׂוֹת: אֵלֶּה תוֹלְדוֹת הַשָּׁמַיִם וְהָאָרֶץ בְּהִבָּרְאָם בְּיוֹם ⁴ עֲשׂוֹת יְהֹוָה אֱלֹהִים אֶרֶץ וְשָׁמָיִם: וְכֹל שִׂיחַ הַשָּׂדֶה טֶרֶם ⁵ יִהְיֶה בָאָרֶץ וְכָל־עֵשֶׂב הַשָּׂדֶה טֶרֶם יִצְמָח כִּי לֹא הִמְטִיר יְהֹוָה אֱלֹהִים עַל־הָאָרֶץ וְאָדָם אַיִן לַעֲבֹד אֶת־הָאֲדָמָה: וְאֵד יַעֲלֶה מִן־הָאָרֶץ וְהִשְׁקָה אֶת־כָּל־פְּנֵי הָאֲדָמָה: וַיִּיצֶר ⁶⁷ יְהֹוָה אֱלֹהִים אֶת־הָאָדָם עָפָר מִן־הָאֲדָמָה וַיִּפַּח בְּאַפָּיו נִשְׁמַת חַיִּים וַיְהִי הָאָדָם לְנֶפֶשׁ חַיָּה: וַיִּטַּע יְהֹוָה אֱלֹהִים ⁸ גַּן־בְּעֵדֶן מִקֶּדֶם וַיָּשֶׂם שָׁם אֶת־הָאָדָם אֲשֶׁר יָצָר: וַיַּצְמַח ⁹ יְהֹוָה אֱלֹהִים מִן־הָאֲדָמָה כָּל־עֵץ נֶחְמָד לְמַרְאֶה וְטוֹב לְמַאֲכָל וְעֵץ הַחַיִּים בְּתוֹךְ הַגָּן וְעֵץ הַדַּעַת טוֹב וָרָע: וְנָהָר יֹצֵא מֵעֵדֶן לְהַשְׁקוֹת אֶת־הַגָּן וּמִשָּׁם יִפָּרֵד וְהָיָה לְאַרְבָּעָה רָאשִׁים: שֵׁם הָאֶחָד פִּישׁוֹן הוּא הַסֹּבֵב אֵת כָּל־אֶרֶץ ¹¹ הַחֲוִילָה אֲשֶׁר־שָׁם הַזָּהָב: וּזֲהַב הָאָרֶץ הַהִוא טוֹב שָׁם ¹² הַבְּדֹלַח וְאֶבֶן הַשֹּׁהַם: וְשֵׁם־הַנָּהָר הַשֵּׁנִי גִּיחוֹן הוּא הַסּוֹבֵב ¹³ אֵת כָּל־אֶרֶץ כּוּשׁ: וְשֵׁם־הַנָּהָר הַשְּׁלִישִׁי חִדֶּקֶל הוּא הַהֹלֵךְ ¹⁴ קִדְמַת אַשּׁוּר וְהַנָּהָר הָרְבִיעִי הוּא פְרָת: וַיִּקַּח יְהֹוָה אֱלֹהִים ¹⁵ אֶת־הָאָדָם וַיַּנִּחֵהוּ בְגַן־עֵדֶן לְעָבְדָהּ וּלְשָׁמְרָהּ: וַיְצַו יְהֹוָה ¹⁶ אֱלֹהִים עַל־הָאָדָם לֵאמֹר מִכֹּל עֵץ־הַגָּן אָכֹל תֹּאכֵל: וּמֵעֵץ ¹⁷ הַדַּעַת טוֹב וָרָע לֹא תֹאכַל מִמֶּנּוּ כִּי בְּיוֹם אֲכָלְךָ מִמֶּנּוּ מוֹת תָּמוּת: וַיֹּאמֶר יְהֹוָה אֱלֹהִים לֹא־טוֹב הֱיוֹת הָאָדָם לְבַדּוֹ ¹⁸ אֶעֱשֶׂה־לּוֹ עֵזֶר כְּנֶגְדּוֹ: וַיִּצֶר יְהֹוָה אֱלֹהִים מִן־הָאֲדָמָה כָּל־ ¹⁹ חַיַּת הַשָּׂדֶה וְאֵת כָּל־עוֹף הַשָּׁמַיִם וַיָּבֵא אֶל־הָאָדָם לִרְאוֹת מַה־יִּקְרָא־לוֹ וְכֹל אֲשֶׁר יִקְרָא־לוֹ הָאָדָם נֶפֶשׁ חַיָּה הוּא שְׁמוֹ:

APPENDIX.

to following nouns because it has art. vii. 6. warag, *and evil*, a. xii. 7. a. the *K'amez* properly a Pathah but lengthened in pause.

10. wĕnahar, *and a river*, s. n. m. yoze', was *going out*, part. m. I. fr. יָצָא ch. i. 12. megeden, xii. 14. lĕhashkoth, *to water*, in. V. cr. fr. שָׁקָה (v. 6). umishsham, *and from thence*. xii. 16. yippared, *was divided*, 3. m. s. F. II. fr. פָּרַד, *separated*, xiii. 60. 6. wĕhayah lĕ-, *and it became*, xii. 6. P. with Waw conv. and therefore equal in time to the former tense and to be construed like it as an imperfect xiii. 62: 'arbagah, *four*. r'ashim, pl. m. of רֹאשׁ *head*.

11. shem, n. m. s. *a name*, ant. to following word. hu', m. pr. *he, that*. hassovev, (is) *the one encircling*, part. I. m. s. with art. xii. 10. a. xii. 16. hazzahav, s. m. n. *the gold*, with art.

12. uzahav, *and the gold of*, cr. of last word with ו ii. 11, xii. 7. hahiw' (pronounced hi') f. pr. 3. pers. xii. 11. habbĕdolah, n. *the beryl*, or *crystal*. we'even, *and the stone of*, u. hashshoham, *the onyx*.

14. haholek, part. I. fr. הָלַךְ *went, the one going*. kidmath, *to the east of*, cr. of קִדְמָה *the east*, a f. form of קֶדֶם (v. 8).

15. wayyikkah, *and he took*, 3. s. m. F. with Waw conv. fr. לָקַח *took*, this is like Vs. in ג. wayyannihehu, *and he placed him*, 3. s. m. F. V. with Waw conv. and af. fr. נוח *rested*. lĕgovdah, *to till it*, in. cr. with ל and af. 3. f. fr. עָבַד *served, tilled*. ulĕshomrah, *and to keep it*, in. cr. with ו, ל and af. 3. f. fr. שָׁמַר *kept*.

16. wayĕzaw, *and He commanded*, 3. s. m. F. ap. III. fr. צוה. See in. Vs. le'mor, see ch. i. 22.

'akol in. abs. fr. אָכֹל Ch. i. 29, xiii. 53. tokel, *thou mayest eat*, 2. m. s. F. same V. xiii. 60. 11. in p.

17. mimmennu, *of it*, xii. 17. 'ăkolka, for in the day of *thy eating.* in. with af. 2. m. moth, in. abs. *to die.* tamuth, *thou shalt die.*

18. hĕyoth, *the being of*, in. cr. fr. הָיָה. lĕvaddo, *by himself*, xii. 17. 'egĕseh-llo, *I will make him*, 1. s. F. followed by prep. with af. and euphonic Dagesh ii. 16. gezer, s. n. *a help.* kĕnegdo, lit. *as before him, according to,* or *like himself, meet for him.*

19. wayyizer, a variant of form in v. 7. wayyave', *and he brought*, 3. s. m. F. V. fr. בוא *to come.* lir'oth, *to see*, in. cr. with prefix from רָאָה *saw.* mah-yyikra'-lo, *what he will call him*, xii. 16. shĕmo, *its name.* shem, with af. xiii. 72. the order must be changed *and as for every living thing that which man calls it is its name.*

20. shemoth, pl. of shem. lo'-maza', *he found not*, impersonally *one did not find, there was not found*, xiii. 48.

21. wayyappel, *and He caused to fall*, 3. s. m. F. V. fr. נָפַל *fell.* tardemah, s. n. *a deep sleep*, fr. r. רדם in H. wayyishan, *and he slept*, 3. s. m. F. fr. יָשֵׁן *slept*, in p. wayyikkah, (v. 15). 'ahath, *one of*, f. of 'chad. mizzalgothayw, *from his ribs*, pl. of צֵלָע *a rib*, with prefix and af. 3. m. s. wayyisgor, *and He closed up*, 3. s. m. F. with Waw conv. fr. סָגַר *he shut.* basar, n. s. m. *flesh.* tahtennah, *instead of it.* tahath, with af.

22. wayyiven, *and He built*, 3. m. F. ap. fr. בָּנָה *he built.* lakah, 3. s. P. m. *he took.* wayĕvi'eha, *and he brought her.* Long Hirik written defectively.

23. zo'th f. of זֶה xii. 16. happagam, lit. *the time*, i. e. *now.* gezem, s. n. *a bone.* megăzamay,

from my bones, vii. 22. *uvasar, and flesh,* xii. 7. mibbĕsari, *of my flesh,* same with af. and מִן. yikkare', 3. s. m. F. II. fr. קָרָא *shall be called.* 'ishshah, *woman.* lukkŏhah-zzo'th, *this was taken.* P. VI. 3. f. anomalous form.

24. gal-ken, *therefore,* xii. 16. yaġăzov-'ish, *a man shall leave,* 3. m. s. F. fr. עָזַב *left.* The Holem becomes Kamez Hatuf before Makkaf. 'aviw', *his father,* for אָב a father with af. viii. 9. 'immo, *his mother,* fr. אֵם, with af. vii. 14. wĕdavak, *and shall cleave.* P. with Waw conv. bĕ'ishto, *to his wife,* fr. אִשָּׁה cr. of אִשָּׁה with af.

25. wayyihyu, 3. m. pl. F. fr. הָיָה *and they were.* shĕneyhem, *both of them,* fr. שְׁנַיִ with af. ġărummim, *naked,* pl. of עֵירֹם. The Dagesh after Shurek is of course anomalous but directed by the masoretic note at the foot of the page. yithboshashu, *they were ashamed.* 3. pl. m. F. vii. fr. בּוֹשׁ *to be ashamed.* Kamez, on account of pause xiii. 60, 6. 66.

CHAPTER III.

1. wehannahash, *and the serpent,* copula, art. n. s. m. garum, a. m. subtle. mikkol, *more than all,* for min xii. 14. 'af ki-amar, *yea hath God said,* xii. 16. lo' tho'kĕlu, *ye shall not eat.* 3. m. pl. F.

2. watto'mer, *and the woman said.* 3. f. s. F. with Waw conv. xii. 64. mippĕri for min pĕri, *of the fruit of,* ant. to gez. no'kel, 1 pl. F. xiii. 60. 11.

3. welo' thiggĕgu, *neither shall ye touch,* 2. m. pl. F. fr. נָגַע *touched.* pen-tĕmuthun, *lest ye die,* 2. m. pl. F. fr. מוּת *to die.* xii. 16. 18.

4. xiii. 53.

5. yodeag, part. m. I. of יָדַע *he knew.* xiii. 20. bĕyom 'ăkolkem, *in the day of your eating,* ant. and con. xiii. 55. in. with af. 2. pl. m. wĕnifkĕhu, *then shall be opened.* 3. m. pl. P. II. with Waw conv. fr. פָּקַח *opened,* xiii. 62. geyneykem, *your eyes,* dual fr. עַיִן *an eye,* with af. 2. pl. m. wihyithem, *and ye shall be.* P. 2. pl. m. fr. היה with Waw conv. ke'lohim, *as yods,* for כְּאֵ xii. 2. yodĕgey, *knowing,* part. m. pl. cr.

6. wattere', *and the woman saw.* F. 3. f. s. with Waw conv. fr. רָאָה. lema'akal, *for food,* n. s. m. wĕki tha'awah-hu', *and that an object of desire it, was.* n. s. f. laŏeynayim, *to the eyes,* dual with art. and prep. wĕnehmad. (ii. 9). lĕhaskil, *to make wise in.* V. fr. שָׂכַל *was skilful,* or taking the word as used Ps. xli. 2. *considering, looking on; to look to,* more proper to the object of *sight.* wattikkah, 3. f. s. F. with Waw conv. fr. לקח, ch. ii. 15. mippiryo, *of its fruit,* s. n. m. af. viii. 9. o. watto'kal, *and she ate,* 3. f. s. F. with Waw conv. in p. wattitten, 3. f. s. F. with Waw conv. fr. נָתַן ch. i. 17. lĕ'ishah, *to her husband,* with af. 3. s. f. gimmah *with her,* xii. 17. wayyo'kal, 3. s. m. F. Waw conv. in p.

7. wattippakahuah, 3. f. pl. F. Waw conv. fr. פָּקַח *opened.* geyney, pl. cr. fr. עַיִן *eye.* shĕneyhem, *the two of them,* ix. 8. wayyedĕgu, 3. pl. m. F. with Waw conv. fr. יָדַע. geyrummim, pl. m. fr. עֵרוֹם *naked.* hem, pr. 3. pl. m. wayyithpĕru, 3. pl. m. F. Waw conv. fr. חָפַר *sewed.* găleh, s. cr. fr. עָלֶה *a leaf,* coll. the'enah, *the figtree,* s. n. f. wayyaŏasu, 3. pl. m. F. lahem, xii. 17. hăgoroth, pl. fr. חֲגֹרָה *a girdle.*

8. wayyishmĕgu, 3. pl. m. F. fr. שָׁמַע *heard.* eth-kol, *the voice of.* mithhallek, part. VII. m. s. fr.

הָלַךְ *went walked.* wayyithhabbe', 3. s. m. F. VII. fr. חָבָא, *hid himself,* x. 10.

9. 'ayyekkah fr. אַיֵּה *where?* xii. 17.

10. kolĕka, kol, with af. 2. m. s. shamagti, 1. s. P. שָׂמֵעַ wa'ira', *and I feared,* 1. s. F. with Waw conv. fr. יָרֵא *feared,* xiii. 64, xii. 7, x. 3. a. 'anoki, pr. 1. s. wa'ehave' 1. s. m. F. II. Waw conv. x. 10.

11. mi, *who?* xii. 16. higgid, V. P. 3. m. s. fr. נגד not used in I., *told.* lĕka, xii. 17. 'attah, pr. hamin, *whether from,* xii. 9. ziwwithika, P. III. 1. s. with af. ch. ii. 16, *I commanded thee.* lĕvilti, *to not — not to,* xii. 17. 'ăkol in cr. *as to the not eating of* 'akalta, *hast thou eaten?* 2. s. m. P.

12. nathattah for nathantah, see the Verbs x. 2. m. s. P. gimmadi, *with me,* xii. 17. nathĕnah-lli, 3. f. s. P. ii. 16. wa'okel, 1. s. F. I. with Waw conv. *and I ate.*

13. la'ishshah, xii. 3. mah-zzo'th, *what is this?* xii. 16, ii. 16. gasith, 2. f. s. P. fr. gasah. hishshiani, 3. m. s. P. V. with af. i. s. *he caused me to forget, beguiled* fr. נָשָׁה *forget,* x.

14. gasitha, 2. m. s. P. 'arur, part. pass. m. s. fr. אָרַר *cursed.* gal-gĕhonĕka, *upon thy belly,* xii. 17 and גָּחוֹן *the belly,* with af. v. 3. thelek, *thou shalt go* fr. יָלַךְ *went,* F. 2. m. s. Verbs in Yod x. wĕgafar, *and dust,* s. n. m. kol-yĕmey, cr. of yamim, *all the days of.* hayyeyka, *thy life,* hayyim with af. v. 3.

15. wĕ'eyvah, *and enmity,* s. f. n. fr. אָיַב *treated as an enemy.* 'ashith, *I will put,* F. 1. s. fr. שִׁית *to put.* zargaka, *thy seed.* zerag, with af. v. 3. yĕshufĕka, *he shall bruise,* F. 1. s. m. fr. שׁוּף *to bruise* with af xiii. 45. tĕshufennu, *thou shalt bruise him,* F. 2. m. s. with af. 3. v. 3. gakev, *on the heel,* xiii. 45.

16. harbah in. V. in. fr. רָבָה *multiplied*, xiii. 53. arbeh F. V 1. s. *gizzèvonek* fr. *gizzavon*, with af. v. 3. *thy sorrow.* heron, *conception*, s. n. fr. הָרָה *conceived.* bégezev, *in sorrow.* tele·li, *thou shalt bear*, 2. f. s. F. fr. יָלַד. van*i*m, *sons, children*, pl. of בֵּן viii. 2. Dagesh not inserted because of preceding quiescent letter iii. 4. 1. *t*êshu*k*athek fr. תְּשׁוּקָה *thirst. desire*, with af. yimshol-bak, F 1. s. m. xii. 17.

17. 'isht*e*ka for 'isht*ê*ka. 'ārurah f. part. (v. 14) xii. 17. *t*o'kálennah, *thou shalt eat* of *it*, 2. m. s. F. with af.

18. ko*z*, s. n. m. *thorn*, coll. dard*a*r, *bramble*, coll. tazm*i*ah, *she*, the ground, *shall cause to shoot forth*, 3. f. s. F. V

19. zegath cr. of זֵעָה *sweat*, vii. 7. 2. 'app*e*yk*a*, pl. of 'af with af. 2. s. m. le*h*em, s. n. m. *bread*, comp. Beth*l*ehem. gad, *until*, xii. 17. shuvèka, *thy returning*, in. cr. lu*k*kahta, VI. P. 2. m. s. *t*ashuv, 2. m. s. F.

20. *h*awwah, a f. form of חַי *alive, living.* 'em, *a mother*, vii. 14.

21. ule'ishto, *and to his wife*, xii. 7. 2. vii. 25. kothnoth, pl. cr. fr. כְּתֹנֶת *a tunic, coat.* gor, *skin.* wayyalb*i*shem, V. F. 3. s. m. with Waw conv. and af. fr. לָבַשׁ *put on* a garment.

22. hen, *behold*, xii. 16. kë*a*had, *like one of*, ix. 10. lad*a*gath, *to know*, in. cr. fr. יָדַע xii. 2. *g*attah, *now*, xii. 16. pən-yishla*h* take care *lest he put forth*, F. 3. s. m. fr. שָׁלַח *put forth, sent*, xii. 16. yado, *his hand*, vii. 16. wëlakah, P. with Waw conv. equal therefore in time to the former tense. gam, *also.* wahay, xii. 7. a. P. of חָיָה defective xiii. 62. golam, *eternity*, s. n. m.

23. wayeshallehehu, 3. s. m. F. III. with Waw conv. and af. notice the *intensive* force of this word compared with the *K*'al in the former verse *He sent him forth not to return*, x. 10. la*g*avod in. cr. with prep. fr. עָבַד *tilled, served*. lukkah, P. IV. mishsham, xii. 16.

24. wayōga*r*esh, 3. s. m. F. iii. fr. גָּרַשׁ *drove out*, xii. 7. wayyashken, 3. s. m. F. V. for שָׁכַן *dwelt*. hakkĕruvim, pl. of כְּרוּב *K*ibbuz for Sh*u*rek, ii. 5. lahat, s. n. m. *flame*. herev, *a sword*, s. n. f. hammith-happeketh, part. f vii. fr. הָפַךְ *turned*. agreeing with *herev, the sword which turned itself*, or see xiii. 22, xii. 10. lishmor, in. cr. of שָׁמַר *kept*. 'eth-derek, *the way of*. Segolate n. definite because the aut. to the following words vii. 4, 22.

CHAPTER IV.

1. wattahar, 3. f. s. F. fr. הָרָה *conceived* with Waw conv. xiii. 64. watteled, 3. f. s. F. fr. יָלַד *bore*. kanithi, P. 1. s. fr. קָנָה *got, acquired*.

2. wattosef, 3. f. s. F. fr. יָסַף *added* with Waw conv. laledeth in. cr. f. יָלַד xii. 2. 'eth-'ahiw, *his brother*, viii. 9. c. rogeh, part. m. cr. fr. רָעָה *fed cattle* vii. 7. 1. zo'n, *sheep*. goved, part. m. s.

3. mikkez, for min, kez, s. n. *the end*. wayyave', 3. s. m. F. V. fr. בּוֹא *to come*. min*h*ah, s. f. n. *an offering*.

4. hevi', P. V. fr. bo'. bĕkor, *the first born*. mehelvehem, *from their fat*, fr. חֵלֶב *fat*, with af. 3. pl. the Yod of pl. is wanting as in ch i. 21, or it may be sing. See Buxtorf s. v. wayyisha*g*, F. ap. 3. s. m. fr. שָׁעָה *looked to, regarded*, x. 11. min*h*atho, af. 3. s. viii. 8.

5. wayyiḥar, F. ap. 3. s. m. fr. חָרָה *was hot, angry*. wayyippélu, F. 3. pl. m. fr. נָפַל *fell*. panayw fr. panim, *face*, with af. vi. 20.

6. lammah, xii. 16. nafélu, 3. pl. m. paneyka (v. 3).

7. halo', *is there not*, xii. 9. 'im-teytiv, *if thou doest well* fr יָטַב *was good*, V. F. 2. m. s. sě'eth, *exaltation*, in. cr. fr. נָשָׂא *bore, lifted*, used as an abstract n. lappeḥath, *at the door*, r. פָּתַח *opened*, xii. 3. ḥatta'th, *sin* or *a sin-offering*, s. n. rovez, *croucheth*, part. m. like an animal fit for sacrifice, but the meaning is doubtful. we'eleyka, *and to thee*, xii. 17. téshukatho af. *his*, ch. 3. 16, which see.

8. After the fourth word some old versions, e. g. Sam. and Syr. had, *Let us go into the field.* bihyotham, *in their being*, i. e. *when they were*, in. cr. with af. fr. הָיָה. wayyakom, F. 3. m. s. ap. fr. קוּם *to arise.* wayyahargehu, 3. m. s. F. with Waw conv. and af. fr. הָרַג *slew, and he slew him.* Dagesh not inserted in ו because of the slight vowel iii. 4. 2 and 6.

9. 'ey, xii. 17, *where?* 'ahika, viii. 9. c. yadagti, 1. s. P. xiii. 59. 3. hashomer, *am I keeping*, part. m. s.

10. meh, *what?* xii. 16. gasitha, 2. m. s. P. démey, pl. cr. fr. דָּם *blood*, vii. 16. zogăkim, pl. part. m. fr. צָעַק *cried out*, agreeing with *blood*, xiii. 22, xii. 17.

11. pazēthah, 3. s. f. P. fr. פָּצָה *opened*. 'eth-piha, vii. 25. lakaḥath, *to receive*. lŏ and in. cr. fr. לָקַח *took*, the la therefore not radical. miyyadeka, vii. 16. yad with min. xii. 14 and af.

12. tagăvod, F. 2. s. m. fr. עָבַד. teth in. cr. fr. נָתַן which see. koḥah, koaḥ, n. *strength* with af. 3. f. s. nag, part. s. m. fr. נוּעַ *to wander.* wanad, xii. 7, part. s. m. fr. נוּד *to flit, wander.* tihyeh, 2. s. m. F. fr. הָיָה.

13. *găwoni* fr. עָוֹן iniquity with af. v. 3. *minněso'*, *than to bear*, in. cr. fr. נְשֹׂא or it may be taken interrogatively *is my iniquity greater than can be forgiven;* the V has both meanings, xii. 14.

14. gerash*ta*, 2. s. m. P. III. ch. iii. 24. *u*mipp*a*neyk*a*, *and from thy face*. *panim*, with af. v. 3. min and W*a*w. 'essather, F. 1. s. II. fr. סָתַר *hid*. *wĕhayithí*, *and I shall by*, P. 1. sing. with W*a*w conv. xiii. 62. *k*olmozë'*t*, *every one finding me*, part. s. m. fr. מָצָא *found*, with af. of object xiii. 50. yaharge*ni*, F. 3. m. s. See (v. 6), Dagesh omitted as above.

15. laken, *therefore*, xii. 16. horeg, part. s. m. shivgathayim, *sevenfold*, ix. 7. *y*ukka*m*, VI. 3. s. m. F. fr. נָקַם *avenged*. wayy*a*sem, *and he put*, 3. s. m. F. with W*a*w conv. fr. שִׂים *to put, set*. 'oth, *a sign, mark*, gave him a token to remind him of the promise continually. hakkoth, in. V. fr. נָכָה *smote*, xii. 17. mozë'*o*, part. with af. v. 3.

16. wayy*e*ze', *and Kayin went out*, 3. s. m. F. W*a*w conv. fr. יָצָא ch. i. 12. milli*f*ney, min-lŏ-pĕn*ey*, cr. of panim, iii. 1. wayy*e*shev, 3. s. m. F. fr. יָשַׁב *dwelt*. *k*idmath, ch. ii. 14.

17. wayyeda*g*, 3. s. m. F. fr. יָרַע. boneh, part. s. m. fr. בָּנָה *built*. gir, *a city*, vii. 25. bĕno, viii. 2.

18. wayyiww*a*led, 3. s. m. F. II. fr. יָלַד. lahănok, xii. 2.

19. she*t*ey, *two of*, ix. 10, iii. 5. nashim, *women, wives*, vii. 25. hashshenith, *the second*, ix. 10.

20. 'avi, *the father of*, viii. 9. b. yoshev, *him dwelling in*, part. s. m. 'ohel, *a tent*, s. n. m. umi*k*neh, *and cattle*, xii. 7 fr. r. קָנָה.

21. *t*ofes, part. s. m. fr. תָּפַשׂ *laid hold of, seized, handled*. *k*innor, s. n. m. *a lute, lyre*. *g*ug*a*v, prob. *a lute*.

22. yalĕdah, 3 f. s. P. lotesh, part. s. m. *one sharpening, instructing.* horesh, part. s. m. of חָרַשׁ *wrought*, in stone work &c. něhosheth *brass.* varzel, *iron,* wa'ăhoth, xii. 7. viii. 9. d.

23. nashayw, *wives,* with af. *his.* shemagan im. ap. 2. f. pl. for שְׁמָעָה. vneshey, vii. 25. ha'ăzennah, V. im. 2. f. pl. the Dagesh shews the last radical doubled by the addition of the termination נָה— 'imrathi fr. אִמְרָה *a word,* with af. *my.* haragti, *I have slain,* P. 1. s. or it may be interrogative, the ki, marking this. lefizgi, lě pezag and af. *to my stroke, hurt.* yeled, *a child, young person.* habburathi, fr. חַבּוּרָה, *a wound,* viii. 8.

24. ix. 10. 5.

25. shath, P. 3. m. s. of שִׁית *to put, place, assign.* 'aher, a. *another.* ki xii. 16. hărago, P. 3. m. s. with af. See p. 135.

26. xiii. 7. yullad, iv. of יָלַד. P. 3. m. s. 'az, xii. 16. huhal, vi. of חָלַל P 3. s. m. *it was begun.* likro', in. cr. with לְ.

CHAPTER V

In this Chapter, see ix. *passim.*

1. sefer, s. n. *a book,* Segolate vii. 22. běro', in. cr. bidmuth xii. 2.

2. běra'am, P. 3. s. m. af. shĕmam, shem, with af. hibbarē'am, ch. ii. 4.

3. wayĕhi, 3. s. m. F. Waw conv. fr. חָיָה, *and he lived.* shěloshim, 30. ix. 10. ume'ath, cr. מֵאָה *and a hundred of.* wayyoled, 3. m. s. F. V. with Waw conv. fr. יָלַד. bidmutho, v. 3. kězalmo, iii. 4. 1. vii. 22. 2. wayyihyu, 3. pl. m. F. Waw conv. fr. הָיָה. 'ahărey, *after.* xii. 17. holido, in. V. af. shě-

monoh, ix. 10. me'oth, pl. ban*i*m *uv*moth, viii. 2. Dagesh omitted in the second word because בּ ceases to be *initial* iii. 4. 1.

6. *t*ĕsh*a*g, cr. of חֵשֶׁע ix. 10. wayy*a*moth, 3. m. s. F. W*a*w conv. fr. מוּת, if this word were not in pause the Waw conv. would make it וַיָּמׇת. xiii. 64.

8. shĕ*t*eym, iii. 5.

22. wayyithhallek, 3. s. m. F. VII. fr. הָלַךְ *went, walked*, Waw conv. 'eth — ha'ĕloh*i*m 'eth, is here the prep. not the mark of the objective case.

24. wŏ'eynonnu, 1 and אַיִן with af. *his* xii. 17, *and he was not*.

29. yĕnah*ă*menu, 3. s. m. F. III. with af. *us* fr. נָחַם in III. *comforted*, this son *shall comfort us*. mimmag*ă*senu, min and mag*ă*seh with af. *our* viii. 7. the r. is עָשָׂה *made, concerning our work.* umegizzĕvon, see ch. ii. 16. cr. s. with 1 and בֵּן prefixed xii. 7. 14. yad*e*ynu, pl. fr. יָד, vii. 16. with af. *our*. 'erārah P. III. fr. אָרַר with af. *her*.

CHAPTER VI.

1 k*i*-hehel, *when man began*, P. V. 3. m. s. fr. חָלַל. l*a*rov in. cr. fr. רָבַב *became numerous*, xi. 7. yullĕdu, P. IV. 3. pl.

2. wayyir'u, 3. pl. m. F. with W*a*w conv. fr. רָאָה. bĕney-ha'ĕloh*i*m, *the sons of God*, viii. 2. tovoth, a. f. pl. hennah, v. 2. wayyi*k*hu, 3. pl. m. F. fr. לָקַח Dagesh suppressed iii. 6. ba*h*aru, 3. pl. P. fr. בָּחַר, *chose*, in pause. x. 3. b.

3. yadon, 3. m. s. F. fr. דִּין, *to judge, strive. Hol*em for Shurek so יָשֹׁב Eccles. 12. 7. Cf. יָבוֹא and יָבוֹשׁ the intermediate form between יָדִין and יָדֹן. So we

have Shurek for *Holem* in F. of the three *Vs.* רֻגַן Prov. xxix. 6. רָצַץ Is. xlii. 4. and שָׂרַר Ps. xci. 6. others invent a r. to satisfy the form of this particular word. *ruhi* fr. רוּחַ with af. *my* v. 3. bĕshaggam fr. בְּ, אֲשֶׁר, גַם, *in as much as* he *also*, xii. 15.

4. hannĕfelím, pl. s. m. prob. the pl. of a Chald. pass. part. fr. נָפַל *the giants*. yavo'u, 3. m. pl. F. בּוֹא *to come, go in*. wĕyalĕdu, *and they bare* P. with Waw conv. equal in time to yavo'u. haggibborim, *the heroes*, pl. of gibbor, *hero, mighty man*. megolam, xii. 14. 'anshey, pl. cr. of אִישׁ. vii. 25.

5. rabbah, f. of a. רַב *many, much, great*, vii. 12. ragath, s. cr. of רָעָה *evil, wickedness*. yezer, s. n. m. *imagination, thought* in cr. with the next word itself in cr. with the next vii. 5. ma*h*shĕvoth, pl. cr. of מַחְשָׁבָה s. n. f. *a thought, device*, ii. 11. libbo, fr. lev, *heart*, vii. 14. rak, *only*, p.

6. wayyinna*h*em, 3. s. m. F. II. with Waw conv. fr. נָחַם, in II. *was grieved, repented*. wayyith*g*azzev, 3. s. m. F. VII. fr. עָצַב, *pained, grieved*.

7. 'emheh, 1. s. F. fr. מָחָה, *blotted out*, xi. 9. bara'thi, P. 1. s. ni*h*amti, 1. s. P. II. fr. נָחַם. gasithim 1. s. P. with af. *them*.

8. maza', ch. ii. 20. hen, s. n. m.

9. zaddik, a. s. m. *righteous*. tamim, a. s. m. *perfect, upright, sincere*. bĕdorothayw, pl. of דּוֹר s. n. m. *a generation* with af. *his*, ii. 19.

11. wa*tt*ishsha*h*eth, 3. f. s. F. II. with Waw conv. fr. שָׁחַת not used in Kal *was corrupted* morally. wa*tt*immalĕ, 3. s. m. F. II. hamas, s. n. m. *violence*.

12. nish*h*athah P. II. 3. s. f. in p. x. 3. b. hish*h*ith, P. 3. m. s. V. darko, vii. 22. 2.

13. *kez*, Ch. iv. 3. *ba'* P. fr. בוֹא, *to come*. lĕfᴀnay, xii. 17. *malē'ah*, P. 3. f. s. mippĕneyhem = min and pᴀnim with af. *their*. hinenɩ xii. 17. mash*h*itham, V. part. with af. *them*.

14. *gᴀseh*, im. 2. m. s. *tevath*, s. cr. of הֵבָה vii. 7. 2. *an ark*, only used of Noah's and that in which Moses was exposed. *gᴀzey*, pl. cr. of עֵץ. *kinnim* pl. of קַן vii. 14, *a nest, cell, chamber*. *tagᴀseh*, 2. s. m. F. wĕkafarta, 2. s. m. P. with Waw conv. fr. כָּפַר, *covered, coated*. bayith, s. n. *a house*, vii. 14. mibbayith *from within*. *huz*, *any open place without* mi*h*uz, *from without, outside*, here Dagesh is *implied* iii. 10. xii. 14.

15. ammah, s. f. n. *a cubit*. 'orek, s. n. m. *length*, here in cr. vii. 4. ro*h*bah, fr. רֹחַב s. n. m. *width* with af. *her* v. 3. *k*omathah fr. קוֹמָה s. n. f. *height* with af. *her* v. 3.

16. *z*ohar, here only s. n. m. *a window*, prob. *t*ekallennah, 2. s. m. F. III. fr. כָּלָה Ch. ii. 1. with af. *her* and N*u*n epenthetic v. 3. milma*g*lah, *from above* = min-le-ma*g*lah. Dagesh implied iii. 6. bĕziddah, fr. צַד *a side* vii. 13. *tas*im 2. s. m. F. ta*h*tiyim, pl. m. of תַּחְתִּי *a lower*. shĕniyim, pl. of שֵׁנִי, ix. 10. shĕlishim, pl. of שְׁלִישִׁי ix. 10. *tag*ᴀsehha, 2. s. m. F. with af. *her*.

17. wa'ᴀnɩ, xii. 7. b. v. 1. mevi', V. part. of בוֹא. mabbul, s. n. m. *destruction*, only used of the flood of Noah. xiii. 45. vii. 6. lĕsha*h*eth, in. cr. III. yigw*ag* 3. m. s. F. of גָּוַע, in p. *expired*, not a hollow V.

18. wahă*k*imothí, 1. s. P. V. with Waw conv. fr. קוּם. See hollow I's. bĕrithi, fr. בְּרִית, *covenant*, with af. *my*. 'ittak. xii. 17. uvatha, 2. s. m. P. *and thou shalt come*, vii. 25. viii. 2.

19. ha*h*ay, iii. 10. *that which liveth, is alive.* taví', 2. s. m. F. beha*h*yoth, in. cr. V. fr. חָיָה ג. 10.
21. ka*h*, im. 2. m. s. fr. לָקַח. ye'akel, 3. m. s. F. II. fr. אָכַל. xiii. 60. 4. wĕ'asa*f*ta, 2. s. m. P. fr. אָסַף, *gathered, collected,* with Waw conv. xiii. 62.

Analysis of the first six Psalms.

PSALM I.

1. 'ashrey, *oh the blessings of, how blessed is,* pl. m. cr. xii. 17. ha'ish, *the man,* iii. 14. 'asher, xii. 16. *who.* lo' halak, *hath not walked,* 3. m. s. P. bagazath, *in the counsel of* s. cr. f. fr. עֵצָה vii. 7. 2. with בְּ xii. 2. rĕshagim, *wicked* men a. pl. m. fr. רָשָׁע. uvĕderek, *and in the way of,* xii. 7. 2. vii. 22. 2. halta'im, *sinners,* pl. m. of חַטָּא vii. 10. gamad, P. 3. s. m. in pause, *he stood.* uvĕmoshav, *and in the seat of,* cr. of moshav, vii. 17. lezim, pl. of lez, *a scorner.* yashav, in p. P. 3. s. m. *he sat.*

2. ki 'im, *but,* xii. 16. bĕthorath *in the law of,* cr. fr. תּוֹרָה vii. 7 2. hefzo, is *his delight,* vii. 22. 1. uvĕthoratho, *and in his law,* xii. 7. 2. v. 3. yehgeh, 3. s. m. F. fr. הָגָה, *meditated.* yomam, adverb. *daily, by day.* wala*y*elah, xii. 7. a.

3. wĕhayah, *and he shall be,* P. with Waw conv. xiii. 62. kĕgez, *like a tree,* xii. 5. n. s. m. shathul, part. pass. m. s. fr. שָׁתַל, *he planted.* gal-palgeymayim *by the streams of water,* xii. 17. vii. 22. 2. viii. 9. a. piryo, *his fruit,* viii. 9. o. yitten, F. 3. s. m. fr. נָתַן, *he gave.* bĕgitto, fr. עֵת *time,* vii. 14.

wĕgalehu, *and his leaf*, fr. עָלֶה viii. 7. yibbol, F. 3. s. m. fr. נָבֵל x. 3. a. wēkol, xii. 17. yagăsch, F. 3. s. m. fr. עָשָׂה *made, did.* yazliah, 3. s. m. F. V. fr. צָלַח *prospered*, V. id.

4. lo'-ken, *not so are*, xii. 16. haréshagim, iii. 14. kammoz, *like the chaff* they are, xii. 3. tiddéfennu, F. 3. s. f. fr. נָדַף, *scattered*, with af. *his* v. 3. ruah, n. s. f. *the wind*.

5. gal-ken, *therefore*, xii. 16. yakumu *they shall stand*, F. 3. m. pl. fr. קוּם *to stand*. bammishpat, xii. 3. *in the judgment*. bagădath, *in the assembly*, s. cr. fr. עֵדָה. vii. 7. 2. zaddikim, a. pl. m. fr. צַדִּיק, *righteous*.

6. yodeag, part. m. s. fr. יָדַע *knew*. to'ved, F. 3. s. f. fr. אָבַד xi. 12. *perished, the way of wicked men shall perish.*

PSALM II.

1. lammah, xii. 16. *why?* ragĕshu, P. 3. pl. fr. רָגַשׁ, *was tumultuous*, goyim pl. of גּוֹי *a nation*. ulĕ'ummim, *and peoples*, pl. fr. לְאֹם. yehgu, F. 3. pl. m. fr. הָגָה Ps. i. 2. rik, a. *a vain thing, empty*.

2. yithyazzĕvu, F. 3. m. pl. VII. fr. יצב only in VII. *stood up, stood fast*. malkey-'erez, *the kings of earth*, vii. 22. 2. pl. cr. of melek vii. 6. rozenim, n. pl. m. *princes*. nosĕdu, P. 3. pl. II. fr. יסד in II. *plotted*. yahad, *together*, in p. meshiho, mashiah, with af. *his*, Messiah xiii. 70. 9.

3. nĕnattĕkah, 1. pl. F. III. fr. נָתַק *drew away*, with ה par. xii. 18. moserothemo, pl. with poet. af. *their*. v. 3. *bonds*. nashlikah, 1. pl. F. V. fr. שָׁלַךְ, *cast away*, with ה par. mimmennu, xii. 17. găvothemo, pl. with af. *their*.

4. yoshev, part. s. m. fr. יָשַׁב, *dwell.* bashsha-mayim, *in the heavens,* xii. 3. yi*s*hak, 3. m. s. F. fr. שָׂחַק, *laughed.* 'ădonay, *my Lord* fr. אָדוֹן pl. with af. *my.* The *K'amez* in this word marks its reference to the Divine Being. yil*g*ag, 3. m. s. F. fr. לָעַג, *scorned.* lamo, xii. 17.

5. *'az*, xii. 16. yĕdabber 3. s. m. F. III. fr. דָּבַר *spoke.* bŏ'appo, *in his wrath* fr. אַף *anger.* uva-*h*ărono fr. חָרוֹן *wrath.* xii. 7. v. 3. yĕba*h*ălemo, 3. s. m. F. III. fr. בהל, not used in *K'*al, *vexed* with af. *them.*

6. wa'ăn*i*, *but I,* xii. 7. nasak*t*i, 1. s. P. fr. נָסַךְ, *anointed, appointed.* malk*i*, vii. 22. 2. har-*k*od-sh*i*, *the mountain of my holiness* fr. קֹדֶשׁ xiii. 39. vii. 23.

7. 'ăsappĕrah, 1. s. F. III. fr. סָפַר *recounted* with ה par. 'el-*h*ok perhaps for 'eth, xii. 6. a. 'amar, P. 3. s. m. *said.* 'elay, xii. 17. bĕn*i*, viii. 2. 'attah, v. 1. hayyom, *the day — to day.* yĕlid*t*ika, P. 1. s. with af. *thee* m. xi. 12.

8. shĕ'al, im. m. s. fr. שָׁאַל *asked* x. 3. c. mim-menn*i* xii. 17. we'ettĕnah, *and I will give*, 1. s. F. with ה par. xii. 18. fr. נָתַן *gave.* goyim, vi. 9. na*h*ălatheka, *as thine inheritance*, vii. 7. v. 3. fr. נָחַל, *inherited* in p. wa'ă*h*uzzathĕka, *and thy possession,* xii. 7. fr. אָחַז *possessed.* afsey-'arez, vii. 22. 2. ii. 21.

9. *t*erogem, *thou shalt break them*, 2. m. s. F. fr. רָעַע, *broke, crushed.* bĕshevet, *with a rod of,* ant. to barzel s. n. m. *iron.* kikl*i*, *like the vessel of,* xii. 2. yo*z*er, part. s. m. of יָצַר *formed, fashioned; a potter.* *t*ĕnappĕzem, 2. m. s. F. III. fr. נָפַץ, *dashed in pieces,* with af. *them* m.

10. we*g*attah, *and now* xii. 16. mĕlakim, *o ye kings* vii. 22. 2. hask*i*lu, im. V. 2. pl. m. *be ye wise.* hiwwasĕru, im. II. fr. יָסַר *corrected; be ye corrected*

וַיֹּאמֶר הָאִשָּׁה הַנָּחָשׁ הִשִּׁיאַנִי וָאֹכֵל: וַיֹּאמֶר יְהוָֹה אֱלֹהִים 14
אֶל־הַנָּחָשׁ כִּי עָשִׂיתָ זֹּאת אָרוּר אַתָּה מִכָּל־הַבְּהֵמָה וּמִכֹּל
חַיַּת הַשָּׂדֶה עַל־גְּחֹנְךָ תֵלֵךְ וְעָפָר תֹּאכַל כָּל־יְמֵי חַיֶּיךָ:
וְאֵיבָה אָשִׁית בֵּינְךָ וּבֵין הָאִשָּׁה וּבֵין זַרְעֲךָ וּבֵין זַרְעָהּ הוּא 15
יְשׁוּפְךָ רֹאשׁ וְאַתָּה תְּשׁוּפֶנּוּ עָקֵב: אֶל־הָאִשָּׁה אָמַר הַרְבָּה 16
אַרְבֶּה עִצְּבוֹנֵךְ וְהֵרֹנֵךְ בְּעֶצֶב תֵּלְדִי בָנִים וְאֶל־אִישֵׁךְ תְּשׁוּקָתֵךְ
וְהוּא יִמְשָׁל־בָּךְ: וּלְאָדָם אָמַר כִּי שָׁמַעְתָּ לְקוֹל אִשְׁתֶּךָ 17
וַתֹּאכַל מִן־הָעֵץ אֲשֶׁר צִוִּיתִיךָ לֵאמֹר לֹא תֹאכַל מִמֶּנּוּ אֲרוּרָה
הָאֲדָמָה בַּעֲבוּרֶךָ בְּעִצָּבוֹן תֹּאכֲלֶנָּה כֹּל יְמֵי חַיֶּיךָ: וְקוֹץ 18
וְדַרְדַּר תַּצְמִיחַ לָךְ וְאָכַלְתָּ אֶת־עֵשֶׂב הַשָּׂדֶה: בְּזֵעַת אַפֶּיךָ 19
תֹּאכַל לֶחֶם עַד שׁוּבְךָ אֶל־הָאֲדָמָה כִּי מִמֶּנָּה לֻקָּחְתָּ כִּי־עָפָר
אַתָּה וְאֶל־עָפָר תָּשׁוּב: וַיִּקְרָא הָאָדָם שֵׁם אִשְׁתּוֹ חַוָּה כִּי 20
הִוא הָיְתָה אֵם כָּל־חָי: וַיַּעַשׂ יְהוָֹה אֱלֹהִים לְאָדָם וּלְאִשְׁתּוֹ 21
כָּתְנוֹת עוֹר וַיַּלְבִּשֵׁם: וַיֹּאמֶר יְהוָֹה אֱלֹהִים הֵן הָאָדָם הָיָה 22
כְּאַחַד מִמֶּנּוּ לָדַעַת טוֹב וָרָע וְעַתָּה פֶּן־יִשְׁלַח יָדוֹ וְלָקַח גַּם
מֵעֵץ הַחַיִּים וְאָכַל וָחַי לְעֹלָם: וַיְשַׁלְּחֵהוּ יְהוָֹה אֱלֹהִים מִגַּן־ 23
עֵדֶן לַעֲבֹד אֶת־הָאֲדָמָה אֲשֶׁר לֻקַּח מִשָּׁם: וַיְגָרֶשׁ אֶת־הָאָדָם 24
וַיַּשְׁכֵּן מִקֶּדֶם לְגַן־עֵדֶן אֶת־הַכְּרֻבִים וְאֵת לַהַט הַחֶרֶב
הַמִּתְהַפֶּכֶת לִשְׁמֹר אֶת־דֶּרֶךְ עֵץ הַחַיִּים:

4.

וְהָאָדָם יָדַע אֶת־חַוָּה אִשְׁתּוֹ וַתַּהַר וַתֵּלֶד אֶת־קַיִן 1
וַתֹּאמֶר קָנִיתִי אִישׁ אֶת־יְהוָֹה: וַתֹּסֶף לָלֶדֶת אֶת־אָחִיו אֶת־ 2
הָבֶל וַיְהִי־הֶבֶל רֹעֵה צֹאן וְקַיִן הָיָה עֹבֵד אֲדָמָה: וַיְהִי 3
מִקֵּץ יָמִים וַיָּבֵא קַיִן מִפְּרִי הָאֲדָמָה מִנְחָה לַיהוָֹה: וְהֶבֶל 4
הֵבִיא גַם־הוּא מִבְּכֹרוֹת צֹאנוֹ וּמֵחֶלְבֵהֶן וַיִּשַׁע יְהוָֹה אֶל־הֶבֶל
וְאֶל־מִנְחָתוֹ: וְאֶל־קַיִן וְאֶל־מִנְחָתוֹ לֹא שָׁעָה וַיִּחַר לְקַיִן 5
מְאֹד וַיִּפְּלוּ פָּנָיו: וַיֹּאמֶר יְהוָֹה אֶל־קָיִן לָמָּה חָרָה לָךְ 6
וְלָמָּה נָפְלוּ פָנֶיךָ: הֲלוֹא אִם־תֵּיטִיב שְׂאֵת וְאִם לֹא תֵיטִיב 7

לַפֶּתַח חַטָּאת רֹבֵץ וְאֵלֶיךָ תְּשׁוּקָתוֹ וְאַתָּה תִּמְשָׁל־בּוֹ:
8 וַיֹּאמֶר קַיִן אֶל־הֶבֶל אָחִיו וַיְהִי בִּהְיוֹתָם בַּשָּׂדֶה וַיָּקָם קַיִן אֶל־הֶבֶל אָחִיו וַיַּהַרְגֵהוּ: 9 וַיֹּאמֶר יְהֹוָה אֶל־קַיִן אֵי הֶבֶל אָחִיךָ וַיֹּאמֶר לֹא יָדַעְתִּי הֲשֹׁמֵר אָחִי אָנֹכִי: 10 וַיֹּאמֶר מֶה עָשִׂיתָ 11 קוֹל דְּמֵי אָחִיךָ צֹעֲקִים אֵלַי מִן־הָאֲדָמָה: וְעַתָּה אָרוּר אָתָּה מִן־הָאֲדָמָה אֲשֶׁר פָּצְתָה אֶת־פִּיהָ לָקַחַת אֶת־דְּמֵי אָחִיךָ 12 מִיָּדֶךָ: כִּי תַעֲבֹד אֶת־הָאֲדָמָה לֹא־תֹסֵף תֵּת־כֹּחָהּ לָךְ נָע 13 וָנָד תִּהְיֶה בָאָרֶץ: וַיֹּאמֶר קַיִן אֶל־יְהוָה גָּדוֹל עֲוֹנִי מִנְּשׂוֹא: 14 הֵן גֵּרַשְׁתָּ אֹתִי הַיּוֹם מֵעַל פְּנֵי הָאֲדָמָה וּמִפָּנֶיךָ אֶסָּתֵר וְהָיִיתִי 15 נָע וָנָד בָּאָרֶץ וְהָיָה כָל־מֹצְאִי יַהַרְגֵנִי: וַיֹּאמֶר לוֹ יְהֹוָה לָכֵן כָּל־הֹרֵג קַיִן שִׁבְעָתַיִם יֻקָּם וַיָּשֶׂם יְהֹוָה לְקַיִן אוֹת לְבִלְתִּי 16 הַכּוֹת־אֹתוֹ כָּל־מֹצְאוֹ: וַיֵּצֵא קַיִן מִלִּפְנֵי יְהֹוָה וַיֵּשֶׁב בְּאֶרֶץ־ 17 נוֹד קִדְמַת־עֵדֶן: וַיֵּדַע קַיִן אֶת־אִשְׁתּוֹ וַתַּהַר וַתֵּלֶד אֶת־חֲנוֹךְ 18 וַיְהִי בֹּנֶה עִיר וַיִּקְרָא שֵׁם הָעִיר כְּשֵׁם בְּנוֹ חֲנוֹךְ: וַיִּוָּלֵד לַחֲנוֹךְ אֶת־עִירָד וְעִירָד יָלַד אֶת־מְחוּיָאֵל וּמְחִיָּיאֵל יָלַד אֶת־ 19 מְתוּשָׁאֵל וּמְתוּשָׁאֵל יָלַד אֶת־לָמֶךְ: וַיִּקַּח־לוֹ לֶמֶךְ שְׁתֵּי 20 נָשִׁים שֵׁם הָאַחַת עָדָה וְשֵׁם הַשֵּׁנִית צִלָּה: וַתֵּלֶד עָדָה אֶת־ 21 יָבָל הוּא הָיָה אֲבִי יֹשֵׁב אֹהֶל וּמִקְנֶה: וְשֵׁם אָחִיו יוּבָל הוּא 22 הָיָה אֲבִי כָּל־תֹּפֵשׂ כִּנּוֹר וְעוּגָב: וְצִלָּה גַם־הִוא יָלְדָה אֶת־ תּוּבַל קַיִן לֹטֵשׁ כָּל־חֹרֵשׁ נְחֹשֶׁת וּבַרְזֶל וַאֲחוֹת תּוּבַל־קַיִן 23 נַעֲמָה: וַיֹּאמֶר לֶמֶךְ לְנָשָׁיו עָדָה וְצִלָּה שְׁמַעַן קוֹלִי נְשֵׁי לֶמֶךְ הַאְזֵנָּה אִמְרָתִי כִּי אִישׁ הָרַגְתִּי לְפִצְעִי וְיֶלֶד לְחַבֻּרָתִי: 24 כִּי שִׁבְעָתַיִם יֻקַּם־קָיִן וְלֶמֶךְ שִׁבְעִים וְשִׁבְעָה: וַיֵּדַע אָדָם עוֹד אֶת־אִשְׁתּוֹ וַתֵּלֶד בֵּן וַתִּקְרָא אֶת־שְׁמוֹ שֵׁת כִּי שָׁת־לִי 26 אֱלֹהִים זֶרַע אַחֵר תַּחַת הֶבֶל כִּי הֲרָגוֹ קָיִן: וּלְשֵׁת גַּם־הוּא יֻלַּד־בֵּן וַיִּקְרָא אֶת־שְׁמוֹ אֱנוֹשׁ אָז הוּחַל לִקְרֹא בְּשֵׁם יְהֹוָה:

5.

א זֶה סֵפֶר תּוֹלְדֹת אָדָם בְּיוֹם בְּרֹא אֱלֹהִים אָדָם בִּדְמוּת 2 אֱלֹהִים עָשָׂה אֹתוֹ: זָכָר וּנְקֵבָה בְּרָאָם וַיְבָרֶךְ אֹתָם וַיִּקְרָא

3 אֶת־שְׁמָם אָדָם בְּיוֹם הִבָּרְאָם: וַיְחִי אָדָם שְׁלֹשִׁים וּמְאַת
4 שָׁנָה וַיּוֹלֶד בִּדְמוּתוֹ בְּצַלְמוֹ וַיִּקְרָא אֶת־שְׁמוֹ שֵׁת: וַיִּהְיוּ
יְמֵי־אָדָם אַחֲרֵי הוֹלִידוֹ אֶת־שֵׁת שְׁמֹנֶה מֵאֹת שָׁנָה וַיּוֹלֶד
5 בָּנִים וּבָנוֹת: וַיִּהְיוּ כָּל־יְמֵי אָדָם אֲשֶׁר־חַי תְּשַׁע מֵאוֹת שָׁנָה
6 וּשְׁלֹשִׁים שָׁנָה וַיָּמֹת: וַיְחִי־שֵׁת חָמֵשׁ שָׁנִים וּמְאַת שָׁנָה
7 וַיּוֹלֶד אֶת־אֱנוֹשׁ: וַיְחִי־שֵׁת אַחֲרֵי הוֹלִידוֹ אֶת־אֱנוֹשׁ שֶׁבַע
8 שָׁנִים וּשְׁמֹנֶה מֵאוֹת שָׁנָה וַיּוֹלֶד בָּנִים וּבָנוֹת: וַיִּהְיוּ כָּל־
9 יְמֵי־שֵׁת שְׁתֵּים עֶשְׂרֵה שָׁנָה וּתְשַׁע מֵאוֹת שָׁנָה וַיָּמֹת: וַיְחִי
10 אֱנוֹשׁ תִּשְׁעִים שָׁנָה וַיּוֹלֶד אֶת־קֵינָן: וַיְחִי אֱנוֹשׁ אַחֲרֵי הוֹלִידוֹ
אֶת־קֵינָן חֲמֵשׁ עֶשְׂרֵה שָׁנָה וּשְׁמֹנֶה מֵאוֹת שָׁנָה וַיּוֹלֶד בָּנִים
11 וּבָנוֹת: וַיִּהְיוּ כָּל־יְמֵי אֱנוֹשׁ חָמֵשׁ שָׁנִים וּתְשַׁע מֵאוֹת שָׁנָה
12 וַיָּמֹת: וַיְחִי קֵינָן שִׁבְעִים שָׁנָה וַיּוֹלֶד אֶת־מַהֲלַלְאֵל: וַיְחִי
13 קֵינָן אַחֲרֵי הוֹלִידוֹ אֶת־מַהֲלַלְאֵל אַרְבָּעִים שָׁנָה וּשְׁמֹנֶה
14 מֵאוֹת שָׁנָה וַיּוֹלֶד בָּנִים וּבָנוֹת: וַיִּהְיוּ כָּל־יְמֵי קֵינָן עֶשֶׂר
שָׁנִים וּתְשַׁע מֵאוֹת שָׁנָה וַיָּמֹת: וַיְחִי מַהֲלַלְאֵל חָמֵשׁ שָׁנִים 15
16 וְשִׁשִּׁים שָׁנָה וַיּוֹלֶד אֶת־יָרֶד: וַיְחִי מַהֲלַלְאֵל אַחֲרֵי הוֹלִידוֹ
אֶת־יֶרֶד שְׁלֹשִׁים שָׁנָה וּשְׁמֹנֶה מֵאוֹת שָׁנָה וַיּוֹלֶד בָּנִים
17 וּבָנוֹת: וַיִּהְיוּ כָּל־יְמֵי מַהֲלַלְאֵל חָמֵשׁ וְתִשְׁעִים שָׁנָה וּשְׁמֹנֶה
18 מֵאוֹת שָׁנָה וַיָּמֹת: וַיְחִי־יֶרֶד שְׁתַּיִם וְשִׁשִּׁים שָׁנָה וּמְאַת
19 שָׁנָה וַיּוֹלֶד אֶת־חֲנוֹךְ: וַיְחִי־יֶרֶד אַחֲרֵי הוֹלִידוֹ אֶת־חֲנוֹךְ
20 שְׁמֹנֶה מֵאוֹת שָׁנָה וַיּוֹלֶד בָּנִים וּבָנוֹת: וַיִּהְיוּ כָּל־יְמֵי־יֶרֶד
21 שְׁתַּיִם וְשִׁשִּׁים שָׁנָה וּתְשַׁע מֵאוֹת שָׁנָה וַיָּמֹת: וַיְחִי חֲנוֹךְ
22 חָמֵשׁ וְשִׁשִּׁים שָׁנָה וַיּוֹלֶד אֶת־מְתוּשָׁלַח: וַיִּתְהַלֵּךְ חֲנוֹךְ
אֶת־הָאֱלֹהִים אַחֲרֵי הוֹלִידוֹ אֶת־מְתוּשֶׁלַח שְׁלֹשׁ מֵאוֹת
23 שָׁנָה וַיּוֹלֶד בָּנִים וּבָנוֹת: וַיְהִי כָּל־יְמֵי חֲנוֹךְ חָמֵשׁ וְשִׁשִּׁים
24 שָׁנָה וּשְׁלֹשׁ מֵאוֹת שָׁנָה: וַיִּתְהַלֵּךְ חֲנוֹךְ אֶת־הָאֱלֹהִים וְאֵינֶנּוּ
25 כִּי־לָקַח אֹתוֹ אֱלֹהִים: וַיְחִי מְתוּשֶׁלַח שֶׁבַע וּשְׁמֹנִים שָׁנָה
26 וּמְאַת שָׁנָה וַיּוֹלֶד אֶת־לָמֶךְ: וַיְחִי מְתוּשֶׁלַח אַחֲרֵי הוֹלִידוֹ
אֶת־לֶמֶךְ שְׁתַּיִם וּשְׁמֹנִים שָׁנָה וּשְׁבַע מֵאוֹת שָׁנָה וַיּוֹלֶד

27 בָּנִים וּבָנֽוֹת׃ וַיִּֽהְיוּ כָּל־יְמֵי מְתוּשֶׁלַח תֵּשַׁע וְשִׁשִּׁים שָׁנָה
28 וּתְשַׁע מֵאוֹת שָׁנָה וַיָּמֹֽת׃ וַֽיְחִי־לֶמֶךְ שְׁתַּיִם וּשְׁמֹנִים שָׁנָה
29 וּמְאַת שָׁנָה וַיּוֹלֶד בֵּֽן׃ וַיִּקְרָא אֶת־שְׁמוֹ נֹחַ לֵאמֹר זֶה יְנַחֲמֵנוּ
 מִֽמַּעֲשֵׂנוּ וּמֵעִצְּבוֹן יָדֵינוּ מִן־הָאֲדָמָה אֲשֶׁר אֵֽרְרָהּ יְהוָֽה׃
ל וַֽיְחִי־לֶמֶךְ אַֽחֲרֵי הוֹלִידוֹ אֶת־נֹחַ חָמֵשׁ וְתִשְׁעִים שָׁנָה וַחֲמֵשׁ
31 מֵאֹת שָׁנָה וַיּוֹלֶד בָּנִים וּבָנֽוֹת׃ וַיְהִי כָּל־יְמֵי־לֶמֶךְ שֶׁבַע
32 וְשִׁבְעִים שָׁנָה וּשְׁבַע מֵאוֹת שָׁנָה וַיָּמֹֽת׃ וַֽיְהִי־נֹחַ בֶּן־חֲמֵשׁ
 מֵאוֹת שָׁנָה וַיּוֹלֶד נֹחַ אֶת־שֵׁם אֶת־חָם וְאֶת־יָֽפֶת׃

6.

א וַֽיְהִי כִּֽי־הֵחֵל הָֽאָדָם לָרֹב עַל־פְּנֵי הָֽאֲדָמָה וּבָנוֹת יֻלְּדוּ
2 לָהֶֽם׃ וַיִּרְאוּ בְנֵי־הָֽאֱלֹהִים אֶת־בְּנוֹת הָֽאָדָם כִּי טֹבֹת הֵנָּה
3 וַיִּקְחוּ לָהֶם נָשִׁים מִכֹּל אֲשֶׁר בָּחָֽרוּ׃ וַיֹּאמֶר יְהוָה לֹֽא־יָדוֹן
 רוּחִי בָֽאָדָם לְעֹלָם בְּשַׁגַּם הוּא בָשָׂר וְהָיוּ יָמָיו מֵאָה וְעֶשְׂרִים
4 שָׁנָֽה׃ הַנְּפִלִים הָיוּ בָאָרֶץ בַּיָּמִים הָהֵם וְגַם אַֽחֲרֵי־כֵן אֲשֶׁר
 יָבֹאוּ בְּנֵי הָֽאֱלֹהִים אֶל־בְּנוֹת הָֽאָדָם וְיָֽלְדוּ לָהֶם הֵמָּה הַגִּבֹּרִים
ה אֲשֶׁר מֵֽעוֹלָם אַנְשֵׁי הַשֵּֽׁם׃ וַיַּרְא יְהוָה כִּי רַבָּה רָעַת הָֽאָדָם
6 בָּאָרֶץ וְכָל־יֵצֶר מַחְשְׁבֹת לִבּוֹ רַק רַע כָּל־הַיּֽוֹם׃ וַיִּנָּחֶם
7 יְהוָה כִּֽי־עָשָׂה אֶת־הָֽאָדָם בָּאָרֶץ וַיִּתְעַצֵּב אֶל־לִבּֽוֹ׃ וַיֹּאמֶר
 יְהוָה אֶמְחֶה אֶת־הָֽאָדָם אֲשֶׁר־בָּרָאתִי מֵעַל פְּנֵי הָֽאֲדָמָה
 מֵֽאָדָם עַד־בְּהֵמָה עַד־רֶמֶשׂ וְעַד־עוֹף הַשָּׁמָיִם כִּי נִחַמְתִּי
8,9 כִּי עֲשִׂיתִֽם׃ וְנֹחַ מָצָא חֵן בְּעֵינֵי יְהוָֽה׃ אֵלֶּה תּֽוֹלְדֹת
 נֹחַ נֹחַ אִישׁ צַדִּיק תָּמִים הָיָה בְּדֹֽרֹתָיו אֶת־הָֽאֱלֹהִים
י הִתְהַלֶּךְ־נֹֽחַ׃ וַיּוֹלֶד נֹחַ שְׁלֹשָׁה בָנִים אֶת־שֵׁם אֶת־חָם
11 וְאֶת־יָֽפֶת׃ וַתִּשָּׁחֵת הָאָרֶץ לִפְנֵי הָֽאֱלֹהִים וַתִּמָּלֵא הָאָרֶץ
12 חָמָֽס׃ וַיַּרְא אֱלֹהִים אֶת־הָאָרֶץ וְהִנֵּה נִשְׁחָתָה כִּֽי־הִשְׁחִית
13 כָּל־בָּשָׂר אֶת־דַּרְכּוֹ עַל־הָאָֽרֶץ׃ וַיֹּאמֶר אֱלֹהִים לְנֹחַ קֵץ
 כָּל־בָּשָׂר בָּא לְפָנַי כִּֽי־מָלְאָה הָאָרֶץ חָמָס מִפְּנֵיהֶם וְהִנְנִי
14 מַשְׁחִיתָם אֶת־הָאָֽרֶץ׃ עֲשֵׂה לְךָ תֵּבַת עֲצֵי־גֹפֶר קִנִּים

APPENDIX

תַּעֲשֶׂה אֶת־הַתֵּבָה וְכָפַרְתָּ אֹתָהּ מִבַּיִת וּמִחוּץ בַּכֹּפֶר: וְזֶה ₁₅
אֲשֶׁר תַּעֲשֶׂה אֹתָהּ שְׁלֹשׁ מֵאוֹת אַמָּה אֹרֶךְ הַתֵּבָה חֲמִשִּׁים
אַמָּה רָחְבָּהּ וּשְׁלֹשִׁים אַמָּה קוֹמָתָהּ: צֹהַר תַּעֲשֶׂה לַתֵּבָה 16
וְאֶל־אַמָּה תְּכַלֶּנָּה מִלְמַעְלָה וּפֶתַח הַתֵּבָה בְּצִדָּהּ תָּשִׂים
תַּחְתִּיִּם שְׁנִיִּם וּשְׁלִשִׁים תַּעֲשֶׂהָ: וַאֲנִי הִנְנִי מֵבִיא אֶת־הַמַּבּוּל 17
מַיִם עַל־הָאָרֶץ לְשַׁחֵת כָּל־בָּשָׂר אֲשֶׁר־בּוֹ רוּחַ חַיִּים מִתַּחַת
הַשָּׁמָיִם כֹּל אֲשֶׁר־בָּאָרֶץ יִגְוָע: וַהֲקִמֹתִי אֶת־בְּרִיתִי אִתָּךְ 18
וּבָאתָ אֶל־הַתֵּבָה אַתָּה וּבָנֶיךָ וְאִשְׁתְּךָ וּנְשֵׁי־בָנֶיךָ אִתָּךְ:
וּמִכָּל־הָחַי מִכָּל־בָּשָׂר שְׁנַיִם מִכֹּל תָּבִיא אֶל־הַתֵּבָה לְהַחֲיֹת 19
אִתָּךְ זָכָר וּנְקֵבָה יִהְיוּ: מֵהָעוֹף לְמִינֵהוּ וּמִן־הַבְּהֵמָה לְמִינָהּ ₂₀
מִכֹּל רֶמֶשׂ הָאֲדָמָה לְמִינֵהוּ שְׁנַיִם מִכֹּל יָבֹאוּ אֵלֶיךָ לְהַחֲיוֹת:
וְאַתָּה קַח־לְךָ מִכָּל־מַאֲכָל אֲשֶׁר יֵאָכֵל וְאָסַפְתָּ אֵלֶיךָ וְהָיָה 21
לְךָ וְלָהֶם לְאָכְלָה: וַיַּעַשׂ נֹחַ כְּכֹל אֲשֶׁר צִוָּה אֹתוֹ אֱלֹהִים 22
כֵּן עָשָׂה:

PSALM 1.

אַשְׁרֵי הָאִישׁ	וְעָלֵהוּ לֹא־יִבּוֹל ₃
אֲשֶׁר לֹא הָלַךְ בַּעֲצַת רְשָׁעִים	וְכֹל אֲשֶׁר־יַעֲשֶׂה יַצְלִיחַ:
וּבְדֶרֶךְ חַטָּאִים לֹא עָמָד	לֹא־כֵן הָרְשָׁעִים 4
וּבְמוֹשַׁב לֵצִים לֹא יָשָׁב:	כִּי אִם־כַּמֹּץ אֲשֶׁר־תִּדְּפֶנּוּ רוּחַ:
כִּי אִם בְּתוֹרַת יְהוָה חֶפְצוֹ ₂	עַל־כֵּן לֹא־יָקֻמוּ רְשָׁעִים בַּמִּשְׁפָּט ₅
וּבְתוֹרָתוֹ יֶהְגֶּה יוֹמָם וָלָיְלָה:	וְחַטָּאִים בַּעֲדַת צַדִּיקִים:
וְהָיָה כְּעֵץ שָׁתוּל עַל־פַּלְגֵי־מָיִם ₃	כִּי־יוֹדֵעַ יְהוָה דֶּרֶךְ צַדִּיקִים 6
אֲשֶׁר פִּרְיוֹ יִתֵּן בְּעִתּוֹ	וְדֶרֶךְ רְשָׁעִים תֹּאבֵד:

PSALM II.

א לָמָּה רָגְשׁוּ גוֹיִם
וּלְאֻמִּים יֶהְגּוּ־רִיק:
2 יִתְיַצְּבוּ מַלְכֵי־אֶרֶץ
וְרוֹזְנִים נוֹסְדוּ־יָחַד
עַל־יְהוָה וְעַל־מְשִׁיחוֹ:
3 נְנַתְּקָה אֶת־מוֹסְרוֹתֵימוֹ
וְנַשְׁלִיכָה מִמֶּנּוּ עֲבֹתֵימוֹ:
4 יוֹשֵׁב בַּשָּׁמַיִם יִשְׂחָק
אֲדֹנָי יִלְעַג־לָמוֹ:
5 אָז יְדַבֵּר אֵלֵימוֹ בְאַפּוֹ
וּבַחֲרוֹנוֹ יְבַהֲלֵמוֹ:
6 וַאֲנִי נָסַכְתִּי מַלְכִּי
עַל־צִיּוֹן הַר־קָדְשִׁי:
7 אֲסַפְּרָה אֶל־חֹק

יְהוָה אָמַר אֵלַי בְּנִי אָתָּה
אֲנִי הַיּוֹם יְלִדְתִּיךָ:
8 שְׁאַל מִמֶּנִּי
וְאֶתְּנָה גוֹיִם נַחֲלָתֶךָ
וַאֲחֻזָּתְךָ אַפְסֵי־אָרֶץ:
9 תְּרֹעֵם בְּשֵׁבֶט בַּרְזֶל
כִּכְלִי יוֹצֵר תְּנַפְּצֵם:
10 וְעַתָּה מְלָכִים הַשְׂכִּילוּ
הִוָּסְרוּ שֹׁפְטֵי אָרֶץ:
11 עִבְדוּ אֶת־יְהוָה בְּיִרְאָה
וְגִילוּ בִּרְעָדָה:
12 נַשְּׁקוּ־בַר פֶּן־יֶאֱנַף וְתֹאבְדוּ דֶרֶךְ
כִּי־יִבְעַר כִּמְעַט אַפּוֹ
אַשְׁרֵי כָּל־חוֹסֵי בוֹ:

PSALM III.

א מִזְמוֹר לְדָוִד בְּבָרְחוֹ מִפְּנֵי אַבְשָׁלוֹם בְּנוֹ:
2 יְהוָה מָה־רַבּוּ צָרָי
רַבִּים קָמִים עָלָי:
3 רַבִּים אֹמְרִים לְנַפְשִׁי
אֵין יְשׁוּעָתָה לּוֹ בֵאלֹהִים סֶלָה:
4 וְאַתָּה יְהוָה מָגֵן בַּעֲדִי
כְּבוֹדִי וּמֵרִים רֹאשִׁי:
5 קוֹלִי אֶל־יְהוָה אֶקְרָא
וַיַּעֲנֵנִי מֵהַר קָדְשׁוֹ סֶלָה:
6 אֲנִי שָׁכַבְתִּי וָאִישָׁנָה

הֱקִיצוֹתִי כִּי יְהוָה יִסְמְכֵנִי:
7 לֹא־אִירָא מֵרִבְבוֹת עָם
אֲשֶׁר סָבִיב שָׁתוּ עָלָי:
8 קוּמָה יְהוָה הוֹשִׁיעֵנִי אֱלֹהַי
כִּי־הִכִּיתָ אֶת־כָּל־אֹיְבַי לֶחִי
שִׁנֵּי רְשָׁעִים שִׁבַּרְתָּ:
9 לַיהוָה הַיְשׁוּעָה
עַל־עַמְּךָ בִרְכָתֶךָ סֶּלָה:

PSALM IV.

לַמְנַצֵּחַ בִּנְגִינוֹת מִזְמוֹר לְדָוִד: א

2 זִבְחוּ זִבְחֵי־צֶדֶק · בְּקָרְאִי עֲנֵנִי אֱלֹהֵי צִדְקִי
וּבִטְחוּ אֶל־יְהוָה: · בַּצָּר הִרְחַבְתָּ לִּי
7 רַבִּים אֹמְרִים מִי־יַרְאֵנוּ טוֹב · חָנֵּנִי וּשְׁמַע תְּפִלָּתִי:
3 נְסָה־עָלֵינוּ אוֹר פָּנֶיךָ יְהוָה: · בְּנֵי אִישׁ עַד־מֶה כְבוֹדִי לִכְלִמָּה
8 נָתַתָּה שִׂמְחָה בְלִבִּי · תֶּאֱהָבוּן רִיק תְּבַקְשׁוּ כָזָב סֶלָה:
4 מֵעֵת דְּגָנָם וְתִירוֹשָׁם רָבּוּ: · וּדְעוּ כִּי־הִפְלָה יְהוָה חָסִיד לוֹ
9 בְּשָׁלוֹם יַחְדָּו אֶשְׁכְּבָה וְאִישָׁן · יְהוָה יִשְׁמַע בְּקָרְאִי אֵלָיו:
ה כִּי־אַתָּה יְהוָה לְבָדָד · רִגְזוּ וְאַל־תֶּחֱטָאוּ
לָבֶטַח תּוֹשִׁיבֵנִי: · אִמְרוּ בִלְבַבְכֶם עַל־מִשְׁכַּבְכֶם
וְדֹמּוּ סֶלָה:

PSALM V.

לַמְנַצֵּחַ אֶל־הַנְּחִילוֹת מִזְמוֹר לְדָוִד: א

6 וַאֲנִי בְּרֹב חַסְדְּךָ אָבוֹא בֵיתֶךָ · אַמְרַי הַאֲזִינָה יְהוָה
אֶשְׁתַּחֲוֶה אֶל־הֵיכַל־קָדְשְׁךָ · בִּינָה הֲגִיגִי:
3 בְּיִרְאָתֶךָ: · הַקְשִׁיבָה לְקוֹל שַׁוְעִי מַלְכִּי
0 יְהוָה נְחֵנִי בְצִדְקָתֶךָ לְמַעַן · וֵאלֹהָי
שׁוֹרְרָי · כִּי־אֵלֶיךָ אֶתְפַּלָּל:
4 הַיְשַׁר לְפָנַי דַּרְכֶּךָ: · יְהוָה בֹּקֶר תִּשְׁמַע קוֹלִי
כִּי אֵין בְּפִיהוּ נְכוֹנָה קִרְבָּם הַוּוֹת · בֹּקֶר אֶעֱרָךְ־לְךָ וַאֲצַפֶּה:
ה קֶבֶר־פָּתוּחַ גְּרֹנָם · כִּי לֹא אֵל־חָפֵץ רֶשַׁע אָתָּה
לְשׁוֹנָם יַחֲלִיקוּן: · לֹא יְגֻרְךָ רָע:
11 לֹא־יִתְיַצְּבוּ הוֹלְלִים לְנֶגֶד עֵינֶיךָ 6 הַאֲשִׁימֵם אֱלֹהִים
שָׂנֵאתָ כָּל־פֹּעֲלֵי אָוֶן: · יִפְּלוּ מִמֹּעֲצוֹתֵיהֶם
7 בְּרֹב פִּשְׁעֵיהֶם הַדִּיחֵמוֹ · תְּאַבֵּד דֹּבְרֵי כָזָב
אִישׁ־דָּמִים וּמִרְמָה יְתָעֵב יְהוָה: · כִּי־מָרוּ בָךְ:

PSALM VI.

א לַמְנַצֵּחַ בִּנְגִינוֹת עַל הַשְּׁמִינִית מִזְמוֹר לְדָוִד:
2 יְהוָה אַל־בְּאַפְּךָ תוֹכִיחֵנִי   אֶשְׂחֶה בְכָל־לַיְלָה מִטָּתִי
וְאַל־בַּחֲמָתְךָ תְיַסְּרֵנִי: בְּדִמְעָתִי עַרְשִׂי אַמְסֶה:
3 חָנֵּנִי יְהוָה כִּי אֻמְלַל אָנִי   8 עָשְׁשָׁה מִכַּעַס עֵינִי
רְפָאֵנִי יְהוָה כִּי נִבְהֲלוּ עֲצָמָי: עָתְקָה בְּכָל־צוֹרְרָי:
4 וְנַפְשִׁי נִבְהֲלָה מְאֹד   9 סוּרוּ מִמֶּנִּי כָּל־פֹּעֲלֵי אָוֶן
וְאַתָּה יְהוָה עַד־מָתָי: כִּי־שָׁמַע יְהוָה קוֹל בִּכְיִי:
5 שׁוּבָה יְהוָה חַלְּצָה נַפְשִׁי   • שָׁמַע יְהוָה תְּחִנָּתִי
הוֹשִׁיעֵנִי לְמַעַן חַסְדֶּךָ:   יְהוָה תְּפִלָּתִי יִקָּח:
6 כִּי אֵין בַּמָּוֶת זִכְרֶךָ   11 יֵבֹשׁוּ וְיִבָּהֲלוּ מְאֹד כָּל־אֹיְבָי
בִּשְׁאוֹל מִי יוֹדֶה־לָּךְ:   יָשֻׁבוּ יֵבֹשׁוּ רָגַע:
7 יָגַעְתִּי בְּאַנְחָתִי

Grammatical Analysis of the first six chapters of Genesis.

The references are to the foregoing pages.
The abbreviations used are as follows:

a. adjective	fr. from	P. Past.
abs. absolute	F. Future	part. participle
af. affix.	im. imperative	pl. plural
ant. antecedent	in. infinitive	pr. pronoun
art. article	m. masculine	r. root
con. consequent	n. noun	s. singular
cr. constructive	o. objective	V Verb
f. feminine	p. particle	v. verse

CHAPTER I.

1. Bĕre'shĭth. bĕ, p. *in* xii. 2, 4. iii. 4. 1. re'shĭth, n. *the beginning* fr. רֹאשׁ *the head.* bara', *he created* V. 3. m. s. P. a r. 'ĕlohĭm n. pl. m. governing bara', xiii. 20. *God.* the s. form of this word is אֱלוֹהַּ. 'eth, sign of o. case, wh. it precedes xii. 17. xiii. 8. hash-shamayim, du. n. with art. prefixed xiii. 9. *the heavens.* wĕ'eth, wĕ *and,* p. xii. 7. ha'arez, n. with art. xii. 9. *the earth.* This word without the art. is 'eruz, but when definite it always takes this form.

2. wĕ ha'arez, *and the earth.* hayĕthah, V. 3. f. s. P. f. r. הָיָה *he was,* see paradigm of verbs ending in ה. thohu, n. *desolation,* iii. 4. 1. wavohu, *and emptiness* n. with ו prefixed xii. 7. a. vĕhoshek, *and darkness* n. here the substantive V. is understood, *was.* gal-pĕney, *upon the face of.* gal, prep. xii. 17. pĕney, n. pl. cr. fr. panim, *the face* vii. 7. thĕhom, n. s. *the deep,* con. to pĕney. weruah, *and the spirit of,* n. f. in

cr. with *elohim*, v. 1. mĕra*h*efcth, part. f. s. III. fr. רָחַף *he fluttered, hovered, brooded.* ɡal-péney, *upon the face of,* see above. hammayim, n. d. with art. xii. 9. *the water.*

3. wayyo'mer, *and he said,* F. apocopated fr. אָמַר 3. m. s. xi. 12. 'elohim, v. 1. yĕhi, 3. m. s. F. fr. הָיָה ap. used as an im. *let there be,* xi. 12. 'or, n. s. *light.* wayĕhi, 3. m. s. F. ap. as before with W*a*w conversive xiii. 64.

4. wayyar', 3. m. s. F. ap. fr. רָאָה *he saw,* xi. 12. k*i*-tov, *that it was good.* k*i*, p. xii. 16. tov, a. m. s. wayyavdel, 3. s. m. F. ap. V. conjugation fr. בָּדַל *he divided,* V. id. beyn, prep. *between,* xii. 17. uveyn, *and between,* xii. 7. ha*h*oshek, n. s. with art. *the darkness* the *h* dispenses with compensation for Dagesh. iii. 10.

5. wayyi*k*ra', *and he called,* 3. m. s. F. fr. קָרָא *he called,* with W*a*w conversive. la'or, the prep. לְ with art. and 'or, *to the light,* that is, *named* the light xii. 3. yom, s. m. n. *day.* wĕla*h*oshek, iii. 10, *and to the darkness* *k*ara' *he called.* r. 3. m. s. P layĕlah s. m. n. *night.* the *K*amez stands for Pata*h* in the first syllable because the word is *in pause* by reason of ethna*h* ii. 21. wayĕhi, v. 3. yerev, n. s. *evening.* voker n. s. *morning.* 'ehad a. *one* ix.

6. wayyo'mer, v. 3. ĕlohim, v. 1. yĕhi, v. 3. ra*k*ia*g*, n. s. *an expanse,* r. ra*k*ag, *he beat out.* bĕthok, prep. *in the midst of* fr. בְּ and תָּוֶךְ *the midst,* cr. תּוֹךְ. vii. 24. hammayim (v. 2). wihi, *and let it be* for וְ, יְהִי the two Shewas coalesce in short *Hirik* xii. 7. b. notice the difference between the word thus pointed and wayĕhi, (v. 3) xiii. 63, 64. mavd*i*l, part. V. m. s. fr. r. בָּדַל v. 4. beyn (v. 4), mayim (v. 2). lamayim, in pause. ii. 21. xii. 2. 17.

7. wayyaga*s*, F. apoc. 3. m. s. with ו conv. fr. r. עָשָׂה *he made* see verbs in ה and table of irregulars and *he made* i. e. *God*. 'eth-ha*r*akia*ǥ*, v. 6. xii. 17. ii. 19. iii. 10. wayyavd*e*l (v. 4). 'ăsher, relative pr. xii. 16. referring to *waters*. mi*tt*a*h*ath fr. מִן and תַּחַת xii. 14. 17, *from underneath*. la*r*akiag, *to the expanse*. me*g*al, *from above* xii. 14. 17. notice the redundancy of preps. xii. 69. wayêhi-ken, (v. 3) and p. xii. 16. *and it was so* iii. 4. 1.

8. wayyikra' (v. 5). sh*a*m*a*yim in pause ii. 21. next five words see (v. 5). sheni a. ordinal numeral *second* m. s. agreeing with yom, ix. *a second day*.

9. yikkawu, 3. m. pl. F. II. fr. r. קָוָה, in II. *was collected, let them begathered together* i.e. *the waters*. mi*tt*a*h*ath (v. 7). 'el-ma*k*om 'el, prep. xii. 17. ma*k*om s. n. *a place* fr. r. קוּם *to stand*. 'ehad, (v. 5) wĕ thera'eh *and let be seen* 3. f. s. F. II. fr. רָאָה *he saw*, hayyabbashah f. n. with art. iii. 14. *the dry land* fr. r. בֹשׁ *was dry*.

10. layyabbashah, (v. 9) xii. 3. 'erez, (v. 1) s. f. n. *earth*. ulĕmi*k*weh *and to the gathering together of* n. cr. of מִקְוֶה vii. 7. with prep. and ן xii. 7. 6. *k*a*r*a' r. 3. m. s. P. *he called* yammim pl. of יָם s. n. *a sea*. for the rest see (v. 4).

11. (vv. 3. 1) *t*adshe', 3. f. s. F. V. fr. r. דָשָׁא, *became green* in V. *produced verdure*. See verbs in א. governed by ha'arcz. *let the earth being forth* xiii. 5, 8. deshe', s. n. *verdure*. gesev, s. n. *herb*. mazriag, V part. fr. זרע, *sowed* in V. *produced seed* agrees with gesev. zera*g*, s. n. *seed* a segolate vii. 22. 2. ge*z*, n. in cr. with péri n. *the tree* of *fruit*. viii. *g*oseh active part. of עָשָׂה, see verbs in ה. *making*, agrees with gez. lĕmino, *according to his kind* fr. מִין, *a species*

with pr. af. v. 3. and prep. âsher, (v. 7) zargo-vo, *his seed* (is) *in him* vii. 22. 2. xiii. 47, 49. for, *whose seed is in him*, the relative being indeclinable xii. 16. ɡal (v. 7).

12. wattoze ha'arez *so the earth brought forth* the V. is 3. f. s. F. V. fr. יָצָא *went out* in V. causative, doubly irregular see xi. 12 next 4 words (v. 11). lĕmīnehu, as before, with different af. v. 3. for rest of v. see (vv. 11. 4).

13. v. 5. shĕlĭshí a. ordinal numeral, *third* ix.

14. v. 3. me'oroth n. pl. fr. מָאוֹר *a place of light* vii. 18. xiii. 29. birkĭaɡ *in the expanse of* cr. of רָקִיעַ, v. 6. with בְּ iii. 1. léhavdel In. V. fr. בדל with pass. hayyom (v. 5) with art. iii. 14. uveyn, b'. (vv. 4. 5). wĕhayu, *and they shall be*, 3. m. pl. P. fr. היה (v. 3) with Waw conv. xi. xiii. 62. lĕ'othoth, *for signs*, pl. of אֹת n. *a sign*. ulemogādim, *and for seasons* xii. 7. 6. pl. of מוֹעֵד *a season* vii. 26. 3. ulĕyamím, *and for days* pl. of yom. vii. 11. distinguish this from pl. of yam (v. 10) and from mayim (v. 2). wĕshanim *and years* pl. of f. n. shanah, *a year* viii. 8 notice ellipse of prep. xiii. 70. 3.

15. lim'oroth, see last v. and xii. 2. lĕha'ir, לְ and in. V. fr. r. אוֹר *was light* in V. *gave light*.

16. v. 7. shĕney, cr. of שְׁנַיִם *two*, ix. art. with mĕ'oroth, iii. 14. haggĕdolim, pl. a. with art. fr. גדל *great* agreeing with me'oroth, xiii. 18. lememsheleth, לְ and cr. of memshalah, n. f. *dominion*, viii. 8. 2. hakkaton, art. with קָטָן a. *little, small*. hakkokavim, art. with pl. of כּוֹכָב n. *a star*.

17. wayyitten, *and he put, placed*, F. 3. s. m. with ו conv. fr. נָתַן *gave, placed, put*, see xi. 12. 'otham, *them*, אֵת with 3. m. pl. af. xii. 17.

18. wĕlimshol, *and to rule*, לְ, וְ and in. cr. fr. מָשַׁל *he ruled* see (v. 16) constructed mediately with בְּ xiii. 51. ulĕhavdel *and to divide* וְ, לְ, xii. 7. with V. in. of בדל (v. 4) for the rest see former vv.

19. rĕvi*gi*, a. m. *fourth* ix.

20. yishrĕzu, *let them being forth abundantly*, 3. m. pl. F. fr. שׁרץ *swarmed with*. sherez, cognate n. collective, *small animals*. nefesh s. f. n. *soul, breath, animal*. *h*ayyah, a. f. fr. חַי alive wĕgof, *and fowl* coll. n. yĕgofef, *let fly*, 3. s. m. F. III. fr. עוּף *to fly*, see xi. 6. *and let fowl fly*.

21. ha*tt*anninim, *the tannins*, art. with pl. of תַּן *a large sea animal* kol—*all* xii. 17. ii. 19. nefesh here may be in cr. with ha*h*ayyah otherwise it should have art. ha*h*ayyah, here s. f. n. *living creature*. haromeseth, art. with part. f. s. fr. רמשׂ *he crept* agreeing with ha*h*ayyah. sha*r*ĕzu, 3. pl. m. P. fr. V. in (v. 20). lĕminehem, *according to their kind*, see (v. 11) with af. 3. pl. m. the Yod is dropped in the pl. af. here which is not usual, but see Ps. cxxxiv. 2. Zech. i. 3. kanaf, n. s. m. *wing* con. to gof.

22. wayĕvarek, 3. m. s. F. III. with ו conv. fr. בָּרַךְ *he blessed*. 'otham (v. 17). le'mor, *saying*, in cr. with לְ fr. אָמַר (v. 3) for לֵאמֹר. pĕru, *be ye fruitful*, 2. m. pl. im. I. fr. פָּרָה *was fruitful;* urĕvu, *and multiply*, xii. 7. 2. m. pl. im. I. fr. רָבָה *was numerous*. umil'u, *and fill*, xii. 7. 2. m. pl. im. I. fr. מָלֵא *was full, filled*. bayyammim, *in the seas*, xii. 3. yirev. 3. s. m. F. ap. fr רָבָה *and let* the fowl *multiply*.

23. *h*amishi a. m. s. *fifth* ix.

24. *t*oze', *let being forth* (v. 12). lĕminah, *according to her kind*, with af. 3. f. s. behemah, n. s. f. coll.

cattle. waremes, *and creeping thing,* xii. 7. a. wehayĕtho, *and the beast of,* irregular cr. form fr. חַיַת xii. 18.

25. ha'ădamah, *the ground.* iii. 14. n. f. s.

26. nagăseh, 1 pl. F. I. fr. עָשָׂה *let us make.* 'adam, n. s. m. *man.* bĕzalmenu, *in our image* fr. אֶלֶם n. s. *image* vii. 22. 2. with בְּ and af. 1. pl. kidmuthenu, *according to our likeness* fr. דְּמוּת *likeness,* with בְּ xii. 5. and at. 1. pl. wĕyirdu, *and let them rule,* 3. m. pl. F. רָדָה *he ruled.* vidgath, *over the fish of* fr. דָּגַת cr. of דָּגָה *fish,* with prep. iii. 4. 2. β. haromes, part. m. fr. ramas, (v. 21) agreeing with remes xiii. 18.

27. wayyivra', c. s. m. F. fr. bara', (v. 1) with Waw conv. xiii. 64. ha'adam, iii. 14. *the man.* bĕzalmo, *in his image,* v. iii. 4. 1. 'otho, *him.* 'eth with aff. 3. m. s. xi. 17 zakar, a. m. s. *male.* unĕkevah, *and female* a. f. s. with וְ xii. 7.

28. lahem, *to them.* lo, with af. 3. pl. m. xii. 17. next words (v. 22) we kivshuha, *and subdue it* sc. the earth. 2 pl. m. im. fr. כָּבַשׁ *he subdued.* see table of F. with af. uredu, *and rule ye,* 2. pl. m. im. from רָדָה (v. 26).

29. hinneh, *behold,* p. xii. 16. nathatti, 1. s. P. *I have given,* (v. 17). lakem lŏ, with af. 2. pl. m. xii. 17. 'asher-bo, *which in it,* i. e. *in which,* xii. 16. zoreag, s. m. part. 1. fr. זָרַע (v. 11.) yihyeh, 3. s. m. F. of הָיָה v. 2. lĕoklah, *for food,* ii. 7. s. f. n. fr. אָכַל *he ate.*

30. ulĕkol, notice the long vowel because without Makkuf, ii. 19. *and to all.* 'eth-kol-yerek, *all the greeness of,* in cr. with gesev, xiii. 35. yerek, a segolate n.

31. mō'od, *very*, xii. 16. hashshishshi, *the sixth,* s. m. s. the art. here is irregular because the n. is without it but the force of it may be *a day* wh. was *the sixth.*

CHAPTER II.

1. wayekullu, *and they were finished,* 3. m. pl. F. IV. fr. כָּלָה *was* complete with Waw conv. xiii. 64. xii. 7. c. next two words Ch. 1. v. 1. we-kol-zēva'am *and all their host* fr. צָבָא *a host,* with af. 3. pl. m.

2. wayēkal *and he finished* 3. m. s. F. ap. fr. kalah. bayyom, xii. 3. iii. 4. 1. hashshēvi*gi, the seventh* a. m. xiii. 18. mēla'kto, *his work* fr. מְלָאכָה *work* with af. 3. m. s. wayyishboth, *and He rested,* 3. s. m. F. fr. שָׁבַת *he rested* with Waw conv. mikkol for min kol xii. 17.

3. wayĕvarek, ch. i. 22. 'eth-yom, should regularly have art. xiii. 18. see last verse of last ch. wayekaddesh, *and he sanctified,* 3. s. m. F. III. of קָדַשׁ *was hallowed,* with Waw conv. xiii. 64. xii. 7. c. 'otho, ch. i. 27. ki, *for,* xii. 16. iii. 4. 1. vo, *in it.* bĕ, with af. xii. 17. iii. 4. 1. lagăsoth, *to make,* in. cr. fr. עָשָׂה xiii. 55. see in. Vs.

4. 'elleh, *these,* pr. xii. 16. tholĕdoth, (are) *the generations* of, *history of,* n. pl. cr. not found in any other form fr. יָלַד, *bore, begot,* ant. to next two words. bĕhibbare'am, *in their being created* iu. II. of ברא with af. 3. pl. m. and prefix. găsoth in. cr. con. to yom, ant. to *Lord God.* xiii. 46.

5. siah, n. s. m. *a plant,* here in cr. with hassadeh, *the field,* s. n. m. with art. iii. 14. terem, *not yet, before.* yihyeh, ch. i. 29. *was not yet,* xiii. 60. 6. yizmah, 3. m. s. F. p. צָמַח *sprouted,* in pause. lo', p. *not,* xii.

or *instructed*. shofetey, pl. m. part. cr. fr. שָׁפַט, *judged*.

11. *givdu*, *serve ye*, 2. pl. m. im. bĕyir'ah, *with fear*, s. f. n. wĕgilu, im. 2. pl. fr. גִיל *to rejoice*. birgadah, xii. 2. *reverence* s. f. n.

12. nashshĕku, im. 2. m. pl. III. fr. נָשַׁק *kissed*. bar, iii. 4. 1. a Chaldee word *son*, prob. and instead of ben to avoid the similarity of sound with the following word. ye'ĕnaf, 3. s. m. F. fr. אָנַף *was angry*, x. 4. 3. tho'vĕdu, 2. m. pl. fr. אָבַד *perished*. yivgar, 3. s. m. F. fr. בָּעַר *burned*. kimgat, xii. 2. 16. *hosey*, part. m. pl. cr. fr. חָסָה *trusted*, xiii. 43.

PSALM III.

1. mizmor, s. n. m. *a Psalm*, fr. זמר in III. *sung*. bĕvorho, in. cr. af. fr. בָּרַח *fled*.

2. mah-rabbu, xii. 16. 3. pl. P. fr. רָבַב. zaray, pl. m. af. *my* fr. צַר *an enemy*. rabbim, pl. fr. רַב, vii. 12. *kamim*, pl. part. m. xij. 17.

3. 'omĕrim, pl. part. m. lenafshi, vii. 22. 2. 'eyn, xii. 17. yĕshugathah, s. f. n. par. form, *salvation*, xii. 18. 2.

4. 'attah, v. 1. magen, s. n. m. *a shield*. bagadi, xii. 17. kĕvodi fr. כָּבוֹד *glory*, with af. umerim, xii. 7, part. V. m. s. fr. רוּם *to be high*.

5. 'ekra', 1. s. F. wayyaganeni, 3. s. m. F. with af. *me* and Waw conv. fr. עָנָה *answered*. mehar, xii. 14. *kodsho*, vii. 23, xiii. 39.

6. shakavti, 1. s. P. *I lay down*. wa'ishanah, *and I slept* fr. יָשֵׁן *slept*, 1. s. F. with ה par. and Waw conv. xii. 18. xiii. 64. hekizothi, 1. s. P. V. fr. קוּץ in V. *awoke*. yismekeni, 1. s. F. af. *me* fr. סָמַךְ *supported*.

7. 'íra', 1. s. F. fr. יָרֵא *feared.* merivěvoth, xii. 14. pl. cr. fr. רְבָבָה *a myriad.* gam, vii. 15. saviv, a. *round about.* shathu, 3. pl. P. שִׁית *to set.*

8. *kumah*, im. 2. m. s. ה pur. קִים *to stand.* hoshigeni, im. V. af. *me* fr. יָשַׁע *saved.* 'ĕlohay, *God,* af. *my.* hikkitha, 2. m. s. P. V fr. נָכָה *smote.* 'oyĕvay, viii. 3. le*hi*, *the cheek,* in p. לְהִי. shinney, pl. cr. vii. 14. shibbarta, 2. s. m. P. III. fr. שָׁבַר *broke.*

9. iii. 14. a. vii. 15. birkatheka, viii. 8. 1. fr. בְּרָכָה *blessing.*

PSALM IV.

1. lamĕnazeah, xii. 3, iii. 6. part. s. m. III. fr. נָצַח in III. *presided, excelled.* nĕginoth, pl. f. *songs, musical instruments.*

2. bĕkor'*i*, in. cr. af. *my.* găneni, imp. 2. m. s. af. *me.* 'ĕlohey, cr. zidki, vii. 22. 3. bazzar, *in affliction,* xii. 3. hirhavta, 2. m. s. P. V. fr. רָחַב *was broad,* ii. 16. *honneni,* im. fr. חָנַן *was gracious,* af. *me.* ushĕmag, xii. 7, x. 3. c. r. שָׁמַע *heard.* tĕfillathi, viii. 8. תְּפִלָּה *prayer.*

3. gad-meh, *till when, how long,* xii. 16. Cf. Ps. x. 13. liklimmah, *for reproach,* xii. 3. te'ĕhavun, 2. pl. m. F. fr. אָהַב *loved.*] par. xii. 18. rik, *vanity.* tĕvakshu, 2. pl. m. F. III. fr. בָּקַשׁ *sought,* iii. 6. kazav, s. n. m. *a lie.*

4. udĕgu, *and know ye,* יָדַע *knew.* hiflah, V. P. *separated.* hasid, a. *pious.* yishmag, 3. s. m. F. xii. 17.

5. rigzu, im. pl. m. רָגַז *trembled.* teheta'u, 2. m. pl. F. חָטָא *sinned.* The F. and not the imp. is used in prohibitions. 'imru, 2. pl. im. m. bilvavkem, bĕlevav, *the heart,* af. *your,* m. mishkavkem fr. מִשְׁכָּב viii. 3. wĕdommu, im. fr. דָּמַם *was silent.*

6. zivhu, im. fr. זֶבַח *sacrificed.* zivhey, pl. cr. vii. 23. 3. *uvithu*, xii. 7. im. fr. בָּטַח *trusted.*

7. 'omĕrim, pl. part. m. yar'enu, F. V. af. *us,* רָאָה. nesah for נְשָׂא or else fr. נָסָה with the same meaning.

8. nathattah, 2. m. P simhah, *joy*, s. f. n. megeth, xii. 14. dĕganam fr דָּגָן *corn.* af. *their.* thirosham, *new wine*, af. *their.*

9. Shalom, s. n. m. *peace.* yahdayw, יַחַד, af. 'eshkĕvah, 1. s. m. F. ה par. levadad, *alone.* lavetah, xii. 2. *in safety.* toshiveni, 2. m. s. F. V. fr. יָשַׁב *dwell.*

PSALM V.

1. hannĕhiloth, pl. f. art. iii. 14. *Flutes.*

2. 'ămaray, pl. of אָמַר vii. 22. 3. af. *my.* ha'ăzinah, im. V. ה par. fr. אָזַן *heard.* binah, im. ה par. fr. בִּין *to understand.* hăgigi, fr. hagig, *meditation*, af. *my.*

3. hakshivah, im. V. ה par. *listen thou.* shawgi fr. שָׁוַע *cry,* af. *my* this word here only. malki, vii. 22. 2. 'ethpallal, 1. s. F. vii. *I make my prayer,* xiii. 60. 4.

4. boker, xiii. 45. tishmag, 2. m. s. F. 'eğĕrok, 1. s. F, *I will set in order* my prayer. wa'ăzappeh, 1. s. F. III. Waw not conv. for then it would have Kamez, *and I will look up, watch,* xii. 7. r. צָפָה *watched.*

5. 'el, God. hafez, *having pleasure*, verbal a. reshag, *wickedness*, vii. 22. lo' yĕgurka rag, evil cannot dwell with *thee*, xiii. 16. 3. m. F. ap.

6. yithyazzĕvu, Ps. ii. 2. holĕlim, part. m. pl. הָלַל *was foolish.* lĕneged, xii. 17. geyneyka, vii. 24. sane'tha, x. 3. s. pogaley, pl. cr. part. 'awon, *iniquity.*

14*

7. tĕ'abbed, 2. m. s. F. III. dovĕrey, pl. cr. part. damim, vii. 16. umirmah, *and deceit.* yĕthagev, xi. 3. fr. תעב in III, *loathed.*

8. *h*asdŏh*a*, vii. 22. 2. 'avo', 1. s. F. 'eshtahăweh, 1. s. F. VII. x. 13. d. fr. שָׁחָה *bowed himself.* heykal, cr. s. vii. 17, *the temple of,* xiii. 39. yir'athekа, *in thy fear,* in p. viii. 8, v. 3, ii. 21.

9. nĕhen*i*, im. af. *me* fr. נָחָה *led.* zidkathek*a*, viii. 8. lĕmagan, xii. 17. shorĕray, *my enemies,* only in part. pl. af. haysher, im. V. fr. יָשַׁר *was straight.* lefanny, xiii. 17.

10. bĕfĭhu, vii. 25, v. 3. nĕkonah, part. II. f. s. fr. כּוּן *to set in order. k*irbam, vii. 22. 3. hawwoth, pl. f. fr. הָיָה *iniquity, mischief. k*ever, *a grave.* pathuah, pass. part. fr. פָּתַח *opened.* gĕronam, *their throat.* viii. 4. lĕshonam, *their tongue,* viii. 4. ellipse of כ xiii. 70. 1. yahălikun, 3. pl. F. V. Nun par. fr. חָלָק *was smooth.*

11. ha'ăshímem, im. V. af. *them* fr. אָשֵׁם *was desolate.* yippĕlu, 3. pl. F. fr. נָפַל. mimmogăzotheybem, מְגוּצוֹת *purposes, plans,* with af. *their.* pishgeyhem, fr. פֶּשַׁע *transgression,* vii. 22. 3. haddihemo, im. V. poet. af. V. 3. fr. נָדַח *drove away.* maru, 3. P. fr. מָרָה *rebelled.*

12. yismĕhu, 3. pl. F. שָׂמַח *rejoiced.* yĕrannenu, 3. pl. F. fr. רָנַן *sung,* xi. 8. thasek, 2. m. F. V. fr. סָכַךְ *covered, protected. g*aleymo, xii. 17. yaglĕzu, 3. pl. F. עָלַז *rejoiced.* 'ohăvey, pl. cr. part. shĕmeka, in. p.

13. tĕvarek, 2. m. s. F. III. kazzinnah, xii. 3, *a large shield,* covering the whole person, larger than magen, which is *a buckler.* razon for bĕrazon, xiii. 70. 1. tagtĕrennu, 2. m. s. F. af. *him* Nun epenth. fr. עָטַר *surrounded.*

PSALM VI.

1. hashshĕmin*i*th, f. s. lit. *the eighth string?* &c. prob. a musical instrument.

2. thoki*h*en*i*, 2. s. m. F. V. fr. יָכַח. V. *reproved.* ba*h*ămathĕka fr. חֵמָה *anger.* theyassĕrenu, 2. s. m. F. III. af.

3. 'umlal fr. אָמֵל *withered, languished,* onom. part. XV. x. 9. 13. b. rĕfa'en*i*, im. af. Cf. xi. 4, רָפָא *healed.* nivhălu, 3. pl. P. II. בָּהֵל *were agitated.* gă*z*amai, vii. 22.

5. shuvah, im. ה par. *h*allĕzah, im. III. *deliver thou.*

6. bammaweth, xii. 3, vii. 24. ˉzikreka, in p. vii. 22. 3. yodeh, F. V. יָדָה *praised.*

7. y*a*g*a*gt*i*, 1. P. יָגַע *was weary.* 'an*h*ath*i* fr. אֲנָחָה *sighing.* 'ashe*h*, 1. F. V. שָׂחָה *swam.* מִטָּה *a bed, couch.* וְדִמְעָה *tears.* ger*e*s, vii. 22. 2. מָסָה V. *caused to melt.*

8. g*a*shĕshah, 3. f. P. *is wasted away.* כַּעַס *grief.* עָתַק *grew old.* zor*ĕ*ray, in p. m. pl. part. צָרַר *distressed, acted as an enemy towards.*

9. *s*uru, im. pl. fr. סוּר *to depart.* biky*i* fr. בְּכִי *weeping* af. *my.*

10. t*ĕh*innath*i*, *my supplication,* r. חָנַן.

11. yibba*h*ălu, 3. pl. F. II. yashuvu, 3. pl. F. yevoshu, 3. pl. m. F. fr. בּוּשׁ *to be ashamed.* reg*a*g, *a moment,* xiii. 70. 1.

Vocabulary to Gen. I—VI. and Ps. I—VI.

The unpointed words are verbs or roots see ch. x. but Hollow verbs are given in their Infinitive forms.

א

אָב A father, viii. 9.
אבד Perished, III. *and* V. Destroyed.
אֶבֶן A stone, vii. 22.
אֵד A mist.
אָדוֹן A lord.
אָדָם A man.
אֲדָמָה The ground.
אהב Loved.
אֹהֶל A tent.
אָוֶן Iniquity.
אור To shine, V. Gave light.
אוֹר Light.
אוֹת A sign.
אָז Then, xii. 16.
אזן III. V. Listened, gave ear to.
אֹזֶן The ear.
אָח A brother, viii. 9.
אֶחָד f. אַחַת One, ix. 10.

אָחוֹת A sister.
אחז Took.
אֲחֻזָּה A possession.
אחר Tarried, delayed.
אַחֵר Another.
אַחַר After, xii. 16.
אַחֲרֵי After, xii. 17.
אֵי Where, xii. 17.
אָיַב Was an enemy.
אֵיבָה Enmity.
אַיִן Is not, was not, xii. 17.
אִישׁ A man, vii. 25.
אכל Ate.
אָכְלָה Food.
אֶל To, xii. 17.
אֵל, אֱלֹהִים, אֱלוֹהַּ God.
אֵלֶּה These, xii. 16.
אִם If, xii. 16.
אֵם A mother.
אַמָּה A cubit.
אמל XV. Withered, languished.

APPENDIX.

אָמַר Said. xi. 12.
אִמְרָה A word, saying.
אֲנִי אָבִי I. v. i.
אֲנָחָה Sighing.
אָנַף Was angry.
אֲנָשִׁים Men, *pl. of* אִישׁ. vii. 25.
אָסַף Collected.
אַף Also, yea, indeed.
אַף The nostril, anger.
אֶפֶס An end. vii. 22.
אַרְבַּע Four. ix. 10.
אָרַךְ Was long.
אֹרֶךְ Length.
אֶרֶץ The earth. vii. 22.
אָרַר Cursed. III. *Id.*
אִשָּׁה A woman. vii. 25.
אָשֵׁם Was desolate. V. Made so.
אֲשֶׁר Who, whom, which.
אַשְׁרֵי O the blessings of! How happy is, are!
אֵת With. *Mark of the objective case.* xii. 17.
אַתָּה Thou. v. 1.

ב

בַּד Single. xii. 17.
בָּדָד Alone.
בדל II. Was separated. V. Separated.
בְּדֹלַח Crystal *or* Beryl.

בֹּהוּ Emptiness.
בהל II. Was agitated. V. Alarmed.
בְּהֵמָה Cattle. A beast.
בוא To come, to enter.
בוש To be ashamed. V. Put to shame.
בחר Chose.
בטח Trusted.
בֶּטַח Confidence.
בין To understand.
בֵּין Between, among. xii. 17.
בַּיִת A house. vii. 24.
בְּכִיר The first born.
בְּכִי Weeping.
בִּלְתִּי Without, except. xii.
בֵּן A son. viii. 2.
בָּנָה Built.
בַּעַד On account of. xii.
בער Burned.
בֹּקֶר The morning.
בקש III. Sought for.
בַּר *Chaldee*, A son.
בַּרְזֶל Iron.
ברח Fled.
ברך Knelt, blessed.
בֶּרֶךְ A knee.
בְּרָכָה A blessing.
בְּרִית A covenant.
בָּשָׂר Flesh.
בַּת A daughter. viii. 12.

ג

- גבר Was strong.
- גִּבּוֹר Strong, mighty.
- גדל Was great.
- גָּדוֹל Great.
- גּוֹי A nation.
- גָּוַע Expired.
- גּוּר To sojourn.
- גָּחוֹן The belly *of a reptile*.
- גיל To rejoice.
- גַּם Also.
- גַּן A garden.
- גֹּפֶר The cypress.
- גָּרוֹן The throat.
- גָּרַשׁ Drove out. III. *Id.*

ד

- דבק Cleaved to.
- דבר Spoke. III. *Id.*
- דָּבָר A word, a thing.
- דָּג A fish. Fish. *Coll.*
- דָּגָה *Id.*
- דָּגָן Corn.
- דּוֹר A generation, an ago.
- דָּם Blood. vii. 16.
- דָּמָה Was like.
- דְּמוּת Likeness.
- דָּמַם Was silent.
- דִּמְעָה A tear, *coll.* tears.
- דין To judge, strive with.
- דַּעַת Knowledge.
- דַּרְדַּר The bramble.

- דרך Walked, trod.
- דֶּרֶךְ A way, road.
- דָּשָׁא Became green. V. Produced verdure.
- דֶּשֶׁא Verdure, the first grass.

ה

- הָגָה Meditated.
- הָגִיג Meditation.
- הוּא He. הִיא She. v. i.
- הַוָּה Calamity, mischief.
- הָיָה Was, happened.
- הֵיכָל A temple.
- הלך Went, walked. III. VII. *Id.*
- הלל Was foolish.
- הֵן Lo, behold.
- הִנֵּה Behold, here is. xii. 17.
- הר A mountain. vii. 16.
- הרה, הָרְתָה Conceived.
- הֵרוֹן Conception.

ז

- זבח Sacrificed.
- זֶבַח A sacrifice.
- זֶה f. זֹאת This. xii.
- זָהָב Gold.
- זכר Remembered.
- זָכָר Male.
- זֵכֶר Memory, remembrance.

APPENDIX.

זרע Sowed. V. Bore seed.
זֶרַע Seed.
זֵעָה Sweat.

ח

חבא II, IV, VII. Hid himself.
הבר Joined.
חַבּוּרָה A wound, scar.
חגר Girded.
חֲגוֹרָה A girdle.
חוּץ Any open place, without.
חָטָא Sinned.
חֵטְא Sin.
חַטָּא A sinner.
חֲטָאָה Sin.
חַטָּאת Sin, a sin offering.
חָיָה, חַי Lived.
חַי Living, alive.
חַיָּה An animal, wild beasts *coll.*
חַיִּים Life.
חָלָב Milk.
חֵלֶב Fatness.
חלל V. Began.
חלץ III. Delivered, freed.
חלק Was smooth. V. Made so.
חמר Desired. II. Was desired.
חֵמָה Heat, anger.
חָמָס Violence.
חֵן Favor.

חנן Was gracious.
חֶסֶד Kindness, grace.
חָסָה Took refuge with, confided in.
חָסִיד Gracious, favored, pious.
חֵפֶץ Desire, delight.
חֹק Statute, custom, duty.
חֶרֶב A sword.
חָרָה Was hot, angry.
חָרוֹן Heat, anger.
חרש Worked *in wood, stone, or metal.*
חשב Thought, devised.

ט

טוב Good.
טֶרֶם Not yet, before.

י

יָבֵשׁ Was dry. x. 3. a.
יַבָּשָׁה Dry land.
יגע Was weary.
יָד A hand.
יָדָה Cast *missiles.* V. Praised.
ידע Knew.
יוֹם A day.
יוֹמָם By day, daily.
יַחַד Together. xii. 17.
יטב Was good. V. Did good to.
יכח V. Reproved.

APPENDIX

יָלַד Bore, begot.
יֶלֶד A child, son.
יָלַךְ *No pret. or part.* Went. V. Led.
יָם A sea. vii. 15.
יסד Founded, established. II. Agreed.
יסר I, III, V. Chastised, corrected.
יצר Appointed, determined.
יצא Went out. V. Brought forth.
יצב VII. Was set up, stood fast.
יצר Formed.
יֵצֶר An Imagination.
יָרֵא Feared. x. 3. a.
יִרְאָה Fear.
יָרָק Greenness, green herbs.
ישב Sat, dwelt. V. *Caus.*
יְשׁוּעָה Salvation.
יָשֵׁן Slept.
ישע II. Was saved. V. Saved.
ישר Was right. III. IV. Made right, direct.

כ

כָּבוֹד Glory.
כבש Subdued.
כָּזָב A lie.
כֹּחַ Strength.

כִּי For, but, if. xii.
כְּכָב A star.
כֹּל All. xii. 17.
כָּלָה Was complete. III. Finished. IV. *Pass.*
כְּלִי Any vessel or instrument.
כְּלִמָּה Disgrace, reproach.
כֵּן So, thus.
כִּנּוֹר A lute, lyre.
כָּנָף A wing, a skirt.
כַּעַס Anger, grief.
כפר Covered, coated.
כֹּפֶר Pitch.
כְּרוּב A Cherub.
כְּתֹנֶת A shirt, tunic.

ל

לְאֹם pl. לְאֻמִּים A people.
לֵב and לֵבָב The heart.
לבש Put on *a garment.* V. Clothed.
לַהַט A flame. vii. 22.
לְחִי The cheek, jaw.
לֶחֶם Bread.
לטש Sharpened.
לַיְלָה m. Night.
לְמַעַן For the purpose that, in order that.
לעג Mocked, scoffed. V. *Id.*
לֵץ A scorner.
לקח Took. xi. 5.

לֶקַח	Instruction, doctrine.	מֶלֶךְ	A king.
לָשׁוֹן	The tongue.	מֶמְשָׁלָה	Dominion, rule.
		מִן	From, out of &c. xii.
		מִנְחָה	An offering.

מ

מְאֹד	Much, very.	מָסָה	V. Caused to melt, moistened.
מֵאָה	A hundred. ix. 10.	מְעַט	A little.
מָאוֹר	Place of light, a light.	מַעְלָה	Above, over, more than, *with* מִן *and* לְ.
מַאֲכָל	Food.	מֹעֵצוֹת	Counsels, plans.
מַבּוּל	Destruction; *only used of* the Flood.	מַעֲשֶׂה	A work.
מָגֵן	A shield, buckler.	מָצָא	Found.
מָה	What? xii. 16.	מִקְוֶה	Collection, gathering together.
מוֹסֵרוֹת	Bonds.	מָקוֹם	A place.
מוֹעֵד	An appointed time, season.	מִקְנֶה	Possession, cattle.
מוֹשָׁב	Seat, place of sitting.	מַרְאֶה	Sight, appearance.
		מָרָה	Rebelled.
מוּת	To die.	מִרְמָה	Deceit.
מִזְמוֹר	A Psalm, hymn.	מָשִׁיחַ	Anointed. Messiah.
מחה	Wiped out, destroyed utterly.	מִשְׁכָּב	A bed.
		משׁל	Ruled.
מַחֲשָׁבָה	A thought, device.	מִשְׁפָּט	Judgment.
מִטָּה	A bed, couch.	מָתַי	When? xii.
מטר	Rained. V. Caused to rain.		

נ

מָטָר	Rain.	נבל	Withered away. x. 3. a.
מִי	Who? xii.		
מַיִם	Water. viii. 9.	נגד	V. Told. VI. *Pass.*
מִין	A kind, species.	נֶגֶד	Before, in front of.
מָלֵא	Was full of. III. filled.	נְגִינָה	A song.
		נגע	Touched.
מְלָאכָה	A work.	נדח	Drove away. V. *Id.*

APPENDIX.

נרף Scattered, dispersed.
נָהָר A river. vii. 19.
נוד To wander.
נוח To rested. V. Gave rest or comfort to.
נוע To wander.
נחה Led, guided. V. Led.
נַחֲלָה An inheritance.
נְחִילוֹת Flutes.
נחם II. Repented. III. Comforted.
נָחָשׁ A serpent.
נְחֹשֶׁת Brass.
נטע Planted.
נכה V. Struck.
נסך Anointed.
נפח Blew, breathed.
נפל Fell.
נְפִילִים Giants. The fallen ones.
נפץ Broke, was dispersed.
נֶפֶשׁ Soul, person, self.
נצח III. Excelled, presided.
נְקֵבָה A female.
נקם Avenged. VI. Was avenged.
נָשָׂא Lifted, set, placed.
נָשָׁא Forgot. V. Caused to forget, deceived.
נְשָׁמָה cr. נִשְׁמַת Breath.
נָשִׁים Women. vii. 25.
נשק Kissed. III. Id.

נתן Gave, put, placed.
נתק III. Broke.

ס

סבב Went round, surrounded.
סָבִיב A round.
סגר Shut.
סור To go aside, forsake.
סכך Covered, protected.
סמך Leaned on: supported.
ספר Numbered. III. Related.
סָפֶר A book.
סחר Concealed.

ע

עבד Served.
עֶבֶד A servant.
עבר Passed over.
וְעֲרוּר with בְּ Because of.
עֲבִית A cord. vii. 26. 1.
עַד Till. xii. 17.
עֵדָה An assembly.
עוֹד Still, yet.
עִילָם Eternity.
עוּגָב A lute, lyre.
עָוֹן Sin, iniquity.
עוף To fly.
עוֹף A fowl Coll.
עוֹר The skin.
עזב Left, forsook.

APPENDIX.

עזר Helped.
עֵזֶר Help: a helper.
עטר Surrounded. III. V. Crowned.
עַיִן Eye.
עִיר City.
עַל Upon. xii. 17.
עָלָה Went up. V. Offered *a burnt offering.*
עלץ Rejoiced.
עַם A people. vii. 15
עִם With.
עמד Stood.
עָנָה Answered.
עָפָר Dust.
עֵץ A tree: *coll.*
עצב Pained. VII. Was grieved.
עֶצֶב Labor, grain.
עִצָּבוֹן Great pain, *as of childbirth.*
עֵצָה Counsel.
עצם Was strong.
עֶצֶם A bone, the same.
עָקֵב The heel.
עֵקֶב The end, because.
ערב Was sweet, became dark.
עֶרֶב Evening.
עָרוֹם and עֵירֹם Naked.
עָרוּם Cunning.
ערך Arranged.
עֶרֶשׂ A bed, couch. vii. 22.

עֵשֶׂב *Coll.* Herbs, Grass.
עָשָׂה Did, made.
עָשָׂר Ten.
עָשֵׁשׁ Became old, wasted away.
עֵת A time.
עַתָּה Now.
עתק Removed: grew old.

פ

פֶּלֶג A channel, stream.
פָּלָה II. Was separated. V. Set apart.
פלל III. Judged. VII. Prayed.
פֶּה A mouth. vii. 25.
פֶּן Lest.
פָּנָה Turned his face towards.
פָּנִים The face. vi. 20. xii. 17.
פָּעַל Did.
פֹּעַל Work.
פַּעַם A time. vii. 22.
פָּצָה Opened the mouth.
פצע Wounded.
פֶּצַע A wound.
פקח Opened *the eyes.* II. *Pass.*
פָּרָה Bore fruit. V. Made fruitful.
פְּרִי Fruit. viii. 9. o.
פרר Broke.

פָּשַׁע Transgressed.
פֶּשַׁע Transgression. vii. 22.
פָּתַח Opened.
פֶּתַח A door. vii. 22.

צ

צֹאן A sheep, flock, vi. 18.
צָבָא A host. vi. 14.
צַד A side.
צַדִּיק Righteous.
צֶדֶק Righteousness.
צְדָקָה Righteousness.
צֹהַר A window.
צִוָּה III. Commanded.
צלח Prospered. V. Made to prosper.
צֶלֶם Image.
צֵלָע A rib.
צָמַח Grew. V. Caused to grow.
צִנָּה A shield *for the whole person.*
צָעַק Cried out.
צָפָה Watched. III. *Id.*
צָרִים Enemies.
צרר Acted as an enemy.

ק

קֶבֶר A grave.
קֶדֶם Before, the East.
קֵדְמָה Towards the East.
קִדְמַת Eastward of.
קדשׁ Was holy. III. *and* V. Hallowed.
קוה I *and* III. Looked for. II. Was collected.
קוֹל A voice.
קִים To stand. V. Made to stand.
קוֹמָה Stature, height.
קוֹץ A thorn-bush.
קָטֹן *and* קָטָן Little.
קֵן A nest. *pl.* קִנִּים Cells. Chambers.
קָנָה Got, possessed.
קֵץ An end.
קָרָא Called. *With* לְ Named.
קרב Approached.
קֶרֶב The midst, the inside.
קָרִיב Near.
קשׁב Listened. V. Regarded.

ר

רָאָה Saw.
רֹאשׁ The head.
רֵאשִׁית The beginning, the first of any thing.
רַב Much, many, enough.
רבב Became numerous.
רְבָבָה Ten thousand.
רָבָה Was *or* became numerous.
רְבִיעִי Fourth.

APPENDIX.

רבץ Crouched.
רגז Shook, trembled.
רֶגַע A moment.
רגש Was tumultuous; here only.
רָדָה Ruled.
רדם II. Was fast asleep.
רוֹזְנִים Princes.
רוּחַ Spirit.
רוּם To be high.
רחב Was broad.
רָחָב Broad.
רֹחַב Breadth.
רחף III. Fluttered, hovered.
רִיק A vain thing.
רמשׂ Crept.
רנן Sang.
רַע Bad, wicked, evil.
רעה *Cattle* fed: fed *cattle*.
רעע Broke, crushed.
רָצוֹן Favor, approbation.
רַק Only.
רקע Stretched out, spread.
רָקִיעַ The expanse, the sky.
רָשָׁע Wicked.

שׂ

שָׂדֶה A field, the open county.
שָׂחָה Swam. V. Caused to swim.

שׂחק Laughed.
שִׂיחַ A plant, bush.
שׂכל Was skilful. V. Looked at, made wise.
ישׂים *and* שׂוּם To place, put, set.
שׂמח Rejoiced, was glad.
שִׂמְחָה Joy.
שָׂנֵא Hated. x. 3. a.

שׁ

שׁאל Asked.
שְׁאוֹל *The abode of departed spirits.*
שֵׁבֶט A rod, staff, tribe.
שְׁבִיעִי Seventh.
שֶׁבַע Seven.
שִׁבְעִים Seventy.
שִׁבְעָתַיִם Sevenfold. ix. 7.
שׁבר Broke. III. Shattered.
שׁבת Rested.
שֹׁהַם The onyx stone.
שׁוּב To return.
שׁוּעַ A cry *for help: here only.*
שׁוּף To strike, bruise.
שׁוֹרְרַי My enemies: *only in this form.*
שָׁחָה Bowed himself. VII. *Id.*
שׁחת II. Was corrupted. V. Destroyed.
שׁית To set, place.

שָׁכַב Lay down, slept.
שָׁכַן Rested, dwelt.
שָׁלוֹם Peace.
שָׁלַח Sent. III. Sent away.
שְׁלִישִׁי Third.
שָׁלַךְ V. Threw, cast.
שָׁלֵם Was at peace, was complete.
שָׁלֵם Perfect.
שָׁלִישׁ Three.
שָׁם There.
שָׁמַיִם The sky, heaven.
שְׁמִינִי Eighth.
שְׁמֹנֶה Eight.
שָׁמַע Heard, obeyed.
שָׁמַר Kept, watched.
שֵׁן A tooth.
שָׁנָה A year.
שֵׁנִי Second.
שָׁעָה Looked, regarded.
שָׁפַט Judged.
שָׁקָה II. Was watered. V. Watered.
שָׁרַץ Swarmed.
שֶׁרֶץ *Numerous* small animals.
שֵׁשׁ Six.
שִׁשִּׁי Sixth.
שָׁתַל Planted.

ת

תַּאֲוָה Desire, object of desire.
תְּאֵנָה A fig-tree.
תֵּבָה An ark: *only used of Noah's ark and of that in which Moses was exposed.*
תְּהוֹם The deep.
תֹּהוּ Desolation.
תּוֹרָה A Law.
תּוֹלְדֹת Birth; posterity: history.
תִּירוֹשׁ New wine.
תָּמַם Was completed. V. Finished.
תָּמִים Complete: perfect *morally*.
תַּנִּין Any large sea animal.
תָּעַב II. Was abhorred. III. Abhorred.
תְּפִלָּה Prayer.
תָּפַר Sewed. III. *Id.*
תָּפַשׂ Laid hold of.
תַּרְדֵּמָה Deep sleep. *See* רדם.
תְּשׁוּקָה Desire.
תֵּשַׁע Nine.
תְּחִנָּה Favor, mercy, prayer for mercy.
תַּחְתִּי Lower.

Texts referred to in the foregoing pages.

Genesis	Page	Genesis	Page
i. 1.	147	iii. 10.	59, 158
2.	12, 130, 147	22.	136
5.	11	iv. 10.	151
6.	128, 138, 163	13.	132
7.	16	15.	158
11.	12	25.	135
14.	152	26.	147
15.	162	v. 18.	52
16.	150	23.	152
20.	158	vi. 3.	133
21.	25	17.	32
22.	151	19.	18
24.	144	21.	161
27.	16	vii. 13.	130
30.	155	20.	157
31.	150	viii. 7.	117, 159
ii. 2.	161	12.	90
4.	158	22.	130, 151
5.	161	ix. 24.	90
7.	90, 157, 159	27.	101, 124
9.	32	xi. 1.	52
10.	161	6.	97, 115
12.	9, 130	7.	97, 113
19.	149, 168	xii. 2.	130
21.	142	xiii. 1.	17
25.	165.	xiv. 10.	147
iii. 1.	132, 135	xv. 18.	161
6.	132	xvi. 14.	158

15

Genesis	Page	Genesis	Page
xvii. 5.	49	xxx. 38.	68
17.	19	xxxi. 6.	25
18.	165	30.	68
xviii. 1.	157	37.	52
5.	136	39.	144
18.	129	49.	134
21.	19	53.	150
xix. 2.	140	xxxii. 9.	152
9.	159	11.	139
xx. 6.	105	13.	163
7.	165	15, 16.	51
13.	150	xxxiii. 10.	136, 161
xxi. 32.	151	11.	105
xxii. 13.	150	14.	138
19.	58	xxxiv. 7.	162
xxiii. 13.	165	27.	134
xxiv. 15.	105	29.	11
27.	147	xxxv. 7.	150
65.	135	xxxvii. 8.	159
xxv. 16.	158	33.	159
32.	68	xxxviii. 5, 9.	163
xxvi. 16.	160	xxxix. 18.	168
27.	131	20.	156
28.	101	xl. 3.	156, 157
xxvii. 1.	132	22.	147
29.	115, 153	23.	148
33.	68	xli. 1.	68, 157
34.	147	21.	25
36.	158	39.	158
38.	9	42.	158
42.	148	51.	67
44.	157	xlii. 1.	59
xxviii. 15.	161	11.	25, 158
xxix. 2.	150	18.	130, 165
3.	114	19.	154
8.	9, 114	28.	166
10.	114	xliii. 24.	144
xxx. 9.	147	xliv. 2.	155
15.	86	xlv. 4.	163
28.	122	19.	165

Genesis	Page	Exodus	Page
xlvi. 3.	122	xvi. 32.	70
4.	159	xvii. 10.	150
22.	152	12.	152
29.	139	xviii. 9.	101
xlvii. 8.	136	25.	52
13.	120, 137	26.	08
xlviii. 1.	158	xix. 12.	159
11.	101	13.	90, 119, 159
xlix. 4.	168	xx. 25.	94
11.	144	xxi. 4.	151
12.	132	28.	149
22.	101,124,144,152,153	29.	150
23.	125	xxii. 10.	134, 150
25.	166	20.	136
l. 20.	101	xxiv. 14.	186
Exodus		xxviii. 17.	157
i. 10.	152	39.	32
21.	152	xxx. 32.	123
ii. 3.	18, 149	36.	114
8.	149	xxxi. 14.	153
iv. 2.	10	xxxii. 1, 4, 8.	150
13.	160	9.	151
v. 16.	151	22.	106
vi. 3.	107	33.	136
28.	157	xxxiii. 13.	25
ix. 19.	151	xxxv. 22.	139
x. 13.	82	xxxvi. 1, 29.	163
xi. 6.	152	23.	52
7.	134	xxxviii. 21.	32
xiii. 18.	123	Leviticus	
xiv. 9, 10.	151	i. 2.	162
11.	160	ii. 2.	37
31.	151	iv. 22.	134
xv. 1.	133	24.	157
2.	144	v. 5.	117
5.	101	12.	37
6.	9	vi. 6.	37, 152
12.	162, 105	13.	157
xvi. 3.	165	18.	156
23.	113	vii. 2.	156

15*

Leviticus	Pages	Numbers	Page
vii. 18.	112	xxii. 5.	138
viii. 7.	113	33.	133, 161
x. 18.	148	xxiii. 23.	12
19.	19	24.	161
xi. 43.	105	25.	160
xii. 4.	120	xxiv. 3, 15.	144
xiii. 55, 56.	119	xxv. 17.	159
xiv. 46.	157	xxvi. 55.	148
xv. 18, 24.	140	xxx. 11.	166
xviii. 29.	134	xxxii. 5.	148
xix. 7.	112	14.	17
xx. 14.	148	25.	153
xxiii. 39.	129	32.	25
xxiv. 22.	51, 155		
xxv. 21.	101	Deuteronomy	
xxvi. 34.	101, 126	i. 30.	138
xxvii. 23.	132	44.	119
		ii. 12.	165
Numbers		24.	119
i. 47.	58	35.	113
iv. 46.	52	iii. 7.	113
vii. 69.	114	24.	134
ix. 6.	152	iv. 1.	89, 119
17.	156	10.	134
xi. 11.	74, 105	12.	138
12.	19	27.	82
15.	159	41.	162
22.	148	v. 12.	159
25.	113	24.	130
xii. 4.	52	26.	165
xiii. 18.	19, 151	27.	152
30.	115	vi. 7.	129
xiv. 2.	161	12.	151
32.	147	24.	129
xvii. 6.	94	vii. 8.	132
10.	126	viii. 13.	101
xx. 3.	165	16.	131
11.	151	ix. 6.	155
xxi. 1.	126	xi. 7.	130
8.	109	xii. 22.	148

IN THE FOREGOING PAGES.

Deut.	Page	Joshua	Page
xiv. 21.	159	xxii. 9.	112
xv. 7.	166	17.	149
xvi. 1.	159	xxiv. 10.	150
16.	148	Judges	
21.	157	iii. 26.	135
xvii. 8.	125, 139	iv. 9.	134
xxi. 8.	58	19.	124
xxii. 24.	156	20.	160
xxiii. 24.	157	21.	164
xxiv. 4.	59	v. 7.	193
xxv. 7.	17	10.	153
xxvi. 5.	157	13.	125, 157
xxviii. 8.	111	23.	159
59.	25	27.	166
67.	165	28.	82
xxx. 11.	144	38.	152
xxxi. 29.	105	vi. 7.	133
xxxii. 13.	30	19.	149
22.	118	20.	135
36.	112	28.	123
37.	101, 110	31.	19
xxxiii. 11.	132, 157	vii. 3.	136
16.	140	8.	157
23.	119	12.	133
29.	30	viii. 19.	161
		ix. 9, 11, 13.	78
Joshua		10.	68
i. 5.	161	53.	37
ii. 17.	152	xi. 39.	151
iii. 14.	32	xii. 5.	19
vii. 7.	78, 123	xvi. 2.	166
15.	148	13.	113
21.	52, 132	14.	32
viii. 15.	154	18.	163
24.	10	xvii. 2.	24
33.	132	xix. 2.	166
x. 12.	133	24.	152
24.	115, 131, 144	30.	163, 166
xiv. 8.	104	xx. 31.	58
12.	140	xxi. 10, 13, 21.	153

TEXTS REFERRED TO

Ruth	Page	1 Samuel	Page
i. 1.	162	xiv. 36.	113
9.	165	xv. 2.	161
20.	25	5.	113
ii. 3.	130	9.	113, 120, 150
8.	68, 145	19.	94
9.	105, 124	xvi. 18.	130
14.	119	xvii. 4.	147
16.	160	35.	163
iii. 2.	25	40.	131
5.	113	50.	137
iv. 1.	94	xviii. 20.	118
		xix. 22.	150
1 Samuel		23.	147
i. 2.	152	24.	158
6.	136	xx. 8.	159
14.	59	12.	168
ii. 4.	151	28.	65
22.	145	30.	17
27.	68	xxi. 2.	144
33.	151	16.	59, 132
iii. 3, 7.	135	xxiv. 6.	148
12.	159	xxv. 14.	94
13.	156, 157	15.	157
iv. 11, 17.	72	xxvi. 12.	30, 147
15.	150	xxviii. 3.	131
19.	118	2 Samuel	
21.	137	i. 19.	32
v. 9, 10.	97	26.	124, 144
vi. 12.	68, 154	iii. 6, 7.	158
ix. 24.	131	13.	157
x. 6.	105, 121	22.	151
13.	105	30.	149
xi. 2.	122	iv. 2.	166
xiii. 18.	154	6.	152
19.	137	11.	149
22.	48	vi. 1.	112
xiv. 15.	147	vii. 23.	150
24.	112	28.	158
30.	112	xi. 2.	158
33, 34.	139	25.	149

2 Samuel	Page	1 Kings	Page
xii. 4.	167	xviii. 13.	147
6.	52	26.	159
xiii. 15.	59	39.	159
18.	163	xix. 11.	150
xv. 4.	139, 165	18.	153
30.	159	xx. 27.	58
31.	159	xxi. 6.	164, 165
xvii. 5.	147	12.	163
11.	112	15.	119
xviii. 6.	149	19.	147
22.	105	xxii. 25.	105
xix. 1.	147	27.	157, 159
2.	164	30.	159
9.	151, 153	xxv. 27.	150
14.	70		
xx. 5.	112	2 Kings	
9.	70	i. 15.	140
10.	59	ii. 10.	69
19.	166	21.	105
xxi. 1.	139	iii. 12.	140
12.	109	25.	139
xxii. 27.	114	iv. 25.	135
34.	156	41.	72
xxiii. 8.	25, 142	43.	159
xxiv. 1.	159	v. 26.	19
24.	140	vi. 6.	148
		vii. 1.	157
1 Kings		viii. 9.	140
i. 26.	147	21.	69
iii. 11.	163	ix. 17.	157
15.	118	25.	149
x. 15.	155	32.	166
21.	160	xi. 3.	166
xiii. 3.	163	4.	125
33.	166	13.	30
xiv. 2.	24	xii. 10.	51
3.	86	xiv. 7, 14.	163
xv. 5.	134	xv. 16.	132
xvii. 10, 11.	72	xvi. 14.	32
14.	105	17.	157

TEXTS REFERRED TO

2 Kings	Page	Ezra	Page
xviii. 36	163	viii. 30, 36.	163
xix. 2.	118	ix. 34, 35.	165
23.	155	x. 14, 17.	131
33.	121		
xx. 9.	146	Nehemiah	
xxiii. 5.	163	ii. 12.	157
15.	114	13.	5
17.	32	ix. 7.	163
xxv. 4.	154	19, 32, 34.	148
10.	166	x. 33.	163
20.	139	xiii. 21.	120
28.	105		
		Esther	
1 Chron.		i. 1.	162
ii. 49.	152	iii. 4.	134
v. 20.	124, 163	iv. 4.	58
xi. 11.	134	viii. 8.	117
xvii. 5.	167	ix. 1.	115
xxi. 1.	158		
xxv. 5.	51	Job	
xxvii. 27.	133	i. 1.	161
		2, 3.	81
2 Chron.		14.	69
i. 4.	131	iii. 3.	161
iii. 1.	52	4.	162
vi. 32.	150	6.	101
xi. 12.	153	10.	149
xv. 9.	157	iv. 2, 5.	120
xvi. 12.	105	6.	166
xxii. 35.	58	12.	142
xxiv. 8.	51	v. 5.	166
xxv. 10.	103	18.	105
xxix. 36.	131	23.	151
xxxi. 1.	110	vi. 2.	159
xxxiii. 8.	127	20.	153
xxxiv. 7.	114	vii. 14.	132
12.	124	viii. 3.	19
		6.	185
Ezra		21.	72, 105
ii. 4.	52	ix. 3.	150
viii. 28.	131		

Job	Page	Job	Page
x. 1	125	xxix. 4.	17
xi. 7.	19	10.	151
20.	142	xxx. 12.	149
xii. 6.	126	14.	59
7.	153	xxxi. 5.	94
11.	166	18.	149
24.	167	27.	124
xiii. 9.	115	31.	134
25.	19	32.	167
28.	166	xxxii. 7.	151
xiv. 10.	184	11.	112
19.	152	18.	74, 105
xv. 22.	101	22.	69
35.	159	xxxiii. 20.	149
xvi. 18.	59	21.	2
xvii. 7.	119	33.	112
16.	154	xxxv. 10.	150
xviii. 21.	157	11.	112
xix. 2.	101, 111	xxxvii. 6.	115
6.	171	20.	135
7.	124	xxxviii. 1.	1
19.	135	21.	151
23.	117	26.	167
29.	166	32.	139
xxi. 5.	127	xxxix. 2.	132
16.	142	24.	105
xxii. 20.	25, 134	xl. 19.	131
xxiii. 9, 11.	136	20.	151
xxiv. 5.	166	22.	166
21.	118	25.	132
24.	126	xli. 9.	59
xxvi. 2.	157	25.	101
5.	167	xlii. 10.	25
xxvii. 4.	150	15.	152
6.	132		
8.	126	Psalms	
20.	153	i. 2.	161
xxviii. 14.	147	6.	151
21.	123	ii. 1.	161
xxix. 3.	149	5.	133

TEXTS REFERRED TO

Psalms	Page	Psalms	Page
ii. 6.	149	xlii. 7.	136
7.	89, 117, 130, 144	xliv. 5.	149
12.	11, 156	23.	154
iii. 8.	157	xlv. 3.	136
v. 2.	11	xlvi. 6.	166
5.	149	l. 1.	67
11.	135	21.	160
vi. 3.	158	li. 7.	62
4.	167	lii. 11.	114
6.	149	lv. 8.	151
viii. 2.	122	13.	59
ix. 7.	131, 147	lvii. 2.	116, 152
16.	25	lviii. 12.	150
19.	167	lix. 6.	157
xvi. 3.	157	lx. 4.	105
5.	66, 127	6.	157
11.	154	lxi. 6.	154
xviii. 23.	142	lxii. 4.	150
26.	127	lxv. 6.	166
27.	114	lxviii. 3.	69, 121
33.	131	24.	142
35.	166	29.	135
xix. 13.	103	lxix. 4.	117
xx. 4.	144	5.	133
xxii. 32.	65	16.	112
xxiii. 1.	66	23.	166
xxiv. 10.	158	27, 33.	166
xxv. 20.	144	lxxi. 7.	156
xxvi. 7.	129	19.	148
xxx. 2.	13	lxxii. 10	119
10.	132	lxxiii. 7.	153
xxxi. 14.	115	26.	150
xxxii. 1.	106, 156	lxxiv. 2.	135
xxxvi. 6.	129	7.	18
7.	147	19.	157
9.	125, 145	lxxvi. 4.	17
13.	114	6.	58
xxxviii. 11.	59	7.	16
17.	137	lxxvii. 18.	116
xl. 15.	16	lxxviii. 44.	111

Psalms	Page	Psalms	Page
lxxviii. 49.	155	cxxxv. 11.	130
lxxix. 2.	144	17.	137
lxxx. 11.	147	cxxxvi. 19, 20.	130
19.	123	cxxxvii. 5.	167
lxxxi. 6.	157	cxxxviii. 6.	117
14.	165	cxxxix. 5.	25
lxxxii. 8.	68	8.	113
lxxxiii. 5.	132	15.	134
12.	149	20.	70, 112
lxxxv. 11.	159	cxli. 5.	121
lxxxviii. 17.	12	cxlii. 4.	135
xci. 4.	123	cxliii. 8.	135, 158
xcii. 12.	167	cxliv. 2.	166
xciv. 21.	114	cxlix. 2.	150
xcv. 11.	134	cl. 2.	37
xcvi. 6.	48		
cii. 4.	117	Proverbs	
27.	149	I. 2.	11
ciii. 3, 6.	144	7.	161
civ. 8.	156	II. 9.	155
29.	29	10, 15.	152
cv. 22.	113	16.	166
cx. 4.	144	iii. 3, 4, 7.	165
cxlii. 5, 6, 7.	144	6.	111
cxiv. 5.	131	18.	153
2.	151	iv. 1.	128
8.	144	21.	94, 120
cxvi. 4, 18.	17	25.	119
12.	144	v. 22.	111, 149
25.	144	vi. 30.	132
cxviii. 7.	167	vii. 5.	111, 129, 166
14, 28.	144	13.	97
23.	20	23.	168
cxix. 22.	114	25.	126, 127
101.	105	viii. 17.	166
cxxii. 3.	157	ix. 5.	148
cxxiv. 6.	133	13.	138
cxxviii. 3.	101	17.	164
cxxix. 6.	157	x. 1.	146
cxxxii. 12.	25, 135	xi. 25.	119, 147

Proverbs	Page	Proverbs	Page
xii. 17.	166	xxxi. 3.	30
27.	168	4.	137
xiii. 1, 6.	167	13.	155
7.	59	27.	101
19.	115	30.	59
21.	148		
xiv. 2.	68, 152	Ecclesiastes	
10.	16	i. 7.	156
25.	167	9, 10, 11.	133
35.	166	ii. 7.	152
xvi. 4.	132	11.	133
33.	148	14.	147
xvii. 4.	112, 167	19.	19
14.	72	iii. 11.	160
xviii. 19.	167	18.	114, 133
xix. 6.	11	21.	136
12.	156	iv. 2, 3.	139
26.	168	vii. 16	67
xx. 1.	146	26.	105
18.	153	27.	151
xxi. 8.	59	28, 29.	18
13.	153	viii. 1.	151
xxii. 19.	147	2.	167
21.	157	12.	105
xxiii. 15.	147	17.	133
22.	135	x. 5.	105
28.	167	17.	25
xxiv. 17.	68	xi. 3.	15, 144, 156
22.	149		
xxv. 13.	150	Canticles	
xxvi. 7.	114	i. 6.	133, 166
xxvii. 6.	124	7.	123
9.	151	8.	129
15.	68	9.	144
16.	153	ii. 11, 17.	166
xxix. 6.	120	v. 10—16.	166
xxx. 1.	40	10.	135
4.	123	vii. 10.	155
12.	82	viii. 6.	17, 147
27.	137		

Isaiah	Page	Isaiah	Page
i. 5.	130	xvii. 10.	155
7.	147	14.	144
21.	161	xix. 3.	97
ii. 11.	151	4.	150
iii. 9.	156	5.	127
15.	10	9.	30
16.	152	xx. 1.	158
iv. 4.	134	4.	30
v. 5.	159	xxi. 1.	157
10.	17	12.	101
11.	156	17.	31, 167
12.	168	xxii. 7.	151, 155
24.	157, 158	11.	30
25.	64	13.	159
vi. 5.	69	17.	58, 157
6.	166	19.	167
9.	169	xxiv. 4.	153
vii. 14.	105	13.	153
15.	159	19.	159
viii. 2.	105	22.	157
6.	156	xxv. 3.	151
ix. 2.	156	10.	94
3.	37, 117	xxviii. 3.	152, 153
6.	5	12.	144
x. 9.	10	28.	159
12.	31	xxix. 1.	157
18.	118	16.	17
27.	37	xxx. 11.	112
xi. 13.	125	29.	157
xii. 2.	144	xxxi. 1.	122
6.	128	xxxiii. 6.	156, 157
xiii. 22.	152	23.	113
xiv. 6.	157, 159	xxxiv. 4.	114
19.	156	6.	58, 115
25.	37	10.	129
xv. 5.	123	xxxv. 2.	156, 157
xvi. 8.	125	6.	133
xvii. 5.	6	xxxvi. 2, 22.	155
6.	166	18.	137
7.	139	xxxviii. 18.	167

TEXTS REFERRED TO

Isaiah	Page	Jeremiah	Page
xl. 21.	166, 167	i. 17.	117
25.	101	ii. 2.	159
xli. 2.	125, 167	8, 11.	166
2, 23.	101	31.	151
5.	162, 105	36.	112
17.	127	iii. 5.	72, 122
xlii. 24.	159, 167	iv. 7.	37
xliv. 16.	153	14.	153
21.	149	v. 13.	131
26.	167	26.	126
xlv. 1.	125	vi. 17.	163, 167
10.	145	19.	117
11.	165	vii. 20.	151
14.	167	viii. 13.	148, 159, 166
xlvii. 2.	16, 117	14.	87
l. 8.	164	22.	132
li. 12.	158	ix. 2.	115
21.	157	4.	159
21.	153	14.	149
lii. 5.	118	22.	162
6.	159	x. 2.	130
liii. 5.	154	6.	140, 144
8.	148	10.	157
10.	101	17.	16
liv. 14.	165	20.	149
lvi. 8.	144	xi. 10, 23.	139
10.	156	xii. 4.	153
lvii. 16.	166	5.	166, 167
lix. 5.	113, 120	9.	16
13.	115	xiii. 16.	153
21.	140	19.	101
lx. 14.	160	xiv. 6.	159
lxiii. 1.	155	xv. 6, 7.	164
3.	121	xvi. 10.	135
11.	166	xvii. 27.	134
lxiv. 10.	167	xviii. 7.	16
		11.	139
Jeremiah		15.	166
i. 6.	150	21.	101, 119
10.	16	xix. 5.	130

Jeremiah	Page	Jeremiah	Page
xlx. 9.	70	li. 29, 48.	153
13.	146	30.	127
xx. 9.	162	34.	105
xxli. 14.	30, 125	46.	137
20.	9		
23.	157	Lamentations	
24.	17	i. 1.	126, 144
xxiii. 21.	153	4.	30, 117
xxv. 9.	130	5.	120
xxvii. 12.	139	8.	94
xxix. 26.	166	14.	157
xxxi. 3.	167	20.	59
28.	16	21.	166
xxxii. 4.	68, 69	ii. 9.	67
35.	105	10.	152
44.	159	11.	59, 115
xxxlii. 25.	134	12.	59
xxxv. 14.	149	13.	131
xxxviii. 14.	150	iii. 1.	166
xxxix. 12.	10	5.	9
xl. 1.	114	iv. 1.	59, 78, 105
5.	167	8.	133
xlii. 6.	25	17.	156
10.	159		
xliv. 18.	162	Ezekiel	
xlvi. 2.	139	iii. 15.	126
8.	112	v. 12.	25
15.	153	vi. 9.	125
18.	150	ix. 2.	160
xlviii. 2.	114	7.	163
5, 36.	157	8.	126
9.	159	11.	160
15.	151	x. 3.	149
41.	135	xi. 7.	159
xlix. 22.	125	11.	107
37.	117	12.	94
li. 9.	105	xii. 10.	166
11.	114	xiii. 11, 20.	25
14.	134	xiv. 1.	152
19.	157	3.	63

Ezekiel	Page	Ezekiel	Page
xvi. 4.	18, 119, 152	xxxiv. 17, 31.	25
13.	118	27.	111
27.	156	xxxvi. 3.	123
31.	25	35.	135
34.	116	xxxvii. 7.	163
47, 52.	142	18.	72
xvii. 7.	17	xxxix. 11.	157
9.	17	20.	134
18.	163	xli. 7.	97
xviii. 4, 20.	116	15.	25, 144
xix. 12.	59, 152	22.	146
xx. 3.	134	xliii. 7.	146
33.	134	xlvi. 9.	138
43.	94	22.	125
xxi. 5.	130	xlvii. 4.	157
17.	156	Daniel	
33.	132	viii. 1, 15.	147
xxii. 20.	69	22.	68
24.	37	ix. 5.	159
xxiii. 5.	78	13.	146
48.	25, 144	23.	167
49.	144, 152	x. 3.	157
xxiv. 3.	72	11, 19.	167
12.	120	14.	163
17.	167	17.	165
xxv. 3.	116	xii. 10.	114
xxvi. 18.	30	Hosea	
xxvii. 5.	30		
xxviii. 8.	130	i. 2.	157
16.	105	9.	167
23.	58, 121	ii. 9.	110
xxix. 3.	149	iii. 2.	19
16.	125	iv. 2.	159
19.	113	15.	113
20.	134	19.	125
xxxi. 3.	123	vii. 12.	118
4.	17	x. 14.	139
6.	149	xi. 3.	59
7.	118	4.	112
xxxii. 27.	132, 149	xiii. 9.	166

IN THE FOREGOING PAGES.   241

Hosea	Page	Micah	Page
xiii. 15.	117	vi. 16.	152
xiv. 1.	152	vii. 12.	166
2.	168	**Nahum**	
2.	167	i. 3.	117
Joel		ii. 3.	114
i. 4.	155	4.	68
20.	152	8.	78
ii. 11.	136	11.	25
iv. 3.	117	iii. 7.	68
Amos		11.	123
i. 11.	144	17.	30
13.	110	**Habakkuk**	
iii. 12.	167	i. 15.	78, 123
v. 15.	116	ii. 10.	160
10.	168	17.	117
vii. 1.	30	iii. 8.	156
2.	134	11.	166
ix. 1.	110	17.	152
Obadiah		**Zephaniah**	
7.	167	ii. 2.	160
13.	152	9.	151
Jonah		iii. 11.	155
i. 7, 12.	133	16.	117
iii. 2.	139	**Haggai**	
3.	147	ii. 7.	152
9.	136	**Zechariah**	
10.	11	i. 9.	155
Micah		iii. 8.	131
i. 2.	168	iv. 10.	113
8.	117	v. 4.	144
15.	113	vii. 5.	147, 149
ii. 4.	115	14.	110
12.	112, 132	x. 2.	167
iv. 8.	112	xiv. 5.	30
v. 4.	168	**St. Mark**	
vi. 6.	119	xii. 11.	20
9.	167	**Acts**	
10.	168	vii. 20.	117
12.	59		

INDEX.

Absolute, p. 31.
Absolute for constructive, 157.
Accent, 11.
Accents, table of, 170.
Adjective, 146.
Anomalies of gender, 152
Antecedent, 31.
Article, 19.
Aspirates, 5.
Concord, 150.
Consequent, 31.
Constructive state, 31. 153.
Constructive for absolute, 157.
Dagesh, 10.
Dagesh, rules for insertion of, 16.
Ellipses, 166.
Emphasis, 147.
'Ethnah, 11.
Feminine, formation of, 28.
Furtive Pathah, 7.
Future, use of, 161.
Future apocopated, 59, 136.
Gutturals, 5, 18.
Hifgil, 58.
Hithpagel, 58.
Hofgal, 58.
Imperative, 165
Impersonal use of verbs, 158.

Infinitive, 157.
Interrogative particle, 131.
Irregular Nouns, 37. 49.
Irregular Verbs, 75.
Italic letters, 4.
Kal, 58.
Kamez Hatuf, 7.
Labials, 5.
Lexicon, use of, 21.
Makkaf, 10.
Mappik, 10.
Nifgal, 58.
Nouns, 27.
Numerals, 51.
Object, 148.
Optative, 162.
Otiose 'Alef, 7.
Paragogic letters, 144.
Paradigm of regular verb, 60.
Particles, 128.
Passive participles, 160.
Past tense, 161.
Pigel, 58.
Pleonasm, 166.
Plural, formation of, 28.
Predicate, 146.
Pregnant meaning of affix, 149
Pronominal affixes, 25.

16*

Pronouns, 24.
Pugal, 58.
Quiescent letters, 4.
Radicals, 20.
Relative, 184.
Segolates, 35.
Shewa, 8. 9. 15.

Silluk, 11.
Slight vowel, 16.
Subject, 147.
Tenses, use of, 160.
Vowels, 6.
Waw conversive, 162.

A List of Works

IN

Classical and School Literature.

LONDON:
JOHN MURRAY, ALBEMARLE STREET.
1867.

CONTENTS.

HISTORICAL CLASS BOOKS.

	Page		Page
The Student's Hume	2	The Student's Ancient Geography	12
,, ,, France	4	,, ,, Old Testament	14
,, ,, Greece	6	,, ,, New Testament	14
,, ,, Rome	8	,, ,, English Language	16
,, ,, Gibbon	10	,, ,, Literature	16

ELEMENTARY SCHOOL HISTORIES.

	Page		Page
James' Fables of Æsop	17	Little Arthur's England	21
Barbauld's Hymns	17	Dr. Wm. Smith's Smaller England	22
Mrs. Markham's England	18	,, ,, ,, Greece	22
,, ,, France	19	,, ,, ,, Rome	22
,, ,, Germany	20	,, ,, ,, Mythology	22

GREEK AND LATIN CLASSICS.

	Page		Page
Dr. Wm. Smith's Latin Course.		Dr. Wm. Smith's Initia Græca	27
Principia Latina, Part I.	24	King Edward VI.'s Grammars	26
,, ,, Part II.	24	Oxenham's English Elegiacs	26
,, ,, Part III.	25	Greek Grammars	27
,, ,, Part IV.	25	Hutton's Principia Græca	27
,, ,, Part V.	25	Bultman's Lexilogus	27
Latin Grammars	26	,, Greek Verbs	27
Lat.-Eng. Vocab.	28		
,, ,, Dictionaries	28		

DR. WM. SMITH'S DICTIONARIES.

	Page		Page
Dictionary of Bible	30	Dictionary of Geography	31
Concise Bible Dictionary	30	School Classical Dictionary	32
Smaller Bible Dictionary	30	Smaller Classical Dictionary	32
Dictionary of Antiquities	31	Smaller Antiquities	32
,, Biog. and Myth.	31	School Prizes	34

Mr. Murray's
HISTORICAL CLASS BOOKS.

"The series of Student's Manuals, Ancient and Modern, issued by Mr. Murray, and most of them edited by Dr. William Smith, possess several distinctive features which render them singularly valuable as Educational Works. They incorporate, with judicious comments, the researches of the most recent historical investigators, not only into the more modern, but into the most remote periods of the history of the countries to which they refer. The latest lights which comparative philology has cast upon the migrations and interminglings of races, are reflected in the histories of England and France. We know no better or more trustworthy summary, even for the general reader, of the early history of Britain and Gaul, than is contained in these volumes respectively.

"While each volume is thus, for ordinary purposes, a complete history of the country to which it refers, it also contains a guide to such further and more detailed information as the advanced student may desire on particular events or periods. At the end of each book, sometimes of each chapter, there are given copious lists of standard works which constitute the 'Authorities' for a particular period or reign. This most useful feature seems to us to complete the great value of the works, giving to them the character of historical cyclopædias, as well as of impartial histories."—*The Museum.*

"Before the publication of these *Student's Manuals* there had been established, by the claims of middle-class and competitive examiners on young men's brains, a large annual demand for text-books that should rise above the level of mere schoolboy's epitomes, and give to those who would master them some shadow of a scholarly knowledge of their subjects. Such books were very hard to find. Mr. Murray now brings out his seven-and-sixpenny manuals. They are most fit for use in the higher classes of good schools, where they may be deliberately studied through with the help of a teacher competent to expand their range of argument, to diversify their views by the strength of his own reading and reflection, and to elicit thought from the boys themselves upon events and the political changes to which they have led. Even the mature scholar may be glad to have on his shelves these elegant manuals, from which he can at a glance refresh his memory as to a name or date, and he will not use them for reference alone. He will assuredly be tempted to read them for the clearness of statement and the just proportion with which there is traced in each of them the story of a nation."—*Examiner.*

THE STUDENT'S HUME;

A HISTORY OF ENGLAND FROM THE EARLIEST TIMES TO THE REVOLUTION IN 1688.

BASED ON THE HISTORY

By DAVID HUME.

INCORPORATING THE CORRECTIONS AND RESEARCHES OF RECENT HISTORIANS, AND CONTINUED DOWN TO THE YEAR 1858.

With 70 Woodcuts. Post 8vo, 7s. 6d.

This Work is designed to supply a long-acknowledged want in our School Literature—a HISTORY OF ENGLAND in a volume of moderate size, for the UPPER AND MIDDLE FORMS. While HUME'S language has been retained, as far as was practicable, *his errors have been corrected, and his deficiencies supplied.* The Roman and Saxon periods have been almost entirely re-written. In the remaining portion of the work very many important corrections and additions have been made from recent Writers.

"The want which this work is intended to supply has long been evident, and no more judicious effort could have been made for the purpose, than to condense Hume's information without damaging his clearness, or the matchless purity of his style."—*John Bull.*

"This work is certainly well done. The additional matter in the form of Notes and Illustrations is, in a literary sense, the most remarkable feature. Many important subjects, constitutional, legal, or social, are thus treated; and, a very useful plan, the whole authorities of the period are mentioned at its close."—*Spectator.*

A Smaller History of England, from the Earliest Times to the Year 1866. By WM. SMITH, LL.D. With 68 Illustrations. Fcap. 8vo, cloth, 3s. 6d., red edges.

Specimen of the Illustrations in

THE STUDENT'S HUME.

Medal commemorating Battle of Plassy.

Stonehenge.

THE STUDENT'S HISTORY OF FRANCE
FROM THE EARLIEST TIMES TO THE ESTABLISHMENT OF THE SECOND EMPIRE IN 1852.

WITH NOTES AND ILLUSTRATIONS ON THE INSTITUTIONS OF THE COUNTRY.

By W. H. PEARSON, M.A.

With 60 Woodcuts. Post 8vo, 7s. 6d.

This work has been written by an English scholar long resident in France, and intimately acquainted with its literature and history. It is intended, like the preceding works in the same series, to supply a long acknowledged want in our literature, namely, a HISTORY OF FRANCE, incorporating the researches of recent historians, and suitable for the higher forms in Schools and for Students at the Universities. It is unnecessary to point out the importance of a knowledge of French history to every one who aspires to a liberal education; but it may not be amiss to remind the reader that the true meaning and effect of the drama of the Revolution, of which we have not yet seen the catastrophe, can be understood only by a far deeper study of the previous condition and history of France than most of our countrymen are disposed to undertake. The author's desire has been to avoid the capital error of writing the history of France from an English point of view, a course which cannot fail to convey an unjust conception of the institutions, government, habits, and character of the people. What is needed is an impartial, genial, and even sympathetic account of French history.—*Editor's Preface.*

"This History of France is the digested work of a thorough French scholar, who, having entered into the spirit of the nation and its history, knows how to generalise and knit into one pertinent whole the sequence of events. It is the best work of its kind accessible to readers of all classes."—*Examiner.*

"This volume is calculated to do much good; by a candid and impartial statement of facts, it may dispel prejudices, and enable the student hereafter, in the ripeness of scholarship, diligently to enlarge and scientifically to methodise the information it affords. The author has collected his authorities with able research, and scrutinised them with unbiassed judgment."—*Morning Post.*

"This work is entitled to the praise of meeting an acknowledged want; a history of France, presented in a comprehensive and perspicuous view. It has, also, the coherency, liveliness, and just comprehension of the facts and their relations, which mark a genuine authorship, in distinction from the work of a mere compiler."—*Nonconformist.*

"We doubt whether there was any greater literary want than a really good English History of France. That want is now supplied by the work before us. The matter is well selected, and well condensed; the style is clear and forcible."—*Gardeners' Chronicle.*

"The style is perspicuous and dignified, though not wanting in vivacity. It is not a history of France written from an English view-point, and designed to flatter the pride of Englishmen. It is quite catholic in spirit, and thoroughly sympathetic in tone."—*The Museum.*

THE STUDENT'S FRANCE.

Specimen of the Illustrations.

Meeting of the States-General in the Salle Bourbon at Paris, October 1614.
From a print of the time.

THE STUDENT'S HISTORY OF GREECE

FROM THE EARLIEST TIMES TO THE ROMAN CONQUEST.

WITH CHAPTERS ON THE HISTORY OF LITERATURE AND ART.

By WM. SMITH, LL.D.

With 100 *Woodcuts. Post 8vo,* 7s. 6d.

My object has been to give the youthful reader as vivid a picture of the main facts of Grecian history, and of the leading characteristics of the political institutions, literature, and art of the people, as could be comprised within the limits of a volume of moderate size. With this view I have omitted entirely, or dismissed in a few paragraphs, many circumstances recorded in similar works, and have thus gained space for narrating at length the more important events, and for bringing out prominently the characters and lives of the great men of the nation. It is only in this way that a school history can be made instructive and interesting, since a brief and tedious enumeration of every event, whether great or small, important or unimportant, confuses the reader and leaves no permanent impression upon his memory. Considerable space has been given to the history of literature and art, since they form the most durable evidences of a nation's growth in civilization and in social progress. A knowledge of these subjects is of great importance to a pupil at the commencement of his classical studies. —*Author's Preface.*

"We are very glad to receive a *History of Greece*, by Dr. William Smith, a man eminently fit for the task he has undertaken. This is to give a readable, interesting, and authentic History of Greece, of sufficient literary merit to attract the sympathies of youthful students."—*Guardian.*

"We have much satisfaction in bearing testimony to the excellence of the plan on which Dr. Smith has proceeded, and the careful scholarlike manner in which he has carried it out."—*Athenæum.*

"The best elementary history on the subject ever written. The excellence of the work is partly dependent on the author's known capacity for the task, on his learning and talent, and partly on the fact of the great work of Grote having made all future attempts at writing Greek history comparatively easy."—*Daily News.*

"Dr. Smith shows himself to be not only thoroughly acquainted with his subject, but what is a much rarer merit, possessed of that practical skill which is indispensable to the production of a good school-book."—*Journal of English Education.*

A Smaller History of Greece, from the Earliest Times to the Roman Conquest. By WM. SMITH, LL.D. 74 Illustrations. Fcap. 8vo, 3s. 6d., cloth, red edges.

THE STUDENT'S GREECE.

Specimen of the Illustrations.

Paris. A Greek Warrior.

The Plain and Tumulus of Marathon.

THE STUDENT'S HISTORY OF ROME

FROM THE EARLIEST TIMES TO THE ESTABLISH-MENT OF THE EMPIRE.

WITH CHAPTERS ON THE HISTORY OF LITERATURE AND ART.

BY DEAN LIDDELL.

With 80 Woodcuts. Post 8vo, 7s. 6d.

"There is no other work at present existing which so ably supplies a History of Rome suited to the wants of the general readers of the present day. To the youthful student, to the man who cannot read many volumes, we should commend it as the one history which will convey the latest views and most extensive information. The style is simple, clear, and explanatory."—*Blackwood.*

"Dr. Liddell has given a lucid, well-marked, and comprehensive view of the progress and revolutions of the Roman State and people. The course of the history is distinctly mapped out by broad and natural divisions; and the order in which it is arranged and presented is the work of a strong and clear mind. There is great skill as well as diligence shown in the amount of facts which are collected and compressed into the narrative; and the story is told, not merely with full intelligence, but with an earnestness and strength of feeling which cannot be mistaken."—*Guardian.*

"Dr. Liddell's History is adapted to the purpose of readers who desire a knowledge of the 'altered aspect which Roman history has assumed.' By means of a skilfully arranged structure, not only the different periods of the history, but their various subdivisions, are presented as distinct parts, yet each having a relation to a larger whole. The general treatment is also judicious. The alleged events, for instance, of the early period, are rapidly touched, while the social, political, and constitutional arrangements are fully expounded."—*Spectator.*

"This excellent History of Rome *will supersede every other work on the subject.*"— *John Bull.*

A Smaller History of Rome, from the Earliest Times to the Establishment of the Empire. By WM. SMITH, LL.D. 79 Illustrations. Fcap. 8vo, 3s. 6d., cloth, red edges.

THE STUDENT'S ROME.

Specimen of the Illustrations.

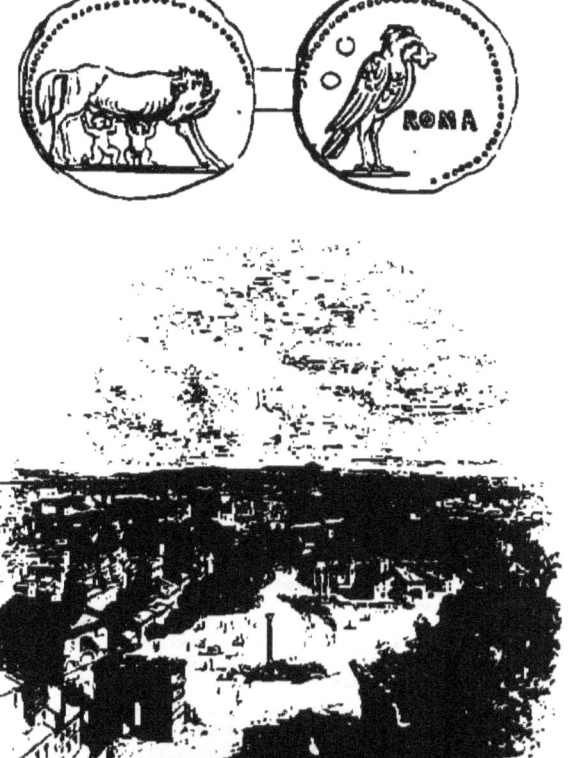

The Forum from the Capitol.

The Student's Gibbon
AN EPITOME OF THE HISTORY OF THE DECLINE AND FALL OF THE ROMAN EMPIRE

By EDWARD GIBBON.

CORRECTING HIS ERRORS AND INCORPORATING THE RESEARCHES OF RECENT HISTORIANS.

With 240 Woodcuts. Post 8vo, 7s. 6d.

"Gibbon's 'Decline and Fall of the Roman Empire' forms the important link between Ancient and Modern history. Its title conveys an inadequate idea of its contents. It contains nearly a complete history of the world for a period of more than twelve centuries, from the time of the Antonines to the capture of Constantinople by the Turks in 1453. Since the history of all ancient nations ends in that of Rome, and the history of modern states of Europe springs out of the Roman Empire, the youthful historical student, after making himself acquainted with the leading facts in the histories of Greece, Rome, and England, cannot employ his time more profitably than in mastering the history of the vast period comprehended in Gibbon's work. It is mainly for the benefit of such students that the present Abridgment has been prepared; but it is believed that it will also prove acceptable to the general reader, whose time or circumstances prevent him from studying so large a work as Gibbon's, but who wishes to make himself acquainted with some of the most memorable events in the history of man."—*Preface.*

"Dr. Smith has already earned the thanks of this generation of scholars by a series o publications. He has now edited *Gibbon* in a single compact volume, with one hundred well-chosen wood engravings of buildings, coins, and other antiquities. Besides abridgment, the chief alterations are the omission of offensive anti-christian sneers, and the incorporation of important notes in the body of the text. Dr. Smith has preserved the main features of the great historian's work."—*Guardian.*

"'Gibbon's Decline and Fall,' will live long as one of the noblest works in the English language; but it is too voluminous for the young student. Dr. Smith has drawn up an admirable abridgment of it, using as far as possible the language of the original, and adopting the plan of omitting or treating briefly circumstances of inferior importance, so that the grand events which have influenced the history of the world may be narrated at length."—*Cambridge Chronicle.*

"The best popular edition of Gibbon extant. It is pervaded by all the warmth, life, and power of the celebrated original; and is just some such volume as Gibbon himself would have issued, had he deemed it proper to send forth a digest of his own immortal performance."—*Christian Witness.*

THE STUDENT'S GIBBON.

Specimen of the Illustrations.

Seal of Frederick II.

Medal of Pope Eugenius IV.

The Triple Wall of Constantinople

THE STUDENT'S
MANUAL OF ANCIENT GEOGRAPHY.

By REV. W. L. BEVAN, M.A.,
VICAR OF HAY.

With 112 Woodcuts. Post 8vo, 7s. 6d.

This Manual presents, in a systematic form, and in a moderate compass, the most important results embodied in the "Dictionary of Greek and Roman Geography." The original work contains a great mass of information derived from the researches of modern travellers and scholars, which have not yet been made available for the purposes of instruction in our colleges and schools.

Besides adapting the larger work, for a different class of readers, many valuable additions have been made, of which the most important are:—

1. A history of Geography in Antiquity, containing an account of the views of the Hebrews, as well as of the Greeks and Romans, illustrated by maps of the world as known to the poets, historians, and geographers.

2. A full account of Scriptural Geography.

3. Numerous quotations from the Greek and Roman poets, which either illustrate, or are illustrated by, the statements in the text.

Great pains have been taken to make the book as interesting as the nature of the subject would allow. The tedium naturally produced by an enumeration of political boundaries and topographical notices is relieved by historical and ethnographical discussions, while the numerous maps, plans, and other illustrations give life and reality to the descriptions. The Retreat of the Ten Thousand Greeks, the Expedition of Alexander the Great, and similar subjects, are discussed and explained. It has been an especial object to supply information on all points required *by the upper classes in the public schools, and by students in the universities.*

"A valuable addition to our geographical works. It contains the newest and most reliable information derived from the researches of modern travellers. No better text-book can be placed in the hands of scholars."—*Journal of Education.*

In Preparation,

The Student's Manual of Modern Geography.

THE STUDENT'S ANCIENT GEOGRAPHY.

Specimen of the Illustrations.

Ruins of Palmyra.

Site of Abydos from the West.

THE STUDENT'S
MANUAL OF OLD TESTAMENT HISTORY;

From the Creation of the World to the return of the Jews from Captivity. With an Appendix, containing an Introduction to the Books of the Old Testament. With 4 Maps and 40 Woodcuts, Post 8vo, 7s. 6d.

II.
MANUAL OF NEW TESTAMENT HISTORY.

With an Introduction containing the connection of the Old and New Testament. With 9 Maps and Plans, and 27 Woodcuts, post 8vo, 7s. 6d.
₊ *See Illustrations opposite.*

The object of these works is to provide Text-books of Scripture History, which, in fulness, accuracy, and scholar-like treatment, may take their place by the side of the Student's Histories of Greece and Rome now in general use in all the best Public and Private Schools.

"Well adapted to the purpose for which it is intended, of a Biblical Manual for the upper classes of our public schools. It will also be found very useful to many persons who have neither money to purchase, nor leisure to consult, the larger and more expensive works on Biblical History and Antiquities."—*Educational Times.*

"All real students of the Bible will delight to possess this. The book will be a real treasure to those whose library is small, as they will find it to be of all but inestimable service."—*Christian World.*

"Useful manuals of history which will no doubt obtain a wider circulation than the similar volumes on the History of Greece or Rome, as the subject-matter is of wider interest. We are glad to say that it will satisfy the more it is examined. Its tone is eminently reverential."—*Churchman.*

"Ample enough to make it a valuable companion to the study table of the clergy at large, and to satisfy most of the wants of intellectual laymen."—*Clerical Journal.*

"We have long needed such a condensed and scholarly view as that which is here given us. The works of Dr. Riddle and Mr. Maclear are both excellent in their own way, but they are brief and rudimentary. The present work is designed for students of a more advanced character, and is admirably suited to its purpose."—*Patriot.*

In preparation,

The Student's Manual of Ecclesiastical History.

Containing the History of the Christian Church from the close of the New Testament Canon to the Reformation. Post 8vo.

The Student's Scripture History.

Specimen of the Illustrations.

Mount Hor.

LITERATURE & LANGUAGE.

Student's Manual of the English Language.
By GEORGE P. MARSH.
EDITED, WITH ADDITIONAL CHAPTERS AND NOTES.
Post 8vo, 7s. 6d.

"This work which Dr. Smith has edited is one of real and acknowledged merit, and likely to meet with a wider reception from his hands than in its original form. It appears that Dr. Smith had projected and commenced a work on the history of the English language in conjunction with the late Dr. Donaldson, so that he was the better prepared for the task he has now executed. Much curious and useful information is given at the end of different lectures, including interesting philological remarks culled from various sources, &c. Dr. Smith has produced a manual of great utility."—*Athenæum.*

Student's Manual of English Literature.
By T. B. SHAW.
EDITED, WITH NOTES AND ILLUSTRATIONS.
Post 8vo, 7s. 6d.

"The reader will find in this manual abundant guidance in his literary pursuits, as will stimulate his own researches, and induce him both to observe and think. As a handy book of reference to the works and biographies of the less famous English writers, the book will be found exceedingly useful, while it supplies a thoughtful and original criticism on those of greater name."—*Guardian.*

Student's Specimens of English Literature.
Selected from the chief English Writers.
By T. B. SHAW.
EDITED, WITH NOTES AND ILLUSTRATIONS.
Post 8vo, 7s. 6d.

"Two objects have been chiefly kept in view in making these selections; first, the illustration of the style of each writer by some of the most striking or characteristic specimens of his works; and, secondly, the choice of such passages as are suitable, either from their language or their matter, to be read in schools or committed to memory. No less than one hundred and fifty-nine authors have been laid under contribution; Caedmon, A.D. 650, supplying the first specimen, and Canning the last. The whole collection seems to have been compiled with much taste."—*Educational Times.*

The Student's Manual of Moral Philosophy.
By WILLIAM FLEMING, D.D.,
Late Professor of Moral Philosophy at Glasgow University.
Post 8vo, 7s. 6d.

JAMES'S EDITION OF ÆSOP.

THE FABLES OF ÆSOP.

A New Version, chiefly from Original Sources.

By Rev. THOMAS JAMES, M.A.

With 100 Woodcuts by TENNIEL and WOLF. Post 8vo, 2s. 6d.

Fable 34.—The House-Dog and the Wolf.

"This work is remarkable for the clearness and conciseness with which each tale is narrated; and the book has been relieved of those tedious and unprofitable appendages called 'morals,' which used to obscure and disfigure the ancient editions of the work."—*The Examiner.*

HYMNS IN PROSE.

By Mrs. BARBAULD.

With 112 Original Designs by BARNES, WIMPERIS, COLEMAN, and KENNEDY. 16mo, 5s.

"Mrs. Barbauld's 'Hymns in Prose' reappears with such beauty of decoration as we did not dream of in our younger days. It is a book to educate the eye as well as the heart."—*Guardian.*

MRS. MARKHAM'S ENGLAND.

A HISTORY OF ENGLAND.

From the First Invasion by the Romans.
With Conversations at the end of each Chapter.

By MRS. MARKHAM.

New and Revised Edition continued down to the Marriage of the Prince of Wales in 1863.

200th thousand. With 100 Woodcuts. 12mo, 4s.

Stonehenge restored.

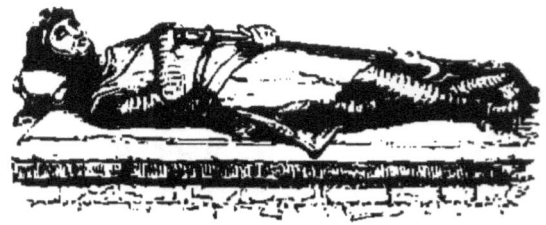

Monument of a Crusader.

"Mrs. Markham's works are constructed on a plan which is novel and we think well chosen, and we are glad to find that they are deservedly popular, for they cannot be too strongly recommended, as adapted for the perusal of youth."—*Journal of Education.*

List of Educational Works. 19

MRS. MARKHAM'S FRANCE.

A HISTORY OF FRANCE.

From the Conquest by the Gauls.
With Conversations at the end of each Chapter.

By MRS. MARKHAM.

New and Revised Edition continued to the Birth of the Prince Imperial in 1856.

With 70 Woodcuts. 12mo, 4s.

ANCIENT TOURNAMENT.

The Bastile.

"Mrs. Markham's Histories are well known to all those engaged in the instruction of youth. Her Histories of England and France are deservedly very popular; and we have been given to understand, in proof of this assertion, that of her Histories *many thousand copies* have been sold."—*Bell's Messenger.*

MRS. MARKHAM'S GERMANY.

A HISTORY OF GERMANY.

*From the Invasion
of the Kingdom by the Romans under Marius.*

By MRS. MARKHAM.

New and Revised Edition continued to the Year 1850.

With 50 Woodcuts. 12mo, 4s.

House in which Albert Durer lived at Nürnberg.

"A very valuable compendium of all that is most important in German History. The facts have been accurately and laboriously collected from authentic sources, and they are lucidly arranged so as to invest them with the interest which naturally pertains to them."
—*Evangelical Magazine.*

LITTLE ARTHUR'S HISTORY OF ENGLAND.
By LADY CALLCOTT.
With 24 Woodcuts. Fcap. 8vo, 2s. 6d.

King John signing Magna Charta.

"I acknowledge myself to be some judge of what suits children, and I never met with a history so well adapted either to their capacities or their entertainment, so philosophical, and at the same time written with such infantine simplicity."—*Mrs. Marcett to Lady Callcott.*

Stories for Children, selected from the History of England, from the Conquest to the Revolution. By JOHN WILSON CROKER. With 24 Illustrations. Square 16mo, 2s. 6d.

DR. WM. SMITH'S SMALLER HISTORIES.

These Smaller Histories have been drawn up chiefly for the lower forms in Schools, at the request of several teachers, who require for their pupils more elementary books than the Student's Histories of England, Greece, and Rome.

1. *A Smaller History of England.* With 68 Woodcuts, 12mo, 3s. 6d.

Sebastopol.

2. *A Smaller History of Greece.* With 74 Woodcuts, 12mo, 3s. 6d.

3. *A Smaller History of Rome.* With 79 Woodcuts, 12mo, 3s. 6d.

4. *A Smaller Classical Mythology.* Illustrated with Translations from the Ancient Poets, and Questions on the Work. With 90 Woodcuts, 16mo, 3s. 6d.

"The object of this work is to give a consecutive account of the Heathen Deities, which may safely be placed in the hands of the young, and which contains all that is necessary to enable them to understand the classical allusions they may meet with in prose or poetry."—*Preface.*

5. *A Smaller Scripture History.* With Woodcuts, 16mo, 3s. 6d. *In preparation.*

DR. WM. SMITH'S SMALLER HISTORIES.

Specimens of the Illustrations.

Site of Ephesus.

The Campagna of Rome.

DR. WILLIAM SMITH'S LATIN COURSE.

PRINCIPIA LATINA, Part I.

A FIRST COURSE.

Containing a Grammar, Delectus, Exercise-Book, and Vocabularies.

12mo, 3s. 6d.

The main object of this work is to enable a Beginner to fix the Declensions and Conjugations thoroughly in his memory, to learn their usage by constructing simple sentences as soon as he commences the study of the language, and to accumulate gradually a stock of useful words. It presents in one book all that the pupil will require for some time in his study of the language.

This Work, which contains a Grammar, Delectus, Exercise-book, and Vocabularies, has been pronounced by the "grinders of small boys" who have used it, to be by far the easiest and best book for beginners in Latin.

PRINCIPIA LATINA, Part II.

A READING-BOOK.

Containing Fables, Anecdotes, Mythology, Geography, Roman Antiquities, and History.

With Notes and a Dictionary, 12mo, 3s. 6d.

This work is intended to furnish a Latin Reading-book suitable for beginners, sufficient in quantity while interesting and instructive in matter, and thus prepare the way for Cæsar or any other classical author. It is believed that it will not only prove interesting, but serve as an introduction to Ancient Mythology, Geography, Roman History, and Antiquities.

It should be used *in conjunction with* the First Part of the "Principia Latina." As soon as the pupil has learnt thoroughly the Declensions and Conjugations, and can translate the simplest sentences, it is important to diversify the somewhat dry and tedious work of the Delectus and Exercise-book, by giving him connected passages containing interesting and instructive matter.

List of Educational Works.

DR. WILLIAM SMITH'S LATIN COURSE—Continued

PRINCIPIA LATINA, Part III.

A POETRY-BOOK.

CONTAINING

1. *Easy Hexameters and Pentameters.* 2. *Eclogæ Ovidianæ.*
3. *Prosody and Metre.* 4. *First Latin Verse-book.*

12mo, 3s. 6d.

This single volume contains subjects usually distributed over two or more separate works; and there can be little doubt that a pupil who has mastered it will have been well grounded in Latin verse, and thus be able to enter upon the study of Virgil and Ovid with greater advantage, than if he had attempted to read those authors without a similar preparatory training.

PRINCIPIA LATINA, Part IV.

PROSE COMPOSITION.

Containing Rules of Syntax, with Examples, Explanations of Synonyms, and Exercises on the Syntax.

12mo, 3s. 6d.

The object of this Work is to supply a series of progressive and systematic Exercises upon the principal rules of the Latin Syntax; there is also prefixed to each Exercise the Syntactical rules which the Exercise is designed to illustrate and enforce. At the beginning of each Exercise is given an explanation of Synonymous words, with passages in which they occur, so that the pupil may, at an early period in his studies, learn to discriminate their use and employ them correctly. At the end of the Work is an English-Latin Vocabulary, containing all the words occurring in the Exercises, in order that the pupil need not have recourse to a Dictionary or any other book in writing the Exercises.

PRINCIPIA LATINA, Part V.

Short Tales and Anecdotes from Classical History, for Translation into Latin Prose.

12mo, 3s.

This work has been added to the Series at the suggestion of the Rev. F. E. Durnford, Master of the Lower School, Eton, and in consequence of the desire expressed by many teachers for a short collection of easy and continuous narratives for translation into Latin Prose. It is in use at Eton, Harrow, and other Public Schools.

LATIN GRAMMARS.

For the Upper Forms.

The Student's Latin Grammar, by WM. SMITH, LL.D. & THEOPHILUS D. HALL, M.A. New and cheaper edition. Post 8vo, 6s.

"This grammar is intended and well calculated to occupy an intermediate position between the large treatises of Zumpt and Madvig, and the numerous elementary school grammars prevalent amongst us. There are very few students who will require more information than is here supplied; and yet, by a skilful arrangement of the materials and typography, the volume is reduced to a very convenient size and form for practical use. The editor's good sense is visible throughout. When he cannot consult the requirements of strictly scientific method, or introduce modern improvements of nomenclature without doing such violence to established usage as to cause serious practical inconvenience, he refrains. At the same time he is not so wedded to existing customs as to retain anything positively erroneous, which the student must afterwards unlearn. Some useful remarks are added on the characteristic styles of the chief prose writers, and the appendix on the alphabet is full of suggestive information."—*Athenæum*.

For the Lower Forms.

Dr. Wm. Smith's Smaller Latin Grammar, abridged from the above. 12mo, 3s. 6d.

King Edward VI.'s First Latin Book. The Latin Accidence, Syntax, and Prosody, with a Translation. 12mo, 2s. 6d.

King Edward VI.'s Latin Grammar. Latinæ Grammaticæ Rudimenta, or an Introduction to the Latin Tongue. 12mo, 3s. 6d.

English Notes for Latin Elegiacs. Designed for Early Proficients in the Art of Latin Versification, with Rules of Composition in Elegiac Metre. By Rev. W. OXENHAM, M.A. 12mo, 3s. 6d.

GREEK GRAMMARS.

For the Upper Forms.

The Student's Greek Grammar, by Dr. GEORGE CURTIUS, Professor in the University of Leipzic. Translated under the Sanction and Revision of the Author. Edited by Dr. WM. SMITH, a new and cheaper edition. Post 8vo, 6s.

"All that refers to the accidence and etymology is of the highest excellence, and there is no Greek Grammar in existence which in so small a compass contains so much valuable and suggestive information. The English translation is a most accurate rendering of the fifth German edition, and we hope that in this country it may ere long be adopted as the standard Greek Grammar, a position which it has already acquired in most of the schools of continental Europe."—*The Museum.*

For the Lower Forms.

Initia Græca, Part I.; a first Greek Course, containing Delectus, Exercise-Book, and Vocabularies. By Dr. WM. SMITH, 12mo, 3s. 6d.

Initia Græca, Part II.; a Reading-Book, containing Short Tales, Anecdotes, Fables, Mythology, and Grecian History. Arranged in a systematic Progression, with a Lexicon. 12mo, 3s. 6d.

A Smaller Greek Grammar, abridged from the "Student's Greek Grammar." 12mo, 3s. 6d.

Principia Græca; an Introduction to Greek, containing a Grammar, Delectus, and Exercise-Book, with Vocabularies. By H. E. HUTTON, M.A. 12mo, 3s. 6d.

Matthiæ's Shorter Greek Grammar. Abridged by BLOMFIELD, revised by EDWARDS. 12mo, 3s. 6d.

Buttman's Lexilogus. A Critical Examination of the Meaning and Etymology of various Greek Words and Passages in Homer, Hesiod, and other Greek Writers. Translated, with Notes, by FISHLAKE. 8vo, 12s.

Buttman's Catalogue of Irregular Greek Verbs. With all the Tenses extant—their Formation, Meaning, and Usage, accompanied by an Index. Translated, with Notes, by FISHLAKE and VENABLES. Post 8vo.

Dr. William Smith's
Latin-English and English-Latin Dictionaries.

For the Higher Forms.

1. *A Complete Latin-English Dictionary.* With tables of the Roman Calendar, Measures, Weights, and Money. *Sixth Edition*, with the References verified, and Additions to the Etymologies (1250 pp.) Medium 8vo, 21s.

"Dr. Wm. Smith's Latin Dictionary is a *most useful book*, and fills for Latin Literature the place now occupied by Liddell's and Scott's Lexicon for Greek."—Sir G. Cornewall Lewis.

"Of Latin and English Lexicons, the best representation of the scholarship of the day is undoubtedly that of Dr. Wm. Smith."—Rev. J. W. Donaldson, D.D.

"Dr. Wm. Smith's 'Latin Dictionary,' is a great convenience to me. *I think that he has been very judicious in what he has omitted*, as well as in what he has inserted."—Rev. Robert Scott, D.D., *Master of Baliol and Author of the "Greek Lexicon."*

"Dr. Wm. Smith's Latin Dictionary is the most useful that I know."—Rev. Dr. Goodford, *Provost of Eton.*

"Dr. Wm. Smith's Latin Dictionary is one of the many obligations which he has conferred upon our public schools."—Rev. Dr. Kynaston, *Head Master of St. Paul's School.*

"Dr. Wm. Smith's Dictionary is, beyond comparison, the best in every point of view."—Rev. Dr. Hodson, *Rector of the Edinburgh Academy.*

"Dr. Wm. Smith's Latin Dictionary is a first-rate work."—Rev. Dr. Badham, *Principal of Edgbaston School.*

"The superiority of Dr. Wm. Smith's Latin Dictionary over all others has been confirmed by increased familiarity with it."—Dr. Schmitz.

2. *A Copious English-Latin Dictionary.* Compiled entirely from original sources. By Dr. Wm. Smith, and Theophilus D. Hall, M.A. Medium 8vo. *Nearly ready.*

For Junior Classes.

3. *A Smaller Latin-English Dictionary.* Abridged from the larger work. Square 12mo, 7s. 6d.

4. *A Smaller English-Latin Dictionary.* Abridged from the larger work. Square 12mo. *Nearly ready.*

5. *A Latin-English Vocabulary*, arranged according to Subjects and Etymology, with a Latin-English Dictionary to Phædrus, Cornelius Nepos, and Cæsar's Gallic War. 12mo, 3s. 6d.

This work is designed to assist beginners in acquiring a copious vocabulary of the Latin language, and in learning the derivation and formation of Latin words.

"Dr. Wm. Smith's Dictionaries form an important element in our modern English scholarship. Probably no modern books have done so much to extend a knowledge of the researches and conclusions of the learned men of our time in the field of antiquity. If the Dictionaries to come are as well executed as their predecessors, the longer Dr. Smith continues to publish the better ordinary scholars will be pleased."—*Guardian.*

DR. WILLIAM SMITH'S
BIBLICAL & CLASSICAL DICTIONARIES.

Comprising :—

1. DICTIONARY OF THE BIBLE.
2. CONCISE BIBLE DICTIONARY.
3. SMALLER BIBLE DICTIONARY.
4. DICTIONARY OF GREEK AND ROMAN ANTIQUITIES.
5. DICTIONARY OF GREEK AND ROMAN BIOGRAPHY AND MYTHOLOGY.
6. DICTIONARY OF GREEK AND ROMAN GEOGRAPHY.
7. CLASSICAL DICTIONARY FOR THE HIGHER FORMS.
8. SMALLER CLASSICAL DICTIONARY.
9. SMALLER DICTIONARY OF ANTIQUITIES.

Dr. William Smith, once a student, and afterwards a master in this School and in this College, was in the course of last spring appointed to the distinguished position of one of the classical examiners to the University of London—appointed, I will say it to his honour, after fair and strict comparison with some scholars of the highest eminence in our national Universities of Oxford and Cambridge. It is an honour to this College to have presented to the world so distinguished a scholar as Dr. William Smith, who has, by his valuable manuals of classical antiquity and classical history and biography, done as much as any man living to promote the accurate knowledge of the Greek and Roman world among the students of this age. I trust that among those names which we have heard mentioned to-day, and to whom my honourable friend has given prizes, there may be found more than one who will aspire to emulate Dr. Wm. Smith's diligent and honourable course, and to render himself in future life the means of conveying to others that knowledge and instruction which he has received within these walls.—*Mr. Grote's Address at the London University.*

A DICTIONARY OF THE BIBLE.

Its Antiquities, Biography, Geography, and Natural History.

BY VARIOUS WRITERS.

INCLUDING THE

Archbishop of York.
Bishops of Calcutta, Ely, Gloucester and Bristol, Killaloe.
Deans of Canterbury, Chester, and Westminster,
Lord Arthur Hervey.
Professors Lightfoot, Plumptre, Rawlinson, Selwyn, etc.

EDITED BY WM. SMITH, LL.D.

With Illustrations, 3 vols., medium 8vo, £5 : 5s.

The object of this Work is to elucidate the Antiquities, Biography, Geography, and Natural History of the Bible, and to present, in a compact form, the researches of the most eminent divines and scholars.

"The work reflects the highest character upon its promoters, and imperatively demands a place upon the study table of every clergyman and of every thoughtful and intelligent student of the Bible. It must always remain in itself a most serviceable library of reference, and a standing monument of the learning, piety, and ability of our Anglican theologians."—*Church of England Monthly Review.*

"By such a work as this, a knowledge of the Bible is brought within easy reach of all commonly well educated persons, and every man of intelligence may become his own commentator."—*Times.*

"Dr. Wm. Smith's Dictionary of the Bible could not fail to take a very high place in English literature: for no similar work in our own or in any other language is for a moment to be compared with it."—*Quarterly Review.*

A Concise Bible Dictionary for Families and Students. Illustrations (1050 pp.) 1 vol., 8vo, 21s.

"This volume is so full and satisfactory that did it not appear as an abridgment it would be accepted as a full and complete Dictionary of the Bible."—*Churchman.*

A Smaller Bible Dictionary for Schools and Young Persons. With 6 Maps, 30 Illustrations, and numerous Woodcuts. (622 pp.) Crown 8vo, 7s. 6d.

"This work has been drawn up for the use of Schools, Sunday School Teachers, and young persons, and contains such an account as a young person is likely to require in the study of the Bible. In short, it seeks to render the same service to the study of the Bible as the Smaller Classical Dictionaries have done for the study of the Greek and Roman Classics in schools."—*Editor's Preface.*

In preparation,

AN HISTORICAL ATLAS OF BIBLICAL GEOGRAPHY.

A Complete
Cyclopædia of Classical Antiquity.

BY VARIOUS WRITERS.

EDITED BY WM. SMITH, LL.D.

1. *Dictionary of Greek and Roman Antiquities.*
   Illustrated by 500 Engravings on Wood. Medium 8vo, £2 : 2s.

2. *Dictionary of Greek and Roman Biography and* Mythology. Illustrated by 564 Engravings on Wood. 3 Volumes, Medium 8vo, £5 : 15 : 6.

3. *Dictionary of Greek and Roman Geography.*
   Illustrated by 534 Engravings on Wood. 2 Volumes, Medium 8vo, £4.

"I have been for some time in the habit of using the Dictionaries of Antiquity and Ancient Biography, as well as the Dictionary of Ancient Geography, and I have no hesitation in saying, from my knowledge of them, that they are far superior to any other publications of the same sort in our language. They are works which every student of ancient literature ought to consult habitually, and which are indispensable to every person engaged in original researches into any department of antiquity."—*Sir G. C. Lewis.*

"I willingly bear testimony to the great value of your Dictionaries of Classical Antiquities, of Greek and Roman Biography and Mythology, and of Greek and Roman Geography. I have had frequent occasion to consult these works, and have derived from them great assistance and instruction. In no other publications known to me is so much trustworthy information got together and rendered easily accessible for elucidating matters of fact connected with the history of Greece and Rome."—*George Grote.*

"The Dictionary of Greek and Roman Geography edited by Dr. William Smith is a work of so much utility to the study of ancient history, and of such general importance to classical education and the progress of knowledge, that its extensive circulation wherever the English language is spoken or read may confidently be anticipated."—*Col. Leake.*

"I have much pleasure in expressing the high estimate which I have formed of Dr. William Smith's many valuable works, which have been for some years past in general circulation."—*Col. Mure.*

In preparation,
AN HISTORICAL ATLAS OF CLASSICAL GEOGRAPHY.

Dr. Wm. Smith's

Classical School Dictionaries

For the Higher Forms.

1. *A New Classical Dictionary of Mythology, Biography, and Geography*, compiled from his larger Dictionaries. With 750 Woodcuts. 8vo, 18s.

For Junior Classes.

2. *A Smaller Classical Dictionary*, abridged from the above Work. With 200 Woodcuts. Crown 8vo, 7s. 6d.

3. *A Smaller Dictionary of Antiquities*, abridged from his larger Dictionary. With 200 Woodcuts. Crown 8vo, 7s. 6d.

"The fame and success of Dr. Smith's Dictionaries are their best recommendation. I consider their publication to have conferred a great and lasting service on the cause of classical learning in this country."—Dean Liddell, *late Head Master of Westminster School*.

"I have much pleasure in expressing my sense of the invaluable services rendered to the cause of Greek and Latin Literature, and of classical education generally, by the great and laborious works of Dr. Wm. Smith, which are extensively used, and with great profit, at Harrow, as in all the public schools of England."—Rev. Dr. Vaughan, *late Head Master of Harrow School.*

"I am extremely glad of the opportunity of expressing to you the strong sense of obligation which I, in common with all teachers and lovers of classical literature, feel to you for your admirable Dictionaries."—Rev. Dr. Hawtrey, *late Head Master of Eton College.*

"I have the pleasure of assuring you that your Dictionaries are in very general use, and are highly esteemed at St. Paul's School. I never lose an opportunity of recommending these most valuable publications to my scholars and friends."—Rev. Dr. Kynaston, *Head Master of St. Paul's School.*

"I do not express myself too strongly when I declare that I consider that the works of which you have been the presiding mind, and to which you have personally contributed so much, have commenced a new era in English scholarship."—Rev. Dr. Hessey, *Head Master of Merchant Taylors' School.*

List of Educational Works. 33

DR. WM. SMITH'S
CLASSICAL DICTIONARIES.

Specimens of Illustrations.

Minerva.

Greek Soldier.

Judgment of Paris.

BOOKS FOR PRIZES.

HERODOTUS; a New English Version. Edited, with copious notes from the most recent sources. By Rev. George Rawlinson. Maps and Woodcuts, 4 vols. 8vo, 48s.

RAWLINSON'S ANCIENT EASTERN MONARCHIES— Chaldæa, Assyria, Babylon, Media, and Persia; their History, Geography, and Antiquities. Maps and Illustrations, 4 vols. 8vo.

GROTE'S HISTORY OF GREECE. From the Earliest Period to the close of the Generation contemporary with Alexander the Great. Portrait and Maps, 8 vols. 8vo, 112s.

GROTE'S PLATO AND THE COMPANIONS OF SOCRATES. 3 vols. 8vo, 45s.

GIBBON'S HISTORY OF THE DECLINE AND FALL OF THE ROMAN EMPIRE. Edited, with Notes, by Wm. Smith, LL.D. Portrait and Maps, 8 vols. 8vo, 60s.

RANKE'S HISTORY OF THE POPES OF ROME; Translated by Sarah Austin. With a Preface by Dean Milman, D.D. 3 vols 8vo, 30s.

ROBERTSON'S HISTORY OF THE CHRISTIAN CHURCH; from the Apostolic Age to the Death of Boniface VIII. A.D. 64–1303. 3 vols. 8vo.

HALLAM'S HISTORICAL WORKS. I. History of England. II. Europe during the Middle Ages. III. Literary History of Europe. 10 vols. post 8vo, 6s. each.

DEAN MILMAN'S HISTORICAL WORKS. I. History of Christianity. II. History of the Jews. III. History of Latin Christianity. 15 vols. post 8vo, 6s. each.

MAHON'S HISTORY OF ENGLAND, from the Peace of Utrecht to the Peace of Versailles, 1713-1783. 7 vols. post 8vo, 5s. each.

DYER'S HISTORY OF MODERN EUROPE; from the taking of Constantinople by the Turks to the close of the War in the Crimea. 4 vols. 8vo.

THE ILLUSTRATED NEW TESTAMENT. Edited, with a short Practical Comment, by Archdeacons Churton and Jones. With 100 Illustrations. 2 vols. crown 8vo, 30s. cloth.

THE ILLUSTRATED PRAYER BOOK. With Borders, Head-Pieces, Initial Letters in red and black, and Historical Engravings. Edited by Rev. Thomas James, M.A. 8vo, 18s. cloth.

THE ANCIENT EGYPTIANS. Their Manners and Customs. By Sir J. G. Wilkinson. With 500 Woodcuts, 2 vols. post 8vo.

HISTORY OF ARCHITECTURE IN ALL COUNTRIES. From Earliest Times to the Present Day. By James Fergusson, F.R.S. With 1500 Illustrations, 3 vols. 8vo.

THE CATHEDRALS OF ENGLAND AND WALES; a concise History of each See, with Biographical Notices of the Bishops. By Richard J. King. With Illustrations. Vols. 1 to 4. Post 8vo.

LIFE AND TIMES OF CICERO. With Selections from his Correspondence and his Orations. By William Forsyth, Q.C. With Illustrations. 8vo, 16s.

THE GERMAN, FLEMISH, AND DUTCH SCHOOLS OF PAINTING. Edited, with Notes, by Dr. Waagen. With Illustrations, 2 vols. post 8vo, 24s.

THE ITALIAN SCHOOLS OF PAINTING. Edited, with Notes, by Sir Chas. Eastlake, R.A. With 150 Illustrations, 2 vols. post 8vo 30s.

HORACE: A New Edition of the Text. Edited by Dean Milman, and Illustrated by 100 Woodcuts. Fcap 8vo.

GREECE; Pictorial, Descriptive, and Historical. By Archdeacon Wordsworth. With 600 Engravings, royal 8vo, 28s.

www.ingramcontent.com/pod-product-compliance
Lightning Source LLC
Chambersburg PA
CBHW052213240426
43670CB00037B/428